AF540275

HINDUSTANI AND PERSIO-ARABIAN MUSIC
An Indepth, Comparative Study

HINDUSTANI AND PERSIO-ARABIAN MUSIC

An Indepth, Comparative Study

DIVYA MANSINGH KAUL

KANISHKA PUBLISHERS, DISTRIBUTORS
NEW DELHI-110 002

KANISHKA PUBLISHERS, DISTRIBUTORS
4697/5-21A, Ansari Road, Daryaganj
New Delhi -110 002
Phones : 2327 0497, 2328 8285
Fax : 011-2328 8285
E-mail : kanishka_publishing@yahoo.co.in

Hindustani and Persio–Arabian Music
First Published-2007
Edition-2022

ISBN: 978-81-7391-923-2

PRINTED IN INDIA

Published by Madan Sachdeva for Kanishka Publishers, Distributors, 4697/5-21A, Ansari Road, Daryaganj, New Delhi-110 002, Typeset by Sunshine Graphics, Delhi, and Printed at Rajdhani Printers, Delhi.

Dedication

To the memory of my great grand father,
the Late Dr. (Major) Ranjit Singh
and
My parents, the Late Saroj Mansingh and
the Late Arjun Deshraj Mansingh
and to,
Dr. (Mrs.) Najma P. Ahmad, but for whom
this book would not have been written

Foreword

I feel delighted to place before the world of music the work entitled "Hindustani and Persio-Arabian Music: An Indepth, Comparative Study" authored by Dr. Divya Kaul, based on her doctoral research work.

The Indian civilization is one of the most ancient in the world. Even though India is one of the few countries that have experienced so many invasions and witnessed so many empires rise and fall, yet it has been able to maintain continuity in its uniqueness.

During the medieval period when Muslims came to India, North Indian music went through a metamorphosis, blending in itself beautifully the Arab, Persian and Central Asian influences. In this process new forms and styles developed which continue to survive even today. The process of intermingling and blending of ideas and techniques was so complete that any attempt to delineate the indigenous and foreign elements would be futile. The Hindustani music that developed as a result of such synthesis was based on rich Indian tradition and its interaction with the Persian, Arabic and Central Asian influences.

During the 13th and 14th centuries, the Sultans Allauddin Khilji (1296-1316 A.D.) and Mohammad Bin Tughlaq (1325-1351 A.D.) profoundly influenced the cultural life of North India. During this period the conflict between the two cultural forces, i.e., the traditional Indian and Persio-Arabic, was transformed first into a position of stalemate and then into reciprocal toleration. It gradually set the stage for interaction, and process of mutual influencing between them; and before long new forces for bringing about a synthesis between two cultural streams took their birth. Mr. Alizadeh Mohammadi had rightly stated in one of his lecture demonstrations on classical music of Iran, that the Persian traditional music has much in common with the modal music of those countries which have similar culture and civilizations, such as that of Turkey, Arabia and to some extent India. The main characteristic performance of Persian traditional music has always been "improvisation." In Persian music each mode, that is called "Mayeh," is similar to the main elements of Indian music, viz. Raga and Tala.

Another major influence on Indian music can be attributed to the Sufis. Sufis have left indelible imprint on Hindustani music. They skilfully blended the Arab and Persian styles with Hindustani musical forms. Music played a central role in all their congregations. Interestingly, the well-known Sufi musician Amir Khusrau enjoyed the patronage of five successive kings who were great patrons of literature and fine arts. According to several Persian texts Khusrau created about twelve new melodies by combining Arabian and Persian Maqamat with Indian Ragas, among which are Zilaf, Muafiq, Ghanam, Farghana, Zangula, Sarparda, Farodast and Sazgiri, etc. The texts further describe that Khusrau chose twelve Ragas out of popular ones and ascribed them new names, such as: The combination of Bairari, Malashri and Hussaini was named "Muwafiq." Similarly, the combination of Sarang, Basant, Farghana and Nawa was named "Ushaq." The prominent Sufi of Suhrawardi sect has also been described as the innovator of several new ragas based on Persian Muqamat.

One of the noteworthy features of the book is that the author has specially emphasized the blending of the two systems of melodic modes, i.e. Persio-Arabian region, and India during the medieval times. She has attempted to examine the similarities in Hindustani music and equally important concepts of Music of Arabian region, like Rhythm (Iqa) musical instruments, forms, emotive effects of Music (Tasir), and other embellishments of singing.

The rhythmic modes of the two systems indicate strong similarities between them. Similarly the analytical description of musical instruments is highly significant in demonstrating the strong comparable traits between the music of the Persio-Arabic region and Hindustani music. The chapter on Tasir and Rasa interestingly discusses the emotive qualities, moods and nature of melodic modes (the Maqamat and Dastgahs) which are similar to the theory of Rasa in Ragas of Indian music. While discussing this point the author perceptively states that the chapter on Tasir and Rasa tells us without any doubt that the emotive qualities, moods and the nature of melodic modes of the Arabian region, the Maqam and Dastgah, are very similar to those of the Ragas of Hindustani music. In both the systems during the process of development and elaboration of the presentation of Maqam or Raga, the use of certain notes, their permutations and combinations and similar other techniques give the required emotional content to the melody.

Dr. Divya Kaul has made a valuable contribution to the field of musicology through this well researched work, which will be a rich source of information and knowledge to the scholars, teachers and students of music.

Dr. Najma Perveen Ahmad

Acknowledgement

I wish to express my sincere gratitude to various people and institutions for their valuable help and encouragement during the process of writing this book.

Foremost, my very sincere and heartfelt thanks are due to my supervisor and guide, respected Dr. Najma Perveen Ahmad, former Dean & Head, Faculty of Music & Fine Arts, University of Delhi, without whose moral support, encouragement, enthusiasm and expert guidance, this work would not have been possible. I want to especially record and appreciate the valuable time which she spared; and the learning process which ensued for me as a result of her knowledge and erudition. She also helped me with the translation of Urdu manuscripts.

My thanks to Mr. Majid Ahmadi of the Iran Culture House, New Delhi, for his help and encouragement. I could attend various Irani Sufi Classical music programmes organized by the Iran culture House, as well as interview a few Irani musicians, on these occasions. This helped me to better understand the Irani Ensemble Form of Presentation. The audio material provided by them helped me a long way in my research work.

I'm grateful to Prof. Mohammad Amin, an eminent historian, for sparing his valuable time, and providing me the correct perspective on the historical developments in the Persio-Arabian Region.

The Library of the Sangita Nataka Academy, New Delhi and American Centre Library, New Delhi, made available to me, much of the material of study and research for this book.

My sincere appreciation and gratitude is due, to the Library of the Faculty of Music and Fine Arts of the University of Delhi, for making available to me the research material for this work. Dr. Mohammad Haroon gave me much help, advice and encouragement. My thanks to him as well as to Dr Kasturi Banerjee, Shri Kuldeep Singh and Shri Maha Singh.

Mr. Gussy Rikh, a musician, teacher and performer on the Guitar, gave me his valuable time and guidance on the subject of Western music and notation.

I'm grateful to Shri Vivek Chaturvedi and Shri Madan Sachdeva of Kanishka Publishers for their enthusiasm, keen interest and for giving me the benefit of their expertise.

My special thanks are due to Mrs. Chitra Santhangopal for helping me with the painstaking typing work; also I record my gratitude to her for her enthusiasm and encouragement.

Last of all, I wish to record my thanks to my sons, Aditya and Mayank, my daughter-in-law, Ekta and my husband Shri Anoop Kaul for their constant support.

AUTHOR

Contents

List of Abbreviations

Harvard Dict.	Harvard Dictionary of Music
New Grove I, IV, IX, XII	The New Grove Dictionary of Music and Musicians I, IV, IX, XII
N.O.H.M.	The New Oxford History of Music, Vol. I
The Genius....	The Genius of Arab Civilization, Ed.J.R. Hayes.
M.S.P.	Music and Song in Persia
P.H.M.	Pelican History of Music (The Music of the Arab World)
Music of the Nations	Music of the Nations, Swami Prajnananand (Music of the Arabs)
A Hist. of Arab. Music	A History of Arabian Music, Dr. H.G. Farmer
Groves Dict. (Old)	Groves Dictionary of Music and Musicians (Old), Eric Blom
LEM	The Larousse Encyclopaedia of Music
The Rise of Music	The Rise of Music in the Ancient World East and West, by Curt Sachs (The Greek Heritage in Music in Psalm)
A Hist. of Ind. Music	A History of Indian Music (ancient period), by Swami Prajnananand
The Mus. of Ind.	The Music of India, by H.A. Popley
Bhart. Sangita	Bhartiya Sangita, Ek Aitihasik Vishleshan, Swatantra Sharma.

Sangita Makarand	A critical study of Sangita Makarand of Narada.
Musalman aur Bhartiya Sangeeta	Musalman aur Bhartiya Sangita, Acharya K.C.D. Brihaspati.
Mousiqui Hazrat Amir Khusrau	Mousiqui Hazrat Amir Khusrau, Ustad Chand Khan
T.H.M.I.	The History of Musical Instruments, Curt Sachs
C.M.I.	Classical Musical Instruments, Suneera Kasliwal
Bharat. Sang. Ka It.	Bharatiya Sangita Ka Itihas, Dr. Jogendra S. Bawra
Mus. Instr.	Musical Instruments, B.C. Deva
C.O.H.M.	The Concise Oxford History of Music, Gerald Abraham.
A.M.	Sitar and Sarod in the 18th and 19th centuries, Allyn Miner.
S.I.N.I.	String Instruments of North India, Vol. I, Sharmishta Ghosh
M.I.W.	Musical Instruments of the World, by Carl Engel
H.D.I.M.	Historical Development of Indian Music, by Swami Prajnanananda.
Saundarya Shastra	Bhartiya Shastriya Sangita Aivam Saundarya Shastra, Dr. Anupam Mahajan
M.S.P.	Music and Song in Persia, Lloyd C. Miller

Transliteration and Corrections

1. In this book the words from Persian, Arabic, Turkish etc. have not been written either in capital letters or in italics. The names of Ragas of Hindustani music and the names of Maqam and Dastgah of the music of the Persio-Arabian Region have been written with the first letter in Capital.
2. Words which have stretched vowel sounds of a, e, i, o and u, in the words of Hindi, Sanskrit and the languages of the Persio-Arabian Region, have sometimes been written as aa or ee; but at other places they are written with a single vowel. *e.g.* Sangita and Sangeet, Vina and Veena.
3. The grammatical indicators for extension of the vowel sound have not been indicated in the words of the music of the Persio-Arabian Region and Hindustani music, *e.g.* Risāla fi'l mūsīqī has been written as Risala fi'l musiqi. Another example is Sārangdeva which has been written as Sarangdeva.
4. There may be two or more spellings for one word at different places in the book; *e.g.* Qaul, Qual, and Qawl, Carnataka and Karnataka, Sudha and Shuḍha. The reason for this is that different books differ in their spellings of the same word.

Introduction

In this book, an attempt has been made to compare the music of the Persio-Arabian Region with Hindustani Music. In order to do this, it was necessary to go into the historical background of the two regions and discover the geographical, political, religious, social and other factors that influenced and made these two systems comparable.

Let us first take a look at the Arabic world that existed at the dawn of the Islamic era. "When the revelations of Muhammad flashed on the world in the seventh century of the Christian era, a message was delivered which could not be confined to the Hijaz, the cradle of Islam. As a result, within three quarters of a century, the banner of the Prophet was planted eastward at the extremities of Transoxiana,[1] southward by the banks of the Indus, northward to the shores of the Black Sea and westward on the slopes of the Pyrenees."[2] From Samarkand (now Uzbekistan in Central Asia) in the East to Cordoba (Spain) in the West, the Arabian Empire encompassed within its fold the wealth, splendour and grandeur of their courts, the erudition of their centres of science and literature, and its rulers were inspired to new artistic life and further development in the field of art and music.

In this background it was inevitable that what was once purely Arabian became influenced by other cultures and in fact was enriched by it. Arabic music is a broad, macro concept, encompassing in its fold the music of the various cultures and communities that came in its contact from the seventh century to the thirteenth century.

In the light of the discussions above we have to state that in the title of this book, the term 'Persio-Arabian Music' refers to the music of all the regions and nationalities of the Middle East that had come within its fold; this area with its inter-oriental character, which 'much too carelessly, we call Arabian',[3] is referred to as the 'Persio-Arabian Region'.

"Islamic music was born and cradled in Arabia; yet under Persian, Syrian and Greek tutelage, it became a universal art."[4] If we look back upon the history of music of the Middle East, we note that it has a direct connection to a series of successive political centres that existed in the Islamic world. These were the Hijaj Region, (in what is now Saudi Arabia), Damascus (Syria), Baghdad (in what is now Iraq), Cordoba (Spain), Istanbul (Turkey), and Isfahan (in what is now Iran). Artists and scholars from these centres contributed towards the music as a whole. However it is convenient to separate three major traditions, Arabic, Turkish and Persian, which have combined to give us the music that is prevalent in countries of the Persio-Arabian Region. Moreover, we cannot ignore the cultural contribution of Afghanistan, Central Asia and the Caucasus.[5]

The music of the Persio-Arabian Region consists of folk music, classical concert music and Muslim religious music. The rich repertoire of folk music can be traced back to the Middle Ages; the practice of classical concert was till the 20th century supported by royal and imperial courts; the third category of music prevalent in these countries is the Muslim religious music, which includes the cantillation of the sacred book the Koran and the call to prayer by the muezzin from the mosques, called Adhhan. Here, we must also mention about the music of the Sufi branch of Islam; this was secular music with sacred overtones in which music was used as a symbolic seeking of union with God by mystic poets and musicians of the Sufi sect.

The diverse influences, mainly Persian, Syrian, Turkish, Spanish and Central Asian that blended homogeneously with the core Arabic elements of music and culture made up the music of the Persio-Arabian Region or the Middle East. Though the individual countries of this Region have now developed their own political independent identities, their geographical proximity and common religious and political past bound them into a common cultural entity and the focus of the book is to compare its music with that of Hindustani Music.

Now we shall look at those factors and events in the history of Hindustani music, which allowed penetration of Islamic faith and

Arabo-Persian influence into the subcontinent; this resulted in the intermingling of the incoming music with the indigenous.

In the history of India major migrations and movements of invaders into the country was possible because of the passes and valleys in the North West mountains and hills. These migrations and historic invasions were of the Vedic Aryans (2nd millennium B.C.), Alexander the Great (327-324 B.C.), Mahmud Ghaznavi (died 1030 A.D.), Muhammad Gori (1193-1205 A.D.), Ibrahim Lodi (1414-1526 A.D.), the Mughal King Babur (1526-1556 A.D.) and Nadir Shah (1739 A.D.). By the 10th, 11th century groups from Afghanistan and Turkistan brought Islam to the subcontinent, and by the 13th and 14th centuries the Sultanate of Delhi had established, through their conquests, the pattern of religious distribution which prevails to this day. Throughout the Indo-Gangetic plain, the ruling class was predominantly Muslim, who ruled over a population comprising of Hindus and Muslims (who were often converts). As early as the 14th century, the Tughlak Sultans of Delhi established Muslim rule in South India; however there were large areas, such as centres like Tanjore and Travancore which never came under Muslim Rule. This explains why North India was more influenced by Muslim culture and art than South India.

Till the period of the reigns of Mahmud Ghaznavi (died 1030 A.D.) and Muhammad Ghori (1193-1205 A.D.), the influence of the incoming culture of the Afghans and Turks was limited to the Punjab; but by the 13th and 14th centuries, almost the whole sub-continent, especially the North was affected by the culture, language and religion of the ruling class. This influence was in the spheres of literature, architecture and music. Thus the Medieval Period stands out in the history of Hindustani music, as it marks the beginning of Muslim rule in India.

According to Acharya Brihaspati, the Muslim rulers were lovers of art and music and gave patronage to musicians attached to their courts; they were specifically interested in the music being popularized by the Sufi saints of the time. The foremost of all Sufi saints in India, who was also a musician, was Hazrat Moinuddin Chishti (died 1235 A.D.). A prominent disciple of his was Muhammad Ghori (1193-1205 A.D.). Further, the ruler Kutubuddin Aibak (1206-1210 A.D.), was a devotee of Sufi Sheikh Kutubuddin Bakhtiar Kaki; during his reign Qawwali singing was encouraged.

Hindustani Music, however, received its greatest impetus during the reign of Allah-ud-din Khilji, (1295-1316 A.D.), whose immense love and patronage of music has been described by the famous historian Ziauddin Barni in 'Taarikhe Fhirozshahi'. Music gatherings of Sufi musicians were held in which experts from all over India participated. He had in his court, the well known scholar and musician Amir Khusrau (1253-1324 A.D.); who also happened to be a solider and statesman. Amir Khusrau was equally proficient in Indian music as he was in Arabo-Persian music. He introduced many Persian Ragas into the Indian Raga system; and by blending them with the Indian Ragas, he formed new Ragas. Some of these are still sung to this day. There is no way to confirm, however, whether the structure of the Ragas during Amir Khusrau's time was the same as it is in modern times. Some of the Ragas which were formed due to the intermingling of Persian and Indian Ragas were Ragas Yaman, Zilaf, Sazgiri, Sarparda, etc. He also helped to introduce and popularize certain Forms of Sufi classical music like Qawwali, Qual, Gazal, Naqsh, Gul and Baseet. The Qawwali performing style could be compared to a form called Nauba, performed in the Turkish, Persian and Arabic speaking regions of the Middle East; this has been mentioned in al-Asfahani's (died 967 A.D.) book Kitab-al-Aghani. This Nauba performing style is popular even today. Therefore Amir Khusrau may not have invented this style, as is opined according to some, but merely introduced it into the Hindustani music genres being sung in those days.

Here we highlight a very important development in the music pertaining to the Medieval period; which is that the two systems of music had started blending and a synthesis was taking place between the Persio-Arabian Music and the existing Indian music. During the reign of Mansingh Tomar of Gwalior (1486-1516 A.D.), Muslim influence had begun to prevail on many aspects of music. A manuscript called Manakutuhala was written; this was a compilation of the discussions and deliberations on music held at the court of Raja Mansingh Tomar of Gwalior, where many famed scholars had been invited. In 1662-1663 A.D., Faqirullah, a statesman musician who lived during Shah-Jahan's and Aurangzeb's period, translated this manuscript into Persian, called Tarjuma-i-Manakutuhala and wrote an additional commentary called Risala-i-Ragadarpana. It is from this treatise, that we get a very good glimpse of the blending of the two systems of music, the incoming and the indigenous.

The Persio-Arabians brought instruments like the Rabab, Tamburchi, Duff and Surnay and these instruments were being played alongside the Bin (Veena) and the Pakhawaj of the indigenous music system. The Qawwals and Kalawants had an equal share of the platform. Some scholars and musicians from Central Asia and Persia, such as Sharqi and Mir Amad Herati, are mentioned by Faqirullah, as some of the talented artists, who came and adapted to playing the local melodies as well as Persian. The Tambura had adapted itself to a structural form which was conducive to Indian music. The same was the case with Rabab, which was being adapted to Indian conditions by Mian Tansen.

The merging of the Raga with the melodic mode Maqam of the Persio-Arabian Region had an echo in the work of the illustrious Sanskrit writer Pundarika Vithala (1599 A.D.), who in his Raga Manjari refers to Parads as Persian airs, which were full of 'gamaks' (embellishment). The same Parads have also been equated with Indian Ragas such as:

- Rahavi with Devagandhara
- Nishapur with Kanhara and
- Mahur with Saranga etc.

Faqirullah himself has mentioned about some Indian Ragas which were blended with the Persian Ragas to make new melodies; *e.g.* Purbi, Gauri and Syama melodically correspond with Farodast (Persian Farudasht). It is significant to note here, that while as this blending and amalgamation of the Indian with Arabo-Persian melodies has been recorded in treatises, as mentioned aforesaid, it is very difficult to determine what was at that time the actual structure and note formation of each of these melodies, whether Indian or of the Persio-Arabian Region.

The contribution of the Mughals towards the development of music, was one of recognition, appreciation, patronage; a favourable atmosphere existed for the blending of the two systems. During the reign of Akbar and Jehangir at Agra and then during Shahjahan's reign at Delhi, the assemblage of artists included Gwaliaris, whose dialect was Gwaliari. They met with an equally developed Dehlavi, with Persian as their language. Against the

Dhrupad, nurtured in the Brijbhasha at the court of Gwalior and Delhi, the Qawwali, Ghazal and Lok Gita was encouraged by the Sufi saints.. The popularity and charm of Indian music was such that it "brought together in its fold, Hindus and Muslims, Sufis and Ulema, Saints and Sultans.....men and women from different castes and social statuses. Music, therefore functioned not only as an esoteric art, or a source of entertainment, but also as a powerful instrument of cultural integration and social harmony".[6] It should be mentioned here that while the process of absorption and blending of the two systems was going on, the basic tenets and roots of Hindustani music remained intact. In fact the Islamic Sufi music was as popular as the Bhakti revival movement of the Hindus.

To sum up, the first point that has been highlighted is, that the music of the Persio-Arabian Region was the product of assimilation of diverse influences and traditions such as those of Persian, Turkish, Arabic, Spanish, Central Asian and Afghanistani. This diversity was because of the geographical and political spread of the Arabian Region, from the 7th century to the 13th century A.D., during the Abbasid rule. This was the Golden Age of music and fine arts, under the mighty Arabian Empire, which "provided a germinal model of Arab music on which future developments, both in the Arab world and in many parts of Asia and Africa, were to be based."[7] The unifying factors or traits of the music of the Arabian Region were the modality of the melodic modes, rhythms, instruments, emotions or Tasir of the modes, embellishment, and Forms or performing style. These common traits can be seen in the presentation style of the different regions: Iraqi Maqam, Turkish Taqsim, Irani Avaz, and the Moroccon Nauba.

The second point that emerges, in view of what has been said before, is that with the Mohemmedan invasions into the sub-continent of India, from the 11th century to the 14th, 15th century, a blending of music and art forms ensued that spawned a period from the 13th century to the 18th century.

As the two music systems intermingled, a clear and distinct realization emerged that the basic concepts of the music of the Persio-Arabian Region and Hindustani music have irrefutable similarities and comparable traits. In fact it is very interesting to note that the areas in which we find these comparisons (*i.e.* in melodic modes, instruments, rhythm, forms, emotions or Tasir, and embellishment) are also the unifying traits within the Persio-

Arabian music, which have made a homogeneous whole of its different components.

OBJECTIVE, RATIONALE AND SCOPE

The objective of this book is to find out the similarities and parallel concepts, between the music of the Persio-Arabian Region and Hindustani Music. These comparisons would be in the area of the Melodic Modes, which are called Maqam in Arabic, also Makam in Turkish, Dastgah and their constituent Gushe in Persian, Mugam in the Caucasus (new Kavkaz and the Bolshoi Mountain Area, in the erstwhile U.S.S.R.) and Shashmaqam in Soviet Uzbekistan. These have similarities with the Indian counterpart, Raga. A special emphasis has been laid on the blending of the two systems of melodic modes of the Persio-Arabian Region and India, during the Medieval period. Besides the melodic mode, an attempt has made to find counterparts in Hindustani Music of equally important concepts of Music of the Persio-Arabian Region like Rhythm, Instruments, Forms, emotive effects of Music like Tasir and embellishments in singing.

Though information was available from many sources on the topic, this had not been systematically compiled in one single work till now. More so, the detailed discussion and comparisons between the two systems of the Arabian Region and Hindustani Music, on Rhythm, Instruments, Forms, as undertaken here, have not been carried out before in one single Research work, according to the information available till now. This work is an humble attempt to address this gap in research material.

SOURCE MATERIAL AND LITERARY SURVEY

Some prominent musicians, scholars and historians have contributed towards the study of the synthesis between the Music of the Persio-Arabian Region and Hindustani Music, in the medieval period in India; these are Faqirullah (Raga Darpana-1662), Amir Khusrau (14th century), Pundarika Vithala (Raga Manjari – 1599 A.D.), Mirza Khan (Tohfat-ul-Hind-1645-1646 A.D.), Mohammed Karam Imam (Madan-ul-Musiqi – middle of 19th century), Ustad Chand Khan (Mousiqui Hazrat Amir Khusrau – 1978) and Pandit V.N. Bhatkhande (20th century). Among the

Western authors, from whom source material has been taken, one of the most prominent is Dr. H.G. Farmer, the scholar on Arabian music. Besides him, authors like Allyn Miner and Curt Sachs (History of Musical Instruments), William Jones, N.A. Williard, Swami Prajnananand, S.M. Tagore, Acharya Brihaspati, Prof. Shahab Sarmadee, Prof. Najma Ahmad, and other eminent Indian and foreign scholars have also provided information in their respective works, on the topic proposed for study. Several dictionaries and encyclopaedias were also very helpful in providing source material. Various programmes and lecture-cum-demonstrations on Irani Sufi Classical Music and Sufi Indian Music, attended by me, enabled me to gather information on instruments like the Rabab and Santoor, as well as on Ragas like Zila of Persio-Arabian origin, played by the Rabab maestro Gulfam Ahmad. I could interview a few Irani musicians, on the occasion of these concerts.

Professor Mohammad Amin, an eminent scholar of History, in a telephonic interview, provided me with the correct perspective on the various influences which contributed towards shaping the traditions and culture of the Persio-Arabian Region.

This book has been divided into eight chapters. The first chapter describes the history of the music of the Persio-Arabian Region as well as that of Hindustani Music. The first part of the chapter deals with the history of the Persio-Arabian Region. Here, emphasis is on the diverse cultures and influences to which this Region was exposed due to its contact with the Persians, the Greeks, the Turks and finally the Europeans. The Arabic conquest of Persia in the 7th century brought not only exposure to Persian influences, but also to the Greek and Mesopotamian culture which had already been imbibed by the Persians. From the 8th to the 15th centuries, Spain was under Arabian rule, which brought the Arabian culture into contact with the West. The occupation of Egypt by France (1798-1801 A.D.) further brought Western notation and instruments to the Arabian Region. The Turkish supremacy over Syria, Palestine, Iraq, the coasts of Arabia and much of North Africa (1517-1917 A.D.) introduced many new forms of presentation, modes – both melodic and rhythmic, and new instruments to the music of the Arabian Region.

These diverse influences merged into a homogeneous whole; the assimilation and contact with cultures bringing into focus a very important realization that along with the diversity, the unifying traits of the music of the Persio-Arabian Region were the same. These are, a common modality in the melodic modes, common modal rhythms, similarity of ornamentation, common emotive elements or Tasir and a basic striking similarity in the instruments. The historical events are divided into different periods of history.

The second part of the first chapter, is on the history of Hindustani Music. Here, there is a division into the three major periods, the ancient, medieval and modern. This book deals with the comparison of the various concepts of the music of the Persio Arabian Region with that of Hindustani music. So, emphasis in this chapter has been given to the various processes of blending and intermingling of the two systems that took place in the medieval period. The music that came with the Mohammedans from the 11th century to the 14th, 15th centuries got imbibed and absorbed, giving rise to an enriched and developed music and culture. The basic tenets and principles of Hindustani music remained intact.

The second chapter is on the melodic modes of the Persio-Arabian Region, which describes the common history of the modes called Maqam till the 15th century, after which the modes of Iran were reconstituted and called the Dastgah. These were found to be similar and comparable to the Indian melodic mode, Raga.

As a parallel to the Maqam or Dastgah of the Persio-Arabian Region, the Hindustani melodic mode, Raga has been discussed in the third chapter, with a sub-chapter on classification of Ragas. In the 14th, 15th century, the Arabian Maqam system was also treated as a parallel concept to the Mela That classification system of Indian music.

The fourth chapter on Blending of the Modes is the most significant chapter of the book; as it brings into focus how the two systems of music, that of the Persio-Arabic Region and India actually blended and amalgamated after the 13th century. Various musicians and scholars, like Amir Khusrau, Faqirullah, Pundarika Vithala etc. contributed to the process.

The fifth chapter compares the rhythmic modes of the Persio-Arabian Region with those of Indian music, and it is found that a strong similarity exists.

The chapter on instruments, which is the sixth chapter of this work is the most enlightening, as it reveals a very close similarity and commonality of traits between the two systems of musical instruments of the Persio Arabian Region and Hindustani Music. It reveals that some historical movements of people and cultures would have taken place in ancient times, as similar instruments have been found in the two regions from ancient times.

The understanding of the music of the Persio-Arabian Region and Hindustani music would be incomplete without analyzing their emotive elements, the Tasir of the music of the Arabian Region and the concept of Rasa 'sidhantha' (principle) in Hindustani Music. This is the subject matter of the seventh chapter.

The eighth chapter deals with the following:

1. Forms or performing styles – many common forms are found in the two systems of music, like the Naubat.
2. Ornamentation: the aesthetic elements of both systems of music are enhanced by embellishments such as 'jawaid' in Arabian music, 'tahrir' in Persian music and the 'gamak' in Hindustani music.
3. Folk styles and presentations have been compared between the two systems of music and have been found to be comparable and similar.

REFERENCES

1. Transoxiana: in Central Asia.
2. N.O.H.M., p. 421.
3. T.H.M.I., p. 244.
4. N.O.H.M., p. 432, 433.
5. Caucasus: now the Bol'shoy Kavkaz Mountains-Between the Black Sea and the Caspian Sea in erstwhile USSR.
6. Hind. Music, p. 10.
7. The Genius...., p. 142.

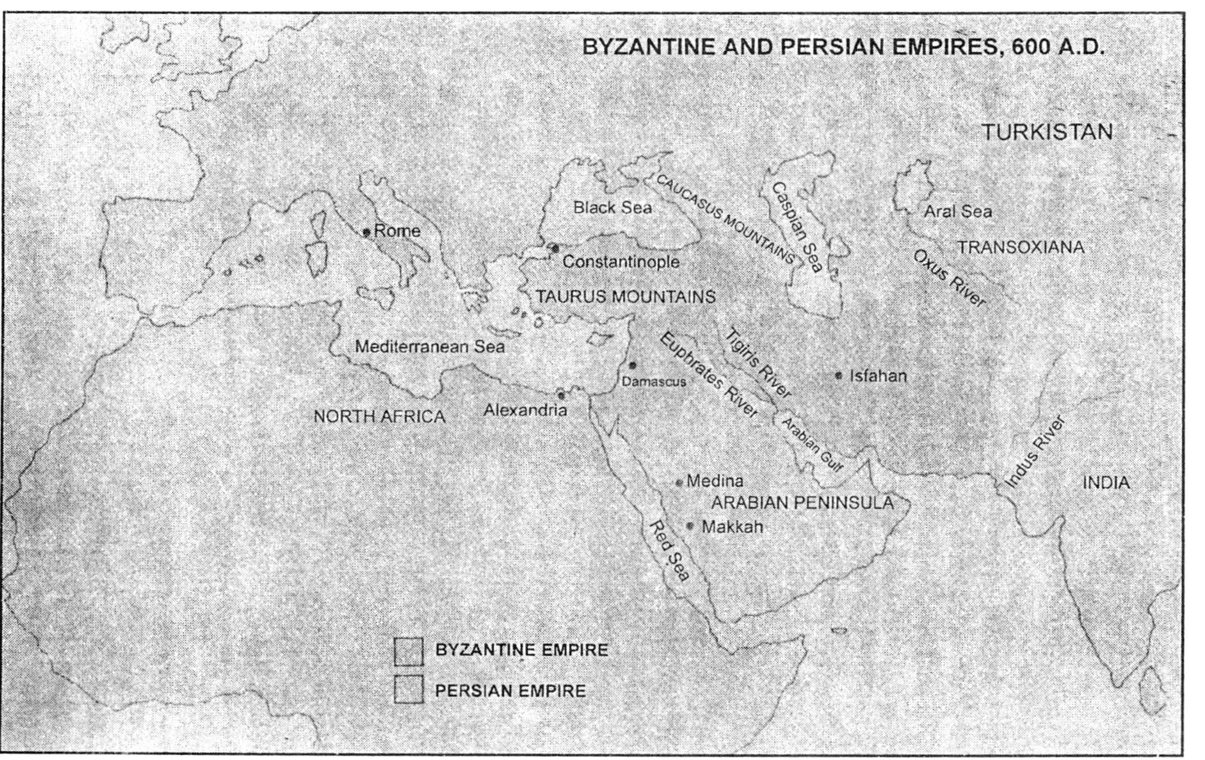
BYZANTINE AND PERSIAN EMPIRES, 600 A.D.
TURKISTAN
Black Sea
CAUCASUS MOUNTAINS
Caspian Sea
Aral Sea
Rome
TRANSOXIANA
Constantinople
Oxus River
TAURUS MOUNTAINS
Tigiris River
Mediterranean Sea
Euphrates River
Isfahan
Damascus
NORTH AFRICA
Alexandria
Arabian Gulf
Indus River
Medina
INDIA
ARABIAN PENINSULA
Makkah
Red Sea
BYZANTINE EMPIRE
PERSIAN EMPIRE

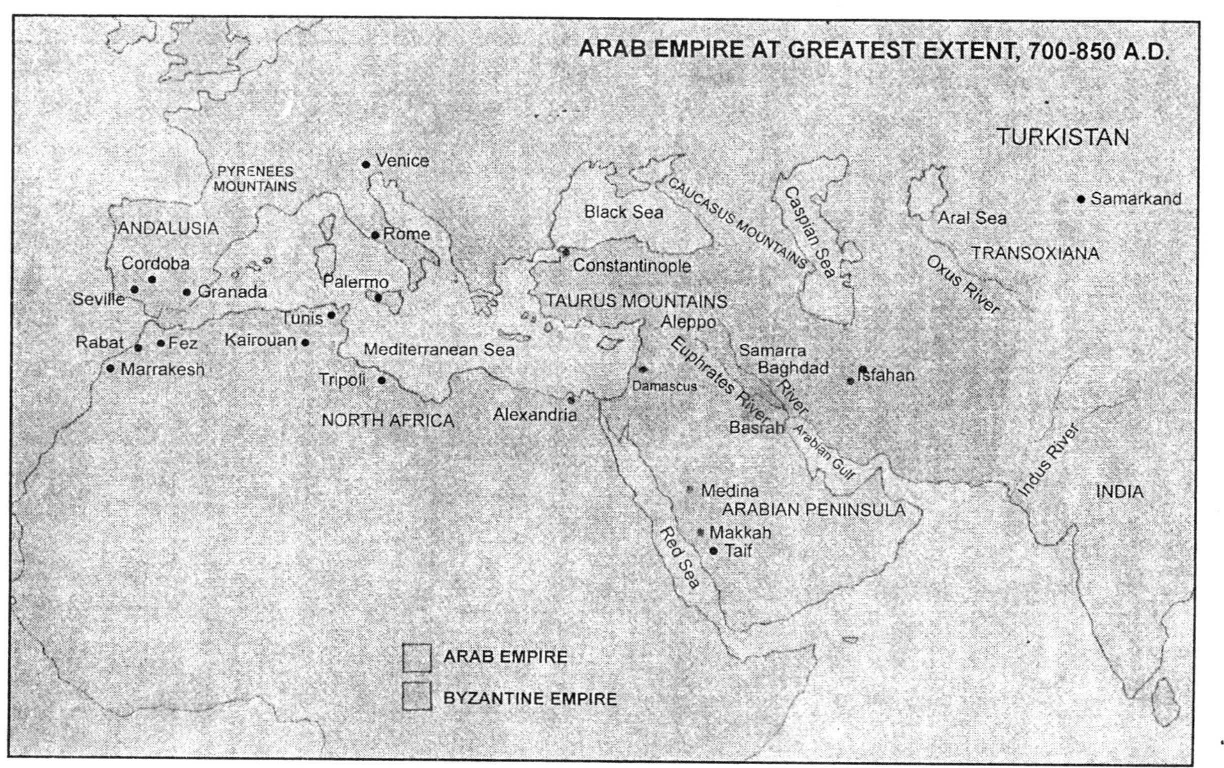
ARAB EMPIRE AT GREATEST EXTENT, 700-850 A.D.
TURKISTAN
PYRENEES MOUNTAINS
Venice
Black Sea
CAUCASUS MOUNTAINS
Caspian Sea
Aral Sea
Samarkand
ANDALUSIA
Rome
TRANSOXIANA
Cordoba
Seville
Granada
Constantinople
Palermo
Oxus River
TAURUS MOUNTAINS
Tunis
Aleppo
Rabat
Fez
Kairouan
Mediterranean Sea
Samarra
Marrakesh
Baghdad
Isfahan
Tripoli
Damascus
Euphrates River
River
NORTH AFRICA
Alexandria
Basrah
Arabian Gulf
Indus River
Medina
INDIA
ARABIAN PENINSULA
Makkah
Red Sea
Taif
ARAB EMPIRE
BYZANTINE EMPIRE

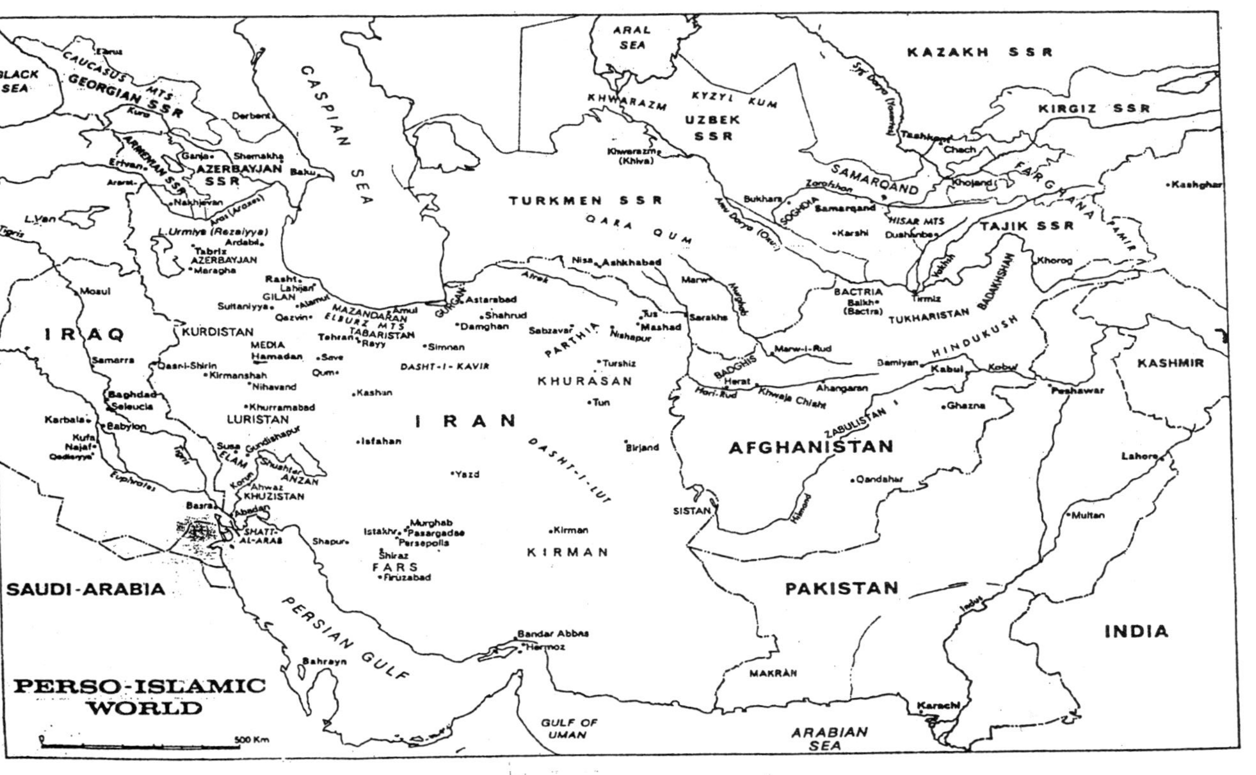

PERSO-ISLAMIC WORLD

1

History and Development of the Music of the Persio-Arabian Region and Hindustani Music

MUSIC OF THE PERSIO-ARABIAN REGION

The countries of the Persio-Arabian Region are located in a geographical area which covers the near and Middle East and North Africa, whose musical culture is dominated by the Islamic Arabic, Persian and Turkish speaking peoples and is made up of a single though heterogeneous system including liturgical, classical, folk and modern popular music. The peoples of Afghanistan, Soviet Central Asia and the Caucasus share in this system peripherally.[1] The Arabian (or Persian) Gulf now includes southern Iraq, Kuwait, the Hasa province of Saudi Arabia, Bahrain, Qatar and the United Arab Emirates.[2] However, in tracing the history and development of the music of the countries of the Persio-Arabian Region, we have to go back to a period when the Arabian influence 'spread over and conditioned a quarter of the then known world'.[3] After Prophet Muhammad's death 'his Arab followers overran the whole Mediterranean coast from the Bosphorus (Turkey) to the straits of Gibralter, conquered Spain'[4] and threatened the Byzantine Emperors.

The modern Arab world consisting of nation-states-that did not exist before the First World War-emerged only about eighty years ago from the ruins of the Ottoman Empire (1517-1917 A.D.). But the countries of the Persio-Arabian Region had a past, which came into prominence in the 7th and 8th centuries, with the Arab conquest of the ancient world. It is this past, reflected in the identity, culture and music of the people, which we have to study, in order to know the historical background of the music of the Persio-Arabian Region. By the 8th or 9th century A.D., the then Arab world 'held sway from the Pyrenees on the border of France to the Pamirs in Central Asia. Spain, North Africa, Egypt, the Byzantine territory south of the Taurus Mountains (Turkey), and the Persian Empire in the East were welded together into an imperial realm that rivalled that of Rome at its peak.'[5]

Assimilation and Contact with Cultures

If we look back upon the history of Arabic Music, we note that it has a direct connection to a series of successive political centres that existed in the Islamic world. These were the Hijaj Region in what is now Saudia Arabia, Damascus in Syria, Baghdad in Iraq, Cordoba in Spain, Istanbul in Turkey and Isfahan in Persia. Artists and scholars from these regions contributed towards the music as a whole; however, it is convenient to separate three major traditions, Arabic, Turkish and Persian, which have combined to give us the music that is prevalent in countries of the Persio-Arabian Region. As we have said before, we cannot ignore areas in Afghanistan, Central Asia and the Caucasus (between the Black Sea and the Caspian Sea) which also contribute to the music tradition of this region.[6]

The common political history of the Near and Middle East (Persio-Arabian Region) brings about similarities between the Arab, Persian and Turkish art music; these are the three major influences in the music of this area. Though, now they are considered distinct from each other politically and in their individual development of their art; as the historical development of the area was marked by immense reciprocal influences, there is much in common in nomenclature, theory, performance practice, modal structure and instruments used.[7] The common Islamic influence has given this region common modal systems, forms and instruments. The music, whether its simple folk music or any other variety has a history with melodic rules and principles, and is dominated by 'theory and conceptualization.'[8] An important point must be mentioned here, that within the Persio-Arabian Region, two major traditions can be distinguished; that of the Eastern Arab world (principally Egypt, Lebanon, Syria and Iraq); and that of the western (Morocco, Algeria, Tunisia). "Both may be said to derive ultimately from the court music that evolved during the Umayyad and early Abbasid periods (7th to 9th centuries), when the Persian influence had already made itself felt. But the North African tradition, although not completely isolated, was less exposed to the subsequent waves of Persian, and later, Turkish influence that had a significant impact in the east, and it is often considered to represent a survival of the Andalusian music of Moorish Spain".[9]

Due to the interrelationship of the various classical music systems of the Region, similar or identical modal identities may have different names in different Regions.[10]

Till now we have talked about the unifying geographical, political and cultural proximity of the various areas of the Persio-Arabian Region, which were once under the Arabian Empire at its peak in the 9th and 10th century (lasted till 1258 A.D.). In fact, even when the Arabian Empire under the Abbasids (750-1258 A.D.) was breaking up, there was seen to be a fusion of the 'common art music idiom over most of the eastern Arab world (but not North Africa and Spain, which must be presumed to have already begun to develop, along slightly different lines)',[11] Persia and some of the major Islamic cultural centers in Central Asia. This fusion included areas such as mode, form and instruments and existed till the 15th century. These areas continued to have a common musical background under the Ottoman Empire (1517-1917 A.D.) when the centre of power shifted to Turkey, as the Arab and Turkish musical systems overlapped considerably. However, with the fall of the Ottoman Empire in 1917, different countries, regions emerged as separate political identities, but continued to have a common cultural and musical background, especially in the areas of modal structure, form and instruments. These were Syria, Iraq, Iran (Persia), Turkey, Jordan, Palestine, Egypt, Libya, Arabian or Persian Gulf (which consists of the present southern Iraq, Kuwait, the Hasa province of Saudi Arabia, Bahrain, Qatar and the United Arab Emirates),[12] Central Asia and Lebanon. In this book, we refer to this area as the Persio-Arabian Region.

Having discussed the commonality of the different geographical areas of the countries of the Persio-Arabian Region, and the assimilation of cultures which resulted, due to a common

Islamic religion, and historical and political reasons, we shall now discuss the different periods of the History of the Region. The contact with different cultures, which got assimilated, will be discussed as we proceed.

Let us briefly refer to the ancient period in History, which throws light on the History of the Persio-Arabian Region and India, the two areas under our study.

ANCIENT PERIOD

As the Aryans or Indo-European settlers came down from Central Asia and settled down in what is now West Asia, Afghanistan and the Indian Sub-continent (2,000 B.C. and 1,000 B.C.), there were constant cultural interchanges and links between the peoples of the area.[13] Mohammad Bagher[14] suggests the idea that 'cultures of early Persia and the Indian sub-continent were continually linked from early times'. As these Aryan tribes moved into the southern part of Persia, called Fars, they came into contact with cultures of the Assyrians and Elamites and other civilizations of Mesopotamia, resulting in cultural and musical interchange.[15]

From the 3rd millennium B.C., not only Syria and Phoenicia, but much of Arabia was under the influence of Mesopotamian culture. This was once a trading centre of the world and the Arabs of the Arabian peninsula "were the inheritors and conservators of much of the great Mesopotamian culture of the past."[16] Here, we may stress on the fact that the rich Mesopotamian culture was a great influence on the then known Arabian world.

PRE-ISLAMIC PERIOD

The Arab world was a centre of civilization from ancient times. In the pre-Islamic period, references to Arabian music mention more about the kind of genre (style or form) that were prevalent. The most ancient form that was sung was the Huda or the caravan song.[17] The Bedouins sang their simple caravan song (huda) to liven their long journeys through the desert. Its rhythm corresponded to the movement of the camel's feet, and this Bedouin music inspired musicians and poets, throughout the ages. This Bedouin music was a prototype of all Arabic metres, and was similar to the music of various pastoral and agricultural tribes in Arabia; it also inspired poets and musicians throughout the ages. The first traceable reference to Arabian music can be seen, in a seventh century B.C. Assyrian inscription which shows the Arab prisoners singing while they worked. There were two types of music – the cult music, where deities were worshipped with hymns and the court or secular music (household music) where singing girls (qaynat), attached to taverns and encampments sang songs of rhythm, vitality and ornate melody.[18]

In poetry the qayna has been portrayed as playing instruments like the lute (Kiran muwattar), and shawm (mizṃar) or frame drum (daff).[19] The male musician (mughanni) and instrumentalist (alati) were not so common.

According to Swami Prajnananand, Mr. Christianowitch says, that in the early days, the music of the Arabs, 'was a sort of recitative with light refrain'[20]. The presence of poetic rhythm in Arabian music was its chief beauty.

A wider category of song form, the 'Ghina', had sub-categories such as the Nasb, the Sinad (characterized as heavy and ornate) and the Hazaj (characterized as 'light' and gay).[21] In Ukaz (now Saudi Arabia), the home of the fair, musicians and poets congregated to recite and sing the 'treasured poems', the Muallaqat.[22]

It would be pertinent here to mention the development of music in Persia separately during the Pre-Islamic days, when the Sasanian dynasty was ruling Persia (224-642 A.D.). Musical activity was flourishing and the Imperial court of Emperor Khosrow (590-628 A.D.) gave exalted status to musicians such as Ramtin, Bamshad, Nakisa, Azad, Sarkash and Barbad. Barbad is credited with devising a musical system consisting of seven royal modes (Khosrovani), 30 derivative modes (lahn) and 360 melodies (dastan), corresponding to the number of days in the week, month, and year of the Sasanian calendar. The exact nature of these modes is not known, but some of their names survive through the writings of Al-Kindi (d.c. 873) and Ibn Zayla (d.1048). The epic poem Khosrow va Shirin by Nezami (Arabic: Nizami; dc 1203), has also recorded the names of some of these modes. There is evidence of many instruments being used during this period, as can be seen from the Rock carvings at Taq-e-Bostan. These are Chang (angular harp played with sound chest uppermost), the Vin (angular harp played with sound chest lower most), the Sorna (shawm), the Barbat, and the Tanbur.[23]

Rock Carvings, Taq-e-Bostan, Iran (Sasanian Period)-224-642A.D.
Musicians in a Boat Playing Chang (Angular Harp)

Persian traditional music had already developed by the Achaemenian period (559-331 B.C.) and was perfected during the later Sasanian era (224-642 A.D.). During the reign of Sasanian ruler Bahram Gur (421-439 A.D.), upto 1200 instrumentalists were invited to Persia from India. It could also be said, that the music of the Sasanian Period gave the foundation for the music that eventually spread to the Islamic world.[24]

During the first centuries of Islam, there was tension between the survival of pre-Islamic pattern of behaviour and the new Islamic norms of social and cultural behaviour. It was a period of considerable upheaval and change. Before the coming of Islam power had centred in Hijaz, particularly the cities of Mecca and Medina.[25]

In Western Arabia, music centered in two towns, in al-Hijaz, namely Ukaz and Mecca. Ukaz became the site of a fair, where 'treasured poems' were recited and sung; Mecca on the other hand became a centre of Arabian cults and a place of pilgrimage. It was here, that Prophet Muhammad, the founder of Islam was born (571-632 A.D.). As the singing girls lead the devotees to forbidden pleasures and pagan ways, secular music received a set back, in the initial period after the advent of Islam; however sacred music like reading the Koran, the call to prayer (adhdan) by the muezzin developed melodically.

The message of the Prophet could not be "confined to Hijaz, the cradle of Islam. As a result, within three quarters of a century, the banner of the Prophet was planted eastward at the extremities of Transoxiana (Central Asia), southward by the banks of the Indus, northward to the shores of the Black Sea, and westward on the slopes of the Pyrenees. Out of this newly won empire arose a civilization which dwindled that of much of the rest of the world into insignificance".[26]

ISLAMIC PERIOD

After the founding of the Umayyad Caliphate (661-750 A.D.), the power shifted to Syria (Damascus), leaving a void of political influence in the Hijaz, now west Saudi Arabia. Entertainment music, previously performed by the qayna (women musicians), was now performed by a group of effiminates called mukhannathun, who were of low social status. This association of music with patterns and attitudes of behaviour which were unacceptable to society, gradually led to it being disapproved or even condemned by the Muslim clergy. This may have been the reason why other type of musical activity also received grudging acceptance. As far as the Muslim clergy was concerned the cantillation of the Koran alone was acceptable.[27]

Persian Arabian Synthesis

The migration of the Arabs, in the 1st., 2nd century A.D. to Syria and Iraq (which retained its Semitic culture), during the Umayyad and Abbasid Caliphates started a process of blending of the culture of the Arabs with the Semitic and Persian cultures, as Iraq was under Persian cultural domination, ever since the 6th century B.C. Let us now dwell, for a while on the Persian influence on Arabian music.[28] The conquest of the Persian Empire by the Arabs began in 642 A.D. and much of the then Iran remained with the Muslim Empire for six centuries. The Arabs valued Persian music and culture, and there was intense exposure to Arab music from Persia and the former Byzantine provinces.[29] By the 7th century, the first male musician and instrumentalist came into the fore. He was a Persian by the name of Tuwais (d.710), who is claimed as the first male musician under Islam. He imitated Persian melodies, which could be heard from the captives who had been brought to Hijaz as slaves. The Persians and Arabians learnt and sang each other's music. The influence of Persian music on Arab practical art was considerable.[30]

According to Dr Farmer, the authority on Arabian music, "Persia helped Arabia with lots of the materials of music, and in favour of this statement, he has forwarded some proofs as:"[31]

- (*a*) "The prisoners, captured in the Persian war, were toiling as slaves on the public works at Al-Medina, and their national melodies began to attract considerable attention.'[32]
- (*b*) '.....the Persians have been claimed as the inventors of Iqa or rhythm by Iban Khirdadbih.'[33]
- (*c*) 'In 684, Abdallah Ibn-al-Zubair brought Persian workers to help in the construction of the Kaba. From these slaves Ibn Turaij borrowed the Persian lute (ud-farisi)'[34]
- (*d*) 'That the Arabs adopted Persian and Byzantine melodies is generally admitted.'[35]

Under the Umayyad Caliphs (661-750 A.D.) secular music

again received encouragement. Under them the Maghrib (the then Western Arab world) and Spain were conquered; and they were lovers of music, who maintained elaborate musical establishments at Damascus (Syria), where power had shifted. The Umayyads brought singing girls from Khorasan, and with them came the long necked Persian Tambur with two strings, on which they presented their vocal and instrumental musical abilities.[36] Vocal music was considered superior to instrumental music till the 10th century and singing solo with the lute was considered a special feature of the music of that time.

With the coming of social change, there were also developments in the musical system itself. The basis of the classical system was established under the Umayyads. The musicians of the 1st century of Islam were portrayed as innovators.[37] Two of the most famous early Umayyad musicians Ibn Misjah and Ibn Muhriz (both d.c.715) were supposed to have travelled through Persian and former Byzantium (areas under former Roman influence) territories and they absorbed and imbibed what they thought could be assimilated into their own traditional music.[38] According to Al-Isfahani's (897-967 A.D.), Kitab al-Aghani al-Kabir (Great Book of songs), it was Ibn Misjah (d.c.715), who first brought Persian song and its rhythmic accompaniment (darb) to Mecca.[39] An outstanding musician of his time, he was the first to codify the theory of Arabian music. "He chose from the scales (nagham) of the (until recently Byzantine–governed) Syrians, the most agreeable sounds, rejecting those which displeased him............ It was he who fixed the order of notes in Arab song and he was the first to make melodies from it."[40] Ibn Misjah may therefore be considered the father of Arabian classical music.

This was a period of transition when the essential character of the music was Arabic, but had the flexibility and capacity to absorb new elements, without compromising on the essential tradition.[41] A feature of art music at this time was the broad distinction between a more serious and 'heavy' style (thaqil) and a 'light' and gayer one (Khafif), the former enjoying more prestige and the latter, more popularity. This may have been a carry over of pre-Islamic days. There was also distancing of art music from folk music, and performances were more professional and artistic.[42]

While the development of musical practice during the Umayyad Period was influenced by Persian music, the classification of the modal system was effected by Byzantine models.[43] Some features of this system which consisted of eight modes are described by Ibn-al-Munajjim (d.912) in his Risala fi'l musiqi (Treatise on music: he uses the Greek word 'musiqi' and not the Arabic 'ghina' for music) and are based on the tuning of the lute in fourths.[44] Ibn al-Munajjim's treatise throws light on the fact that the Arab classical scale was the same as the Pythagorean scale of the Greeks. These modes were described in terms of the diatonic lute fretting to which their names relate. Each of these modes was classified according to its 'course' (majra) either with the middle finger (wusta) on the lute, giving the minor third, or with the third finger (binsir), giving the major third.[45] These finger modes dominated Arabian practical theory until the 11th century, when Persian ideas took a firmer hold on Islamic culture. The complicated melodic style of Arab music known as jawa'id, tahasin, zuwwaq originated from these modes.

The final formulation for this system was post – Umayyad. During the reign of the Abbasid Caliphs (750-847 A.D.), who came to power after overthrowing the Umayyads in 750 A.D., the centre of power shifted again from Syria (Damascus) eastward to Iraq (Baghdad).[46] The Abbasids made Baghdad the capital in 768 A.D. and they were great enthusiasts for music. The Byzantine as well as Persian influence infiltrated into Arab music to form a 'classical' style. The Abbasid ruler Harun-al-Rashid patronised not only Court music but also encouraged music among the general public. A form of music called the Nauba-Central Asian in origin – was adopted by Islamic music during the reign of the Abbasids.[47]

At this point in the History of Persio-Arabian Music, two groups emerged among the prominent musicians of the time; either supporting Arab cultural supremacy (defending tradition) or opposing it (thereby encouraging change and innovation). The chief upholder of the classical Arab heritage was Ishaq-al-Mawsili (d.849 A.D.) the son of Ibrahim al-Mawsili (742-804 A.D.), a teacher and composer. Ishaq was a scholar and poet and a great musician. The father and son were musicians during the time of Harun-al-Rashid, the Abbasid ruler of the time. The group encouraging Persian influence in the classical Arab style was headed by Ibrahim Ibn al-Mahdi [48] (779-839 A.D.), who happened to be the brother of Harun-al-Rashid, and had an extra-ordinary voice. His sister Princess 'Ulaiya was a noted singer and had a

Byzantine organ. During this time Caliph Al-Ma'mun, encouraged cultural contact with Byzantium. Byzantine scholars were invited to Baghdad and earlier Greek treatises of Aristotle and Plato, dating back to approx. 500 B.C., were translated into Arabic; and Arab musicians were familiar with Greek theories which leaned too much on mathematical applications like precise measurement of micro-intervals.[49] Ancient Arabian music was treated as a subsidiary under Mathematics. Students of Philosophy studied Music. Al Farabi was a recognized scholar in the field.

Perhaps because of these legendary musicians during the Abbasid period, this period has been termed the 'golden age' of Arab music.

Theorists

Between the 9th and 13th centuries, some two hundred books on music were written, and many theorists deserve mention. Ishaq al-Kindi (c.790-c.874) gives us valuable information about actual Arab music of this period. He advocates a fifth string for the fretted lute. He also describes a system of eight rhythmic modes quite foreign to the Greeks, and suggests nine letters for notes possible within the octave, but these were not actually notation for music.[50] Al Kindi utilized concepts derived from Greek theory, and his treatment of scale was expressed in terms of fretting of the lute. Al Kindi also focussed on correlation of number sets (*i.e.* numerology), and the four strings of the lute were related to the zodiac, the elements, the seasons and the humours.[51] Al Farabi (d.950 A.D.) and Ibn Sina (Avicenna) (980-1037 A.D.) also wrote extensively on music borrowing from Greek heritage, and stressed on the 'codification of various tetrachord types and the numerical analysis of their constituent intervals.' There was a concentration on theory for its own sake; at that time music was viewed as one of the mathematical sciences, and this emphasis on theory was an extension of the purely speculative side of music.[52] Al-Farabi used letters of the Arabic alphabet for the 15 notes corresponding to the Greek Perfect System. He also found corresponding names of Greek modes (aeolian, dorian etc.) in Arabic .

No Arabic music was written down even alphabetically before the 13th century, everything was transmitted orally and the proficiency of an artist lay in exhibiting the ornamental nature of the music prevalent then with all its trills and grace notes.[53]

Al Farabi describes Tumbur Baghdadi and Tumbur Khurasani as being two instruments whose scales appeared to be different from that of the Ud. The Tumbur Khorasani scale included neutral intervals, and had steps of limma, limma and comma, a model that was taken up and extended in the 13th century. Of all the theorists of this period, Al-Farabi, in his Kitab al-Musiqi al-Kabir is the most profound and wide ranging in his scope of subjects.[54]

It may be noted that Arabic and Persian music became influenced by Greek and Byzantine music, and its chief quality was profusion of ornamentation. Gradually the Abbasid Caliphate became divided. In 909 A.D. a rival Fatimid Caliphate was established in North Africa (capital at Cairo) and in 929 A.D. another one was established in Spain. However, even now the Caliph of Baghdad remained the spiritual head of the Islamic world and the music of the Baghdad Caliphate retained its position of prestige till its fall in 1258 A.D. to the Mongols.[55] Thus ended an era of one of the great and splendid civilizations of history. Egypt and Syria by virtue of the Arabic language continued to remain the pivot of the intellectual life of Islam.[56]

As the Caliphate at Baghdad was weakening, the Saljuqs from Turkistan became virtual masters of the Caliphate, and a fresh cultural influence began to show itself in Persia, Syria and Mesopotamia. The Ayybid Sultans (1169 A.D.) and Momluk Turks (1252-1517 A.D.) brought with them a Turkomanian influence which was reflected in the fine arts in general. They maintained elaborate court music and military bands till the Ottoman Turks conquered Egypt in 1517 A.D.[57].

The early 11th century presents a transitional stage in the History of development of music of the countries of the Persio-Arabian Region. The early diatonic system still survived but the transition was taking place (incorporating elements from varied sources) to a more complex, more varied system described by Arab and Persian theorists of the 13th century onwards.[58]

We get further information about theory and instruments in Persia from the treatise Al-Shifa (The cure) of Ibn Sina (Avicenna) (980-1037 A.D.).[59] Ibn Sina's writings discussed not only 'the theory of music but also the ancient concept of ethos (ta'thir), the therapeutic effects of music, and the notion of harmonic dissonance and consonance.' Ibn Sina named the 12 primary modes of his time; these were Rahawi, Husayni, Rast, Busalik, Zankula, Ushshaq, Hijazi, Iraq, Isfahan, Nawa, Buzurk, Mukhalif. These modes are still found in modern Persian art music, but they do not necessarily have the same melodic form as they had in Ibn Sina's time.[60] As we can see, these names were non-technical; Ushshaq meant passion; Nawa was melody or sound; Iraq, Isfahan were names of places. We come to know from Ibn Sina's treatise that as a result of foreign contacts, new instruments were also included, and purely instrumental music was gaining importance in the Islamic world. At this time the Seljuk Turks brought the Kemancha, a one stringed instrument from Central Asia to Persia and Syria.[61]

Contribution of Persian Theorists

Here we may mention an important factor about Islamic music and its development. The contribution to Islamic music by Persian musicians is sometimes credited to Arab scholars, as these Persian scholars bore Arabic names and wrote in Arabic, the lingua franca of the time. During the Abbasid period (750-1258 A.D.), the seat of the Caliphate having shifted to Baghdad, former Persian territory, Persian musicians and scholars played an important role in shaping the development of music in the Persio-Arabian Region. Among the Persian musicians of fame, we have already discussed are, Ibrahim al-Mawsili, Ishaq al-Mawsili, Al-Farabi and Ibn Sina. Among the later musicians of the 13th century, are Safi al-Din (d.1294) and Qutb al-Din (d.1312), a pupil of Safi al-Din.[62] The last great theorist of this era was Abd-al-Qadir (d. 1436 A.D.) whose Jami al-Alham (Compiler of melodies) contains the earliest notations of Persian music which have survived.

With the Safavid dynasty (1501-1722 A.D.) coming to power in Persia, its destiny moved in a different direction from that of the other Islamic countries of the Persio-Arabian Region. As the Safavids were Shiites and the attitude of the religious leaders towards music was hostile, music suffered in Persia from the 16th century to the 20th century.[63]

Till the 20th century, Persian music like Arabo-Turkish music was based on improvising a melody structure within the framework of a Maqam, the Melody Mode or Scale of notes. The 12 Modes put forward by Ibn Sina in the early 11th century were in use during the Abbasid Period. By the 16th century, many more than the original 12 modes of Ibn Sina were in common use. In Persia, the Dastgah system was developed in the 20th century, which was a heritage from the Qajar period of rule there (1785-1925 A.D.). In this system Maqamat are used in groups, each group making up one Dastgah. The final organization of the 12 Dastgah is credited to Mirza Abdollah (1845-1918 A.D.), an eminent Setar player and teacher.[64]

The period from 1050 to 1250 A.D. is devoid of any major texts, and so no developments can be traced during this time in the musical system. However, there grew at this time 'a single broadly unified art music idiom embodying a synthesis of Arab and Persian elements............texts of the 13th to 15th centuries make no reference to differences between Arab and Persian practice.'

With the decline of the Abbasid Caliphate, power became decentralized and local dynasties and commanders usurped power in their hands. However, this fragmentation led to an increase in artistic activity. With regard to the melodic modes, forms and instruments, by mid 13th century, complete synthesis had taken place between Arab and Persian music systems. This common music idiom spread to most of the Arab world (except North Africa and Spain), Persia and major Islamic cultural centres in Central Asia.[65] After the fall of Baghdad, Persian instead of Arabic became the lingua franca. The Mughal rulers as we shall see later were softened by Islam and Persian culture, and became patrons of the arts.

Safi al Din and the Melodic Modes

The Arabian Caliphate gradually lost its territorial influence, and Al-Mustasin, a lover of music, was the last Khalifa. Safi al-Din (c1230-1294 A.D.), an outstanding musician and theorist was the chief musician at his Court. He escaped from the sack of Baghdad, and was taken into the service of the conqueror, Hulagu Khan, grandson of Jenghiz. He was the author of two important treatises, Risalat al-Sharafiyya (Treatise for Sharaf, his pupil), and Kitab al-Adwar (Book of Mode). He was an inventor of instruments, which included a Bass Lute, Mughni and a rectangular 64 stringed Qanun, Nuza.[66] He described the subject of melodic modes, describing the intervals of each mode in accordance with a detailed theoretical scale, similar to the one found in the Khorasanian Tumbur, described by Al-Farabi. Accordingly, each Pythagorean whole step in the seven tone scale was divided into two limmas (90 cent intervals) and a small remainder or comma (a 24 cent interval). Thus it was possible to accommodate the neutral intervals found in certain modes. Safi-al-Din's contribution to modal theory greatly influenced Persia and Turkey. Al Kindi and Safi al-Din have given notations to song pieces, based on alphabetical symbols.[67]

The Systematist School

The two treatises of Safi al-Din (d.1294) form the basis of the framework which was followed by music theorists for the next two centuries. He founded what came to be known as the Systematist school of theory. Taking as the basis, the division described by Al-Farabi, 'the octave was arranged in symmetrical layers: it was divided into two conjunct tetrachords and a whole tone, each tetrachord being made up of two limmas and a comma'. He explained rhythm in a clear and unambiguous way. Qutb al-Din (1236-1311 A.D.) the next Systematist theorist and Al-Ladhiqi (end of 15th century) tended to reproduce the corpus of modes recorded by Safi al-Din. The rhythmic cycles were also evolving and additions to the number of time units were being made. The influential works of Abd al-Qadir (d.1435) deal with major musical forms, classification and description of instruments.[68]

From the 13th to 15th centuries, music continued to evolve through the introduction of new modes, rhythms, forms and instruments and when the Turkish Ottoman Empire (early 16th century to early 20th century) held sway over the Persio-Arabian Region, this process continued.

There was a dominant style of Turkish art music, which itself was based on earlier composite Arab and Persian tradition. At this point of time, after the 15th century, due to the hostility between Safavid Persia and the Ottomans, the history of Persian music began to develop along slightly different lines.[69]

While the Ottoman Turks held sway over Syria and Egypt, Persia and Mesopotamia, music and song continued in the Courts; and Arabic and Persian works were translated into Turkish.

In the 20th century, a Lebanese theorist, Mikhail Mashaqa (Risala al-Shihabiyya...............) introduced a new system for analyzing scale: according to which an octave was divided into 24 intervals of a quarter tone.[70]

In 1932, the Cairo Congress on Arab music was held, where an attempt was made to codify and classify the melodic modes used in Arab countries. The most comprehensive list of 119 maqamat used in eastern Arab countries has been drawn up by d'Erlanger (1949). The Maqamat of the Western Arab countries (*i.e.* those of North Africa) are similar in broad structural principle.[71]

MODERN PERIOD

Countries with Arabian Influence

Increasing contacts with the Western world since the late 19th century have had a profound influence on the music of the countries of the Persio-Arabian Region. In Egypt and Lebanon, conservatories and music academies have been established where classical Arab and Western music are taught. Some musicians continue to perform traditional types of forms like the taqsim, on traditional instruments but introduce some Western elements of melody and occasionally introduce harmony also. The music composed by Sayyid Darwish (1892-1923 A.D.), Muhammad'Abd al Wahhab and Farid al-Altrash has become famous throughout the Islamic world. Um Kalthum (1908-75) was famous as a singer. The music of these composers, although rooted in tradition, has some features of Western music also.[72]

In modern music, compound forms like the Syrian 'Fasil', North African 'Naubah' and Iraqi 'Maqam' are popular. These are musical compositions in which instrumental and vocal pieces from the same mode are alternated.[73]

Persian Music

With the Napoleonic conquest (1798-1801 A.D.) of Egypt, and subsequent political interaction during the 19th and 20th centuries, European musical influence began to be felt. Military bands were the first western music to be heard by the Persians. Western notation was introduced and gradually became widely used. The school of National Music was started by Ali Naqi Vaziri in the 1920s. He was an excellent performer on the Persian tar (long necked lute) and a musician of the old school.[74]

A modern performance of Irani Sufi Classical music is based on classical modes called Dastgah. The presentation is in the form of an ensemble. There are one or two vocalists, a few chorus singers, and three or four instrumentalists. The repertoire proceeds by alternating different forms of Persian ensemble forms like the Pishdaramad, Reng, Avaz, the Tasnif, which is a vocal form, and Chaharmezrab, which is a piece for the solo performer. The Chaharmezrab is in fast tempo. The Avaz (vocal) is similar to the Alap of Indian music. The texts consist of poems of great Persian poets like Hafiz, Sa'di, Rumi, which embody Sufi mysticism themes.[75]

HINDUSTANI MUSIC

The purpose of this work is to compare the various facets of the music of the Persio-Arabian Region and Hindustani Music. Since the various aspects like Ragas, instruments, Forms, Rhythms, etc., will be covered separately with their corresponding features in the music of the Persio-Arabian Region, this chapter on history and development of Hindustani Music covers the various periods of history, briefly, laying stress on the Medieval Period, when there was an intermingling between various aspects of the two Systems.

The primary historical sources for the history of Hindustani Classical music are authoritative traditions of existing musical practice (sampradaya) and genuine recognized works on theory (shastra). Performing traditions were, and continue to be passed down orally by the Guru-shishya Parampara; also authoritative treatises are available on the teaching of music since centuries.

There are 4 major periods in the history of Indian music:[76]

1. Ancient Period (Vedic Period) – 2000 B.C. to 1000 B.C.
2. Ancient Period (Post Vedic Period) – 1000 B.C. to 1300 A.D.
3. Medieval Period (Muslim Period) – 1300 A.D. to 1800 A.D. [According to some sources the Medieval Period starts from 1001 A.D.]
4. Modern Period – 1800 A.D. onwards

VEDIC PERIOD

It is said that at the instance of the Devatas, Lord Brahma took the text from Rig-Veda, music from Samveda, drama and acting from Yajur-Veda and Rasa from Atharva Veda, and created the Natya Veda, which is also called the 5th Veda. The singing of the Veda Mantras was done by Sama Gana which consisted of 3 notes. The singer was called Udgata. In every household music was used as a means of worship.[77] Sacrifices were carried out according to Vedic rites and music was an inherent component of these ceremonies.[78] It is said that Samveda may have been the prime source of all music. Present day temple singers of the Sama sing the music which has an oral tradition dating back to the ancient period of history. The instruments used were the following:[79]

Percussion:	Dundubhi, Adambar and Bhumidundubhi
Cymbal:	Aghati
String:	Vana: lute of 100 strings. Vina was a general name for string instruments
Wind:	Tunava (wooden flute), Nadi (reed flute)

Music in the Epic Times

In course of time, Vedic music gradually was replaced by the more developed form of Gandharva or Marg type of music. This variety of giti was known as 'laukik', as compared to 'Vaidic' or Vedic music. Marga style of music was based on the Samgana, and possessed seven pure (shudh) jatis, which were like Ragas; hence they were called Jati rags.[80]

The earliest reference to musical theory appears to be the Rikpratisakhya (c.400 B.C.) in which mention is made of the three voice octaves and the seven notes. This was the time when Pythagoras was introducing the musical system of the Greeks (510 B.C.).[81]

Panini's Astadhyayi (500 B.C.) mentions the use of musical instruments like the madduka, jharjhara, the former being a skin covered drum; music, dance and drama were prevalent.[82]

Patanjali in his commentary, Mahabhashya (300 – 200 B.C.) has mentioned instruments like Mridanga, Veena and Dundubhi. Drama was performed on a 'manch' (stage) and the actors were called 'nata'. The temple dancing girls (devadasis) existed during this time.[83]

Buddhist Period

Gautama Buddha was born in the year 566 B.C. The Buddhist literature of the period comprising Avadanas, Jatakas, and Pithakas is full of references to music, instruments and dances with their hand poses (mudras). Buddhist hymns were sung by Bhikshus and Bhikshunis (male and female monks). In the Matasya Jataka, mention is made of meghagiti; which perhaps could be the forerunner of Megha Raga of today, as the Ragas were called gitis then. However, this is only a conjecture. The Saptatantri Veena of the Jataka and the Chitra Veena of the Natyashastra are ancestors of the modern day Setar, according to one opinion. This counters the belief that the Setar was introduced to Indian music in the 13th, 14th centuries by Amir Khusrau, the famed musician in the court of Allaud-din-Khilji.[84]

The Ramayana (approx. 400 B.C. to 200 A.D.) was composed by Rishi Valmiki and is an important epic of the Post Vedic period. There is evidence that during this period music had permeated every aspect of social life. The art of ballad singing existed during this time, since Rama and Lakshmana sang a poem composed by Valmiki, before King Dasratha. The precursor of Ragas, Jatis is also mentioned in the Ramayana; they were seven in number. Among the musical instruments mentioned are:

1. Bheri, Dundubhi, Mridanga, Pataha, Ghata, Panava, Adambara and Dindima among the percussion instruments.
2. Mudduka (brass trumpet) among the wind instruments.
3. Vina was the general name for all string instruments.[85]

The Mahabharata (approx.500 B.C. – 200 A.D.) was written by Veda Vyas and it is not considered to be a musical treatise; however it gives a good indication of the musical activity prevalent at that time. The types of musical compositions popular were Geet and Gandharva and all sections of society were engaged in musical activity *i.e.* vocal, instrumental music as well as dance: music was considered to be an important aspect of cultural education. Shri Krishna and Prince Arjun were accomplished musicians. The term used for musicians is Gandharva and Tumburu, Ativahu, and Naṛad were foremost among them.[86]

The Gupta period (320-550 A.D.) is considered to be the Golden Age for the Arts. Kalidas (400 A.D.) makes frequent references to music in his dramas. Shakuntala and Meghdoot are well known dramas written by him. The rulers of the time had court musicians; the temple and the stage were the forum for the presentation of music.[87]

Bharat's Natyashastra is a major treatise on dramaturgy, and consists of 36 chapters; 6 chapters (28 to 33) out of these are devoted directly to music. In the 28th chapter very valuable information on swar, shruti, instruments, gram, murchhna, jatis and their 'laxans' are given. The time period for Natyashastra is considered to be approx. from the 2nd century A.D. to the 4th, 5th century A.D. Some scholars place its time to be before Christ. In the 6th and 19th chapters the topic on Rasa has been discussed. A type of music composition called Dhruva Geet has been given prime importance in the enactment of drama.[88]

In Matanga's Brihaddeshi (8th, 9th century) the word Raga has been mentioned and defined for the first time. The monumental treatise was written, it would appear to describe the Desi Ragas prevalent at that time. The Deshi Ragas were the melodies accepted by the people and which had no restrictions or rules, as compared to the Marg category of music, which was bound by rules.

Here, we may draw a parallel with the music of the Persio-Arabian Region, where also two categories of music existed in the 8th century during the time of Ibn Misjah (d.c.715); the heavy style was called 'thaqil' and the light one, 'khafif'.[89]

According to Matang, Gram Ragas evolved from Jatis and he gives the 10 'laxans' (identifying features) of a Jati, which are prevalent even today, though with modifications.[90] In Brihad-deshi, Matang has talked about theories of sound from the angle of metaphysics and physiology as related to Tantric Yoga.[91]

Naradiya Shiksha (10th to 12th centuries) is not connected with the name of the great Rishi, Narada, but nevertheless, its author was one Narada. He gives an account of seven Gram Ragas. This is a considerable development upon Natyashastra in the area of Raga systems.[92]

'Sangita Makaranda' of Narada (7th to 9th century A.D.) is a work on music and dance; here music comprising vocal and instrumental music, as well as dance. The Deshi Music described here is based on supposedly, Tantra concept. The terms used in music evolve around the male female concept of the universe, which is the basic concept of Tantra-Purush and Prakriti.[93] The treatise deals with the topics of nada, shruti, swar, gram-murchhna, tanas, classification of Ragas and Nritya.

At the end of the 12th century, Jaydev a well known poet and musician wrote 'Gita Govind', a Sanskrit treatise, in which verses are written in 'ashtapadi'[94] form and glorify Lord Krishna and Radha. These verses are based on Raga and Tala. Sir Edwin Arnold translated this under the title, 'The Indian Song of Songs'; so impressed was he by its lyrical beauty.[95] These compositions were called Prabandhas.[96]

Sangita Ratnakar was written by Sarangdeva, (1210-1247 A.D.) a court musician with the Yadava dynasty of Devagiri (Daulatabad), in the Deccan. Probably he had been exposed to the music of both North and South India, as references to both styles of music are made in this very significant work. The fundamental scale (sudha Raga) of Sarangdeva is Mukhari, the modern Kanakangi, which is the Sudha scale of Carnatak music today. This seven chapter treatise carries forward the basic viewpoints put forward by Matang in Brihad-deshi (8th cent. A.D.) and Bharat in Natyashastra (4th, 5th century A.D.), but introduces new concepts also. There are detailed discussions on Swar, Raga, Prabandha, Tala, Vadya and Dance; and descriptions of 264 Ragas, with a proposed classification into Gram Raga, Upraga, Bhashanga, Raganga etc. The ancient theory (sastra) was available to future theorists through this monumental work. During Sarangdeva's time Bharat's Jatis and Matanga's Deshi ragas were not in use; instead 'Adhuna Prasidha' Ragas were popular.

There are two commentaries on this treatise: Simhabhupal's Sudhakar, (1330 A.D.) and Kallinath's Kalanidhi (1450 A.D.).[97]

MEDIEVAL PERIOD

The 11th century stands out in the history of Hindustani music, as it marked the beginning of the political occupation of North India by the Turks, Afghans and Mughals. During the time of Mahmud Ghaznavi (1030 A.D.) and Muhammad Ghori (1193-1205 A.D.) the main influence of the rulers was in Punjab. But, by the 13th century, almost the whole of the sub-continent especially northern India, was affected by the Muslim culture, in the spheres of Literature, Architecture and Music.

We have to take into consideration certain developments taking place during the very crucial period of the 14th and 15th centuries. According to Acharya Brihaspati, the Muslim rulers were lovers of art and music, and had musicians attached to their courts; they specifically took interest in Sufi music.[98] The Delhi Sultanate was expanded to the South, and in the Deccan, Muslim Courts were established; the Hindu Vijaynagar Kingdom was established in 1336 A.D., under the able guidance of Vidyaranya. When the Delhi Sultanate was fragmented by Timur's invasion of 1398 A.D., the musicians fled to regional centres; independent rulers of Bengal, Jaunpur, Gujarat and Gwalior became the chief patrons of music. Sultan Hussein Sharqi of Jaunpur (1458-1477 A.D.) revived the Khayal style of presentation.

There was constant exchange of musicians between the Northern Muslim and Hindu Rajput Kingdoms and the Muslim and Hindu Vijaynagar Kingdoms in the South. It has been widely accepted that, during this period a distinct difference started to emerge between the Hindustani and Carnataka styles of music, due to political as well as geographical factors. The core centres of the two styles of Hindustani and Carnataka Music were Delhi (influenced by Muslims) and Tanjore (influenced by Hindus), respectively.[99]

Here, it would be relevant to mention the views of the well known musicologist, Dr. Shahab Sarmadee.[100] He says that according to Faqirullah, the author of Ragadarpana (approx. 1662 A.D.), which is a translation and commentary on the treatise Manakutuhala (15th, 16th century), the Karnata and Desa Ragas (being sung in the South and North India, respectively) were both equally popular in the kingdom of Vijayanagar. The Dhrupad style of the North also had an acceptance in the South; moreover a few Ragas of the two regions had similar swar patterns, and this situation continues even in modern times.

During the reign of Allah-uddin Khilji (1296-1315 A.D.) the development of music received an impetus, as he was a great patron of music. His Court musician Amir Khusrau, (1253-1324 A.D.) was a musician, scholar, soldier and statesman. He helped to popularize certain forms of Sufi classical music like Qawwali, Qual, Gazal, Naqsh, Gul and Baseet. There is a controversy regarding his having invented these styles, as similar performing styles were prevalent in Persian, Arabian and the Turkish regions. He was equally proficient in the music of the Persio-Arabian Region as he was in Indian music; he introduced many Persian Ragas into the Indian mainstream melodies, to form new Ragas like Raga Yaman, which is still sung today. The others are Zilaf, Sazgiri, Sarparda etc.. Amir Khusrau will also be remembered as an outstanding disciple of the Sufi Saint Nizamuddin Auliya.

Amir Khusrau also made contributions to the development of melody forms like Khayal, Tarana, Chaturang and Trivat as well as to the Tala system.[101]

A significant factor in the development of music during the 15th and 16th centuries (Lodi Period 1414-1526 A.D.) was the steady progress in the improvement of the status of music. The Muslim musicians intermingled with the Hindus to achieve this state. Sikander Lodi encouraged the development of Indian music and respected its musicians.

Raga Tarangini

This treatise was written by Pandit Lochan in the 15th century A.D. approximately. The That classification system was adopted instead of the Raga-Ragini classification system. He accepted his Shudh that as being similar to the Kafi that, followed the past scholars in accepting 22 shrutis.[102]

Lahjat-I-Sikander Shahi

During Afghan King Sikander Lodi's reign (1487 A.D. to 1517 A.D.), the Delhi Court became a centre for music activity. The Arabian Maqam Huseini was the King's favourite; this is listed as a Raga in the 16th century treatises. A Persian treatise on Indian music Lahjat-I-Sikander Shahi – a monumental work belonging to the Lodi period (1414-1526 A.D.) was written and was dedicated to Sultan Sikander Lodi. This was the first of many Persian works based on earlier Sanskrit manuscripts.[103]

Mughal Rule

The beginning of the 16th century marks the dawn of the Mughal

Empire in India. Babur, the first Mughal Emperor was a lover of music and gave patronage to musicians; many famous singers were invited from Gwalior to Delhi during his rule.

The Bhakti revival in Bengal took place under Chaitanya (1483 A.D.-1533 A.D.) and was accompanied by a great deal of musical activity. Performing styles known as Sankirtan and Nagarkirtan were introduced at this time.[104]

The 16th century was important for the development of the Bhakti movement and its associated poetry.

1. Surdas (1535-1640 A.D.)—He wrote the famous treatise on poetry, which was composed in Ragas, thus popularising music through his verses. His poetry dealt with the everyday life of the people.
2. Tulsidas (1554-1680 A.D.)—He wrote the 'Ramcharit Manas', in which he combined devotional poetry with music. His poetry was composed in Ragas in a way, which brought out the devotional or Bhakti Rasa (ethos) of the verses.
3. Kabirdas (1456-1575A.D.)—He was one of the most illustrious poets of the Bhakti movement. Being a poet and musician his poetry is composed in 24 Ragas and it also expresses Hindu-Muslim unity.
4. Mirabai (1560-1630 A.D.)—Her Bhajan compositions are steeped in devotion to Lord Krishna and represent the folk style of Gujarat and Rajasthan. She composed in Braj Bhasha, Gujarati and Rajasthani, and she stands out as an illustrious exponent of the Bhakti movement.[105]

During Akbar's reign (1556-1605 A.D.) music and other arts flourished because of a stable political set up and royal patronage. During this period, there lived in Brindavan, a great saint and musician Haridas Swami, who was born in 1512 A.D. He had as his pupils, Tansen and many other musicians, who popularized music far and wide.

Tansen (c 1500-1589)

Tansen was a court musician in the State of Rewa; Akbar brought him to Delhi, after hearing of his proficiency in music. Abul Fazl, in Ain-I-Akbari, acclaims him as a 'Sangita Samrat'. He was specially competent in the art of Dhrupad singing, which was the performing style of music, in Akbar's period. 300 of his Dhrupad compositions are found in manuscripts. Tansen was knowledgeable in the concept of 'Murchhna' and well versed in the Muqam Padyati.[106] His disciples were divided into two groups: the Rababiyas and the Binkars. Their descendants went to the court at Rampur State which gave patronage to many illustrious musicians. The representative of the Binkars was Muhammad Wazir Khan and that of the Rababiyas was Muhammad Ali Khan.[107]

Raja Mansingh Tomar of Gwalior (1486-1516 A.D.)

He is acclaimed as having introduced the Dhrupad style of singing. At this time Muslim influence had begun to prevail on many aspects of music. The traditional performing style called Prabandh was being sung at this time in Sanskrit. With the purpose of popularising this style of music, he introduced the form called Dhrupad in the popular local language Brijbhasa, which was well received among the music lovers of the period. The devotional Form called Vishnu-pad was also popularized during this period.

The popularity of folk music among the masses continued along with the development of court music.

The best known musicians and scholars of the period used to visit the court at Gwalior, among whom were Sikander Lodi, Nayak Bakshu, Nayak Bhannu, Nayak Pandvi of Telengana, Mahmood, Lohang, Karna and Sultan Husain Shah of Bengal.

During the medieval period, one aspect of music, which must be taken note of, is the one arising from devotional and spiritual sources. This was the Sufi music at the gatherings in Dargahs and Sufi mazars; and the music popularized by the Bhakti movement being performed in temples and social gatherings of the Hindus.

The 17th and 18th centuries were most crucial in the history of music development in India. The Mughal Empire rose to its heights of grandeur and then gradually declined till its end in the middle of the 18th century. The Empire had reached "the peak of political and military greatness" under Akbar, and of cultural glory under Jehangir (1605-1627 A.D.) and Shahjehan (1628-1658).

However the music retained its vigour and vitality.[108] During Akbar's reign music flourished as is borne out by Abul Fazl in Ain-i-Akbari (1597 A.D – an account of the music life at Delhi and Agra) due to the patronage given by the Emperor. The following are the names of some illustrious musicians of the time: Miya Tansen, Sujan Khan, Baba Ramdas, Baz Bahadura, Tansen's sons, Bilas Khan and Tantrang Khan, Surdas, son of Baba Ramdas, Rangsen of Agra, Ustad Yusuf of Herat, Pirzada of Khorasan etc. This list includes persons belonging to all religions and regions such as Hindus, Iranis, Turanis, Kashmiris; they also belonged to varied castes and social background.[109]

During Aurangzeb's reign (1658-1707 A.D.) there was a decline of music, but after the accession to the throne of Muhammad Shah 'Rangiley' (1719 A.D.), music was again revived and attained great heights of maturity and popularity. Muhammad Shah was a singer of good standing and during this time women, both of royal and humble descent participated in the music life of society.[110]

Nawab Dargah Quli Khan of Hyderabad who visited Delhi in 1738 A.D. has described the vibrant music life at the mazars of Sufi saints and other public places, especially during Vasant Utsav, in his book Muraqqa-e-Delhi.[111]

So, the Indian music prevailing at that time included the Hindus with their kirtans and Bhajan singers, the Muslims with their singers of Qawwali and Qawl; and hence it was a means of cultural integration and social harmony. The traditional ancient musical forms and varieties continued to flourish and be preserved.[112]

Books in Sanskrit were translated into Persian as it was the official language of the Courts and the upper classes. Ghunyat-ul-Munya (1374 A.D.) and Lahjat-e-Sikander Shahi (Lodi Period 1414-1526) were the earliest Persian books on Indian music.[113]

Pundarika Vithala

He was brought to Delhi by Akbar in 1599 from Khandesh (situated on the banks of the Tapti River-modern Gujarat). He was knowledgeable in both the Hindustani and Karnataka systems of music, and wrote four treatises: Sadragchandrodaya, Ragamala, Ragamanjari and Nartananirnaya. He accepted 14 shrutis in the octave to describe his Ragas and adopted 12 frets for the Vina. The northern Ragas were described by him taking the Sudha scale of the Karnataka music.[114]

Between 1550 A.D. and 1800 A.D. many technical treatises were written. In some books, verse iconographies[115] have been found; such as the structured sets of miniature paintings called Raga Mala. Subhankara's Sangita Damodara (1500 A.D.) gives a list with verbal iconography for each Raga; so does Pundarika Vitthala's Ragamala (1576 A.D.)[116]

Ramamatya

He wrote 'Swarmela Kalanidhi' in approx. 1550 A.D. which was based on the Carnataka music style. For the first time an adequate description of Indian Ragas is given. He accepted 7 'shudh' and 7 'vikrit' Swar, and classified Ragas according to 20 'thats' according to their 'shudh' and 'vikrit' Swar. The Ragas and 'thats' described by him are not found in the current Hindustani style of music in their original form.[117]

Somnath

In 1609 A.D., Somnath, a Telegu Brahmin wrote Ragavibodha, one of the important land marks in the treatises which were written in Indian music. He discussed the theory of sound, types of Vinas, the names and positions of 22 shrutis etc. The Raga classification proposed by him was the Janak and Janya classification.[118]

Ahobal

In the 17th century Pandit Ahobal wrote Sangita Parijat; this treatise was translated into Persian in 1724. He accepted 29 shrutis in the octave but used only 12 to describe the Ragas. The relationship between Swars and the length of the strings of ihe Vina was also discussed by him. An account of 122 different Ragas was given by him. This is an important treatise of Hindustani system of music.[119]

Bhavbhatt

Pandit Bhavbhatt was a musician during Shah Jehan's period.

Between 1674 A.D. and 1709 A.D. three treatises were written by him: (*a*) Anoop Vilas, (*b*) Anoopankush and (*c*) Anoop Sangitratnakar.

He belonged to the Carnataka tradition of music; his shudh that was Mukhari; and all Ragas were classified by him under 20 thats.[120]

Pandit Vyankatmakhi

In 1660 A.D. Pandit Vyankatmakhi wrote the Chaturdandi Prakashika. This treatise forms the base of the present day Southern system of music. He introduced the Mela[121] Raga classification using 12 notes, in which all existing Ragas were classified into 72 Melas on mathematical principles; this was a landmark in the history of development of music. Out of these 19 Melas are popularly used in Carnataka music; 55 Ragas originate from them.[122]

In 1625, Damodar Misra wrote Sangita Darpana, where most of the information given is based on Sangita Ratnakara. This was during Jehangir's rule.[123]

Muhammad Shah (Rangiley)

Muhammad Shah (Rangiley)[124] (1719 A.D. to 1748 A.D.), the last Mughal Emperor, was a lover, composer and patron of music. He had many famous musicians at his Court, the foremost being Sadarang (Nemat Khan) and Adarang (Feroz Khan), who popularized the Khayal performing style and trained many pupils. They were also prominent instrumentalists and played the Vina. During this period, a new type of Khayal presentation was introduced which was sung in the tradition of the Qawwali. Also, the Sehtar was becoming popular in place of the Vina.[125]

Ghulamnabi Shori, who belonged to Punjab, initiated the singing of the Tappa style of music. This form requires the voice to be very well trained in embellishments like 'Kampan', 'Tana' and 'Gitkiri'.[126]

MODERN PERIOD

Some eminent people contributed towards the development of music during this period.

Mohammad Reza

A nobleman from Patna, Mohammad Reza, wrote Naghmat-e-Asaphi in 1813 A.D. He rejected the old Raga-Ragini system of Raga classification and propounded a system whereby Ragas were brought together into a group because of the existence of certain common features they had. The Bilawal scale was adopted as the Shudha scale; till this day this practice continues.[127]

Maharaja Pratap Singh of Jaipur

A conference of musical experts was held in Jaipur, under the patronage of Maharaja Pratap Singh of Jaipur (1779-1804 A.D.), and the deliberations collected in a publication, the Sangita Sar, which tells us about the existing musical practices of that time. The Bilaval scale had been accepted as the Hindustani Shudh Scale.[128]

Shri Sourindra Mohan Tagore from Bengal wrote a number of books on music, between 1867 A.D. and 1896 A.D; the most prominent among them being "The Universal History of Music". He continued to accept the Raga Ragini Putra system of Raga classification.[129]

Pandit V.N. Bhatkhande and Pandit V.D. Paluskar

Two stalwarts among musicians greatly contributed towards the popularising of music in the modern day period. Both of them also wrote authentic treatises to carry forward the music for future generations as well as make it available to the masses. Till then music had been the privilege of the rich and higher classes; but now colleges and institutions were started, so that the general public could learn the art. These two great musicians and propagators were Pandit V.N. Bhatkhande and Pandit V.D. Paluskar.

Pandit V.N. Bhatkhande (1860 A.D. to 1936 A.D.) travelled extensively, collecting compositions and material on music from scholars and musicians all over the country. He established music academies in Vadodara (1916 A.D.) and Lucknow and wrote many books: the Kramik Pustakmalika (6 parts), Bhatkhande Sangita Shastra (4 parts), etc. He introduced a simple notation system, which is still being followed.

Pandit V.D. Paluskar (1872 A.D. to 1931 A.D.) was an illustrious pupil of Pandit Balkrishna Bua and was an excellent singer and teacher. His pupils, during and after his death went to all parts of India to spread and teach music. He started the first school of music, Gandharva Mahavidyalaya at Lahore in 1901, and then at Bombay in 1908. After his death, his pupils established the Akhil Bharatiya Gandharva Mahavidyalaya, which has now branches all over India. His books include the Raga Vigyan (seven parts), Sangit Balbodh, etc. His pupil Prof. Narayan M. Khare proposed the Raganga classification system for Ragas, which has been widely accepted.

REFERENCES

1. Harvard Dict., p. 528.
2. New Grove I, p. 513.
3. NOHM, p. 421.
4. COHM, p. 190.
5. The Genius..., pp. 5-6.
6. Harvard Dict., p. 529.
7. New Grove I, p. 514.
8. Harvard Dict., p. 532.
9. New Grove I, p. 514.
10. Harvard Dict., p. 530.
11. New Grove I, p. 518.
12. *Ibid.*, p. 513.
13. MSP, p. 1.
14. Mohammed Bagher, '*The influence of Persian in the Indian Subcontinent*' Historical studies of Iran, No. 1, September 1971 (Tehran: Ministry of Information Press), pp. 29-32.
15. MSP, p. 3.
16. NOHM, Vol. I, pp. 422-23.
17. New Grove I, p. 515.
18. PHM, p. 119.
19. New Grove I, p. 515.
20. Music of the Nations, p. 107.
21. New Grove I, p. 515.
22. NOHM, p. 423.
23. New Grove IX, p. 292.
24. MSP, pp. 3, 5-6.
25. New Grove I, p. 515.
26. NOHM, p. 421.

27. New Grove I, p. 515.
28. *Ibid.*
29. New Grove IX, p. 292
30. NOHM, p. 428.
31. Music of the Nations, pp. 127-28.
32. A Hist. of Arab. Music, p. 48.
33. *Ibid.*, p. 49.
34. *Ibid.*, p. 73.
35. *Ibid.*, p. 76.
36. COHM, p. 191.
37. *Ibid.*
38. New Grove I, p. 515.
39. COHM, p. 191.
40. *Ibid.*
41. New Grove I, p. 515.
42. *Ibid.*
43. *Ibid.*
44. COHM, p. 191.
45. NOHM, p. 448.
46. New Grove I, pp. 515-16.
47. COHM, pp. 191-92.
48. New Grove I, p. 516.
49. COHM, p. 193.
50. *Ibid.*, p. 194.
51. New Grove I, p. 516.
52. *Ibid.*, p. 517.
53. COHM, p. 194.
54. New Grove I, p. 517.
55. COHM, p. 195.
56. NOHM, p. 431.
57. *Ibid.*, p. 430.
58. New Grove I, pp. 517-18.
59. COHM, p. 195.
60. New Grove IX, p. 292.
61. COHM, p. 195.
62. New Grove IX, p. 292.
63. *Ibid.*, p. 293.
64. *Ibid.*
65. New Grove I, p. 518.
66. COHM, p. 196.
67. The Genius..., p. 124.
68. New Grove I, p. 518.
69. *Ibid.*, p. 519.
70. *Ibid.*, p. 521.

71. New Grove I, pp. 522-23.
72. *Ibid.*, p. 526.
73. The Genius..., p. 134.
74. New Grove IX, p. 293.
75. Personally attended a few programmes on Iranian Sufi classical music (Presented as an ensemble) organised by the Iran Culture Centre, New Delhi.
76. *Bhart. Sang. Ka. It.*, p. 6 and Sangit Visharad, p. 16.
77. *Bhart. Sang. Ka It.*, p. 6.
78. *A Hist. of Ind. Music*, p. 90.
79. *The Mus. of Ind.*, p. 8.
80. *A Hist. of Ind.Music*, pp. 97-98.
81. *The Mus. of Ind.*, p. 9.
82. *A Hist. of Ind. Music*, p. 98.
83. *Ibid.*
84. *Ibid.*, pp. 99-101.
85. *The Mus. of Ind.*, pp. 9-10.
86. *Bhartiya Sangita Ka Itihas*, Dr. Thakur Jaidev Singh, pp. 186-88.
87. *The Mus. of Ind.*, p. 12.
88. *Sangita Visharad*, p. 20.
89. *New Grove I*, p. 515.
90. *Sangita Visharad*, pp. 20-21.
91. New Grove IX, p. 78.
92. The Mus. of Ind., p. 14.
93. *Sangita Makarand*, pp. 13-14.
94. A song form consisting of eight verses.
95. *Bhart. Sangita*, pp. 56-57.
96. *The Mus. of Ind.*, p. 14.
97. *The Mus. of Ind.*, pp. 14-15 and Sangita Visharad, pp. 23-24.
98. *Musalman Aur Bharatiya Sangeet*, pp. 57-58.
99. New Grove IX, p. 77.
100. *Tarjum-I-Manakutuhala...*, Intr., pp. XXX to XXXII.
101. *Bhart. Sangita*, pp. 61-62 and The Mus. of Ind., p. 15.
102. *Bhart. Sangita*, pp. 71-72.
103. New Grove IX, pp. 80-81.
104. The Mus. of Ind., p. 16.
105. *Sangita Visharad*, p. 27 and Bhart. Sangita, pp. 86-91.
106. *Bhart. Sangita*, p. 86.
107. *The Mus.* of Ind., p. 17.
108. *Hind. Music*. p. 3.
109. *Ibid.*, p. 5.
110. *Ibid.*, pp. 8-9.
111. *Ibid.*, p. 9.
112. *Ibid.*, p. 10.

113. *Ibid.*, p. 2,11.
114. *The Mus. of Ind.*, pp. 17-18.
115. Iconography: illustration of subject by drawing.
116. New Grove IX, p. 82.
117. *Sangita Visharad*, p. 26.
118. *The Mus. of Ind.*, p. 18.
119. *Ibid.*, pp. 19-20.
120. *The Mus. of India*, p. 20.
121. *Mela: Primary Mode or scale of the Carnataka music system*, corresponding to the 'that' of the Hindustani music system.
122. *Sangita Visharad*, p. 29, The Mus. of India, pp. 18-19.
123. *The Mus. of India*, p. 19.
124. A title which he earned because of his fondness for the music and the Arts.
125. *Bhart. Sangita*, p. 115.
126. *Ibid.*, pp. 115-16.
127. *The Mus. of India.*, p. 21.
128. *Ibid.*, p. 22.
129. *Bhart. Sangita*, pp. 120-21.

2

Melodic Mode of the Countries of the Persio-Arabian Region

The early History of the music of the Persio-Arabian Region or the Middle East shows a common Islamic influence mainly by the existence of common modal systems and instruments. "The chief characteristics of Islamic music were and are modal homophony, fioritura and rhythm".[1] The music of this Region as found today – whether it is religious music, classical art music or simple folk, reflects a historical past steeped in rules and principles of melody. The principal position of melody in the Persio-Arabian Region and absence of complex polyphony (standing for different sounds) distinguishes the music of this part of the world and India from European music.[2]

We have seen in the chapter on the history of Persio-Arabian Music, that different regions and its people dominated the political and cultural life of this Region as a whole, at different periods of history. The geographical area denoted here "covers an area of West Asia and North Africa whose musical culture is dominated by the Islamic Arabic, Persian and Turkish speaking peoples and is made up of a single though heterogeneous system including liturgical, classical, folk and modern popular music. The peoples of Afghanistan, Soviet Central Asia and the Caucasus (Between the Black Sea and Caspian Sea; Kavkaz and Bol'shoy Mts in erstwhile USSR) share in this system peripherally."[3]

Before describing the various Melodic Modes which existed in the regions dominated by the Arabic, Turkish and Persian people, we will first proceed to discuss the history of the Melodic Mode. We may at the outset mention here that the modes have more specific names in different areas. It is called, Maqam, Makam in Arabic and Turkish areas and was also called Maqam in the Persian dominated areas till the 20th century, after which it came to be called Dastgah (with its component Gusheh). In the Caucasus it is known as Mugam and as Shashmaqam in Soviet Uzbekistan.[4]

While as in different historical periods and geographical areas the interpretations may vary, in general a Maqam "has a scale and a hierarchy of pitches whose distribution in the lower tetrachord is the main characteristic. Scaler intervals include those approximating tempered whole and half, three quarter and five quarter tones although there is variation and theoretical controversy regarding their precise tuning."[5] Maqams also have characteristic melodic patterns, motifs and interval sequences. All these attributes of a Maqam make it very similar to the Indian Raga system.

Let us take a brief look at the history of the melodic modes practiced in the area of the Persio-Arabian Region, primarily influenced by the Arabic, Persian and Turkish people. Some regions of Central Asia and the Caucasus also share in the common cultural ethos.

HISTORY OF MODES DURING DIFFERENT PERIODS

Pre-Islamic Period

According to one opinion, the sources from which we can gather information on the early history of the music of the Persio-Arabian Region, are not earlier than the 9th century; and these often need to be treated with caution.[6] However, we do have information that the Sasanid dynasty (224-642 A.D.) was a glorious era for music. The musicians associated with this era are Barbad, Shirin, Azada. Al Masudi has credited Barbad with having devised the 'seven royal modes', which bore similarity to the ones mentioned by Muhammad B. Ahmad al Khwarizmi (10th century). There is reason to believe that they may have originated from the musical scales of the ancient Semites of Babylonia – Assyria.[7]

Islamic Period

During the Umayyad Period (661-750 A.D.) the development of musical practices, especially art music, were very much influenced by Persian music. However, the organization and particularly the classification of the modal system during the period was based on Byzantine models.[8]

The systematization of modal music, as practised during the Umayyad Period was done by Ibn Misjah (d.c.715). He learnt from Syria and Persia what was acceptable to him and rejected that which he disliked.[9] The modal system finalized by him consisted of eight 'finger modes' (asabi), and the classification of these modes was done on the basis of its 'course' (majra) either with the middle finger (wusta) on the lute, giving the minor third, or with the third finger (binsir), giving the major third. These modes may have been similar, but not identical to the Syrian Ikhadias, as assumed by Al Kindi. These finger modes dominated Arab theory for the art music till the 11th century. They have been fully described by Ibn al-Munajjim (d.912) in his Risala fi'l-musiqi (Treatise about Music).[10]

1. *Muṭlaq fī majrā al-wusṭā*	G. A. B♭. c. d. e. f. g.
2. *Muṭlaq fī majrā al-binṣir*	G. A. B. c. d. e. f. g.
3. *Sabbāba fī majrā al-wusṭā*	A. B♭. c. d. e. f. g. a.
4. *Sabbāba fī majrā al-binṣir*	A. B. c. d. e. f. g. a.
5. *Wusṭā fī majrāhā*	B♭. c. d. e. f. g. a. b♭.
6. *Binṣir fī majrāhā*	B. c. d. e. f. g. a. b.
7. *Khinṣir fī majrā al-wusṭā*	c. d. e♭. f. g. a. b. c'.
8. *Khinṣir fī majrā al-binṣir*	c. d. e. f. g. a. b. c'.

Eight finger modes-Ibn-al- Munajjim
(Ref. New Oxford History of Music, page 448)

With one exception (No. 7) they are identical with the Greek and church modes. They are given with the fourth string taken as base ('imad'). Al-Munajjim (d.912) discussed them in terms of the diatonic lute fretting, which corresponded to their names. This fretting was based on the Pythagorean fretting, which produced scales of whole tones (204 cents) and limmas (90 cents). The systematic naming of these modes took place, post Umayyad period.[11] 'In Persia, the melodic modes were known by fanciful names rather than by descriptive ones.' Ibn Sina's (980-1037 A.D.) Al-Shifa (The cure) tells us that the number of modes were increased and their names had become non-technical: Ushshaq (passion), Nawa (melody or sound), Iraq, Isfahan etc.[12]. Some of these names were borrowed by the Arabs. We get more information from Ibn Sina (d.1037) regarding the relationship of modes and tetrachords. Some of the modes described by him could be broken up into conjunct tetrachords, but no clear structural pattern emerged.[13]

By the time of Ibn Sina (d.1037) and Ibn Zaila (d.1048) twelve modes were in use. By the 13th century these twelve modes were called Maqamat, and six secondary modes existed called Awazat. The Turkoman and Mughal influence introduced branch modes or modal formulas called Shu'ab and by the fifteenth century there existed a total of forty-eight modes, now called Shudud. In Muslim Spain, the melodic modes were twenty-four in number, called Tubu'. They were supposed to have a cosmic relationship with the four elements.[14] Let us now discuss the system of modes as it finally evolved in the 13th century, during Shafi-al-Din's time when it acquired the name of Maqam (plural Maqamat). As we have said before, the Arabs had been using 4 principal plus 8 subsidiary modes, a total of 12 modes. In addition to this, by mutual combination 6 more additional modes had been derived, taking the existing total number to eighteen. Finally, there evolved 12 principal modes called Maqam, each of them having 2 modes under them, called Shobhas which were 24 in number, each of them had Raginis under them called Gusvas which were 48 in number. According to Swami Prajnananand "the Arabian Maqams, Shobhas and Gusvas really correspond to "that" or "mela", ragas and 'raga-angas' of Indian music".[15]

The greatest contribution to modal theory was made by Safi-al-Din (d.1294 A.D.) who was the author of two important treatises, Risalat-al-Sharafiyya (Treatise for Sharaf, his pupil) and Kitab-al-adwar (Book of Modes). He may be considered to be the founder of the Systematist school of theory, which treated the scale in a different, analytical way, and was removed from the Hellenistic Theory of Greek influence which had dominated Arabian music till that time.[16]

Shafi-al-Din proposed, based on the scale of the Systematists, the 12 primary modes (maqamat) mentioned before, seven of which had Persian names, which prevailed upon the music of the then known Arabo-Persian world from the 13th to the 16th century. Shafi al-Din took as his basis the "division described by al-Farabi for the first tetrachord of the Tunbur Khurasani, so that the neutral intervals, difficult to reconcile with the traditional stress on the primacy of simple ratios, were now treated virtually as just intonation intervals. The octave was arranged in symmetrical layers: it was divided into two conjunct tetrachords and a whole tone, each tetrachord being made up of two whole tones and a limma, and each whole tone of two limmas and a comma."[17] For a clearer apprehension of these new modes, given below, a common tonic has been chosen.

'Ushshāq	c. d. e. f. g. a. b♭. c¹.
Nawā	c. d. e♭. f. g. a♭. b♭. c¹.
Būsalīk	c. d♭. e♭. f. g♭. a♭. b♭. c¹.
Rāst	c. d. f♭. f. g. b♭♭. b♭. c¹.
'Irāq	c. e♭♭. f♭. f. a♭♭: b♭♭. b♭. d♭♭. c¹.
Iṣfahān	c. d. f♭. f. g. b♭♭. b♭. d♭♭. c¹.
Zīrāfkand	c. e♭♭. e♭. f. a♭♭. a♭. b♭♭. c♭. c¹.
Buzurk	c. e♭♭. f♭. f. a♭♭. g. a. c♭. c¹.
Zankūla	c. d. f♭. f. a♭♭. b♭♭. b♭. d♭♭. c¹.
Rahāwī	c. e♭♭. f♭. f. a♭♭. a♭. b♭. c¹.
Ḥusainī	c. e♭♭. e♭. f. a♭♭. a♭. b♭. c¹.
Ḥijāzī	c. e♭♭. f♭. f. a♭♭. b♭♭. b♭. c¹.

List of 12 Modes (Safi Al-Din) – NOHM, pages 449, 450

The Maqamat have been named after places, or musical terminology, which refers to fretting of instruments etc.. For example Hijaz (Arabia), Nahawand (Iran), Kurd (the Kurds) and Saba (Sheba) are names of places. Bayati is a poetic term, Rast is Persian for right or straight, Jahargah (fourth place), and Sigah (third place) are also Persian words which refer to fretting of instruments or scale degrees (notes). These names indicate the Persian influence on the music of the Arabic Region.[18]

Awazat

Shafi-al-Din has also mentioned in his 'Risalat-al-Sharafiyya' about Awazat, which are similar to Maqams, and are the Persian names of the melodic modes. There existed 6 Awazat in Shafi-al-Din's time; they were – (1) Kwasht, (2) Kardania, (3) Nauroz, (4) Nihaft, (5) Muḥaiyyar, (6) Hijaz. In other treatises some more names are given (1) Salmak, (2) Maya, (3) Shahnaz. According to some Arabian musicians there exists a classification, where Maqamat are the principal modes, and Awazat, the subsidiary modes derived from them. This has similarity to the Raga-Ragini Classification of the North Indian Hindustani Sangeet Padyati. As we mentioned before, the modes proposed by Safi al-Din influenced the music scene from the 13th to the 15th century. By the 16th century, under Persian influence the old Pythagorean scale,-which was the old Arabian system already flourishing in the Persian Region since the 14th century – was again imbibed by the music of the Near and Middle East. This implied that not only the notes of the maqamat, avazat, and shuab were changed, but an alteration occurred in their form also. "They were now no longer 'modes' in the commonly understood sense of the term (*i.e.* scales within the gamut of which melodies were composed) but melodic patterns which became matrices for composition."[19]

Intervals

In Egypt and Levant in the 20th century, theorists divide the octave scale into small microtones, comparable to the practice at the time of Al-Farabi (11th century) and Shafi-al-Din. Several types of micro-intervals have been advocated, including the comma division (roughly one-ninth of a whole step) which is found in some Syrian theories. Generally the Maqamat are based on a referential octave scale consisting of 24 equal quartertones. Now Western notation has become fully established and extra symbols are used to suit the melodic nature of the music. In addition to the regular flat and sharp signs, the symbol '𝄳' lowers a note by approximately a quarter tone; while the symbol '≠' raises a note by roughly a quarter tone. Following is the list of Maqamat popularly used in Egypt and the Levant.[20] (given on the next page)

As we have mentioned before, there is an inter-relationship of the various classical music systems of the Arabo-Persian Region. Melodic compositions follow a system of modes. These modes have more specific names in the different regions and languages of the countries of the Persio-Arabian Region. In Arabic it is called Maqam, Makam in Turkey, Dastgah and Gusheh in Persian, Mugam in the Caucasus and Shashmaqam in Soviet Uzbekistan.[21]

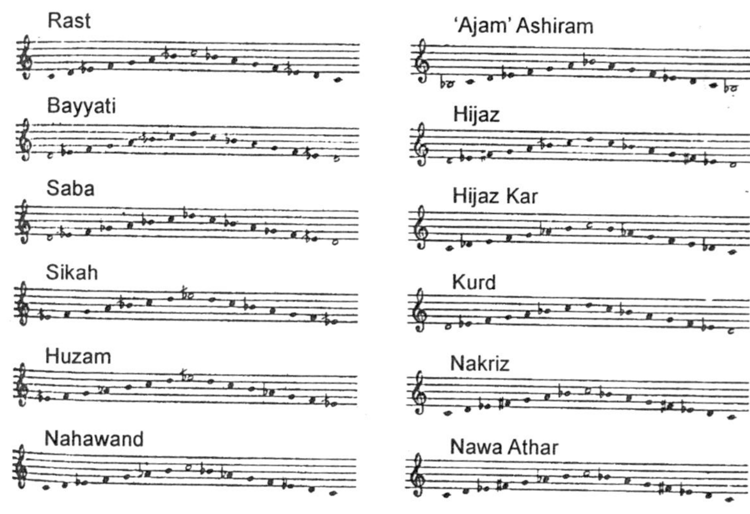

List of Maqamat (Egypt, Levant),
(The Genius..., page 131)

Now we proceed to discuss the modal system of the Persio-Arabian Region taking note of the differences in names and form which existed in the regions dominated by Arabic, Turkish and Persian people. Melody in Arab music also incorporates microtonality, *i.e.* intervals that do not conform to the half step and whole step divisions of traditional Western art music. The concept of melody is commonly connected with modality, a conceptual organizational framework widely known under the name Maqam (plural Maqamat).[22] In Iran, after the 20th century, these modes were called Dastgah and their constituent Gusheh.

Melody Mode from the Arabo-Turkish Region

The meaning of the word Maqam is a stage. It specifically referred to the stage on which performances took place before the Caliph. According to Larousse Encyclopaedia,[23] "the generic term 'maqam' has been used to designate the notion of the mode". According to

Curt Sachs,[24] Maqam is 'a pattern of melody, based though with a certain freedom on one of the modal scales, and characterised by stereotype turns, by its mood, and even by its pitch middle, high and low.'. The initial note too is important; for example, the Maqam Rast starts from the tonic and Mahur from the fifth; Rast is slow and sombre, while Mahur is faster. Different Maqams give stress on different notes, for example, Bayat stresses the fourth and Sikah the third below the tonic.

"In theory, the maqam is a characteristic scale in which certain notes are stressed; these notes, or degrees of the mode are often repeated and serve as supports for the melody; sometimes playing a role comparable to that of the keynote in European music."[25]

"Its modal meanings ultimately derive from a basic meaning of 'tone' or 'degree of the scale' – that is, a particular place in the general scale of all pitches available in the system". In the countries of the Eastern Mediterranean, which have Arabic speaking people, 'Maqam' as well as the word Naghmah (tune, voice) denote 'modal entity' (which is the technical term).[26] In Persia the 'modal entity' are called Gusheh or Avaz (plural Avazat) depending on the importance and scope of the modal entity in question. 'Mode' and 'Maqam' refer to the type of scale, while as Naghmah is considered equivalent to Gusheh or Avaz. The Persian word Perdeh (curtain) has become obsolete as a term denoting 'modal entity'; it may continue to be used in the musical sense of 'fret' or key (of a piano), and in this basic sense it is parallel to the meaning of Maqam, both referring to a 'determined position in an overall background system of available pitches'.[27]

In Arab, Persian and Turkish music, alike, the modal entities constitute a scale made up of a limited number of notes, which are considered to be drawn out of a general background collection.

At present about 30 Maqamat are used in Arabic music. The following chart gives the lower tetrachords of the eight principal groups (after Touma, 1975), 'whose constituent Maqamat are differentiated in the upper tetrachord'.The Western notation used, is the one commonly found in Middle Eastern publications *i.e.* 'ƀ' for a quarter tone sharp, and 'p' for a quarter tone flat.[28]

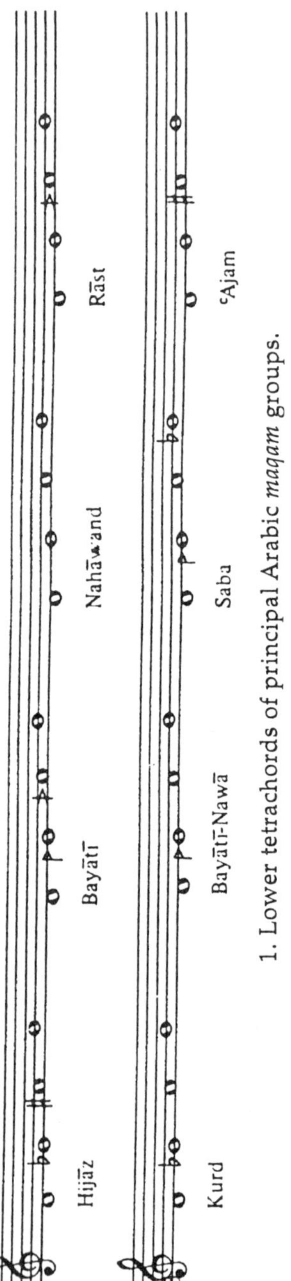

1. Lower tetrachords of principal Arabic *maqam* groups.

(Harvard Dict., page 530)

Turkish

The melodic modal base here is also called the Makam. Intervals have been standardized by adopting "a 24 tone scale of unequal intervals generated by the circle of fifths and used as the basis of permanent frets on the chief stringed instrument, the tambur."[29]

The Turkish Makam now consists of an open-ended system of several dozen modal entities. Signell (1977) suggested that 60-70 Makams are recognized today; Oransay (1966) quoted a 19th century Turkish source claiming that 92 Makams are in use and 62 more, are not in common use.[30]

Persian

Although close to Arabic practice before 1880 A.D., Persian music started developing independently only in the 19th, 20th century. Persian music was reconstituted by rebuilding from "traditional assemblages of Gusheh of all kinds, performing style Gusheh as well as modal nuclei. The prime concern has been to assemble authoritative sequences of gusheh into larger systems, that is, to determine one or more series (radif) for a small number of Dastgah".[31] This 20th century system of the 12 Dastgah-ha has been inherited from the Qajar period (1785-1925 A.D.). Till this time Persian music, like Arabo-Turkish music "was based on improvisation or composition within the structure of a Maqam". In the Dastgah System Maqamat are used in groups, each group of these Maqamat constituting a Dastgah. The final organisation of the 12 Dastgahs is credited to Mirza Abdollah (1845-1918), who is an eminent Setar (long necked lute) player and teacher.[32]

In the Dastgah system, there are 12 Dastgahs, seven primary and five secondary (called Avaz or Naghmeh). The system has tried to balance between an important traditional number, which closes the future expansion of the system; and allowing one or two important Gusheh such as Shushtari to break away and give rise to secondary Gusheh, which could form a new Dastgah thus opening the doors for future expansion.[33]

The introduction of the Dastgah System in Iran was an attempt at refurbishing the traditional system along Western lines, with the standardization of the Radif by Mirza Abdollah and Darvish

Khan in 1900. The modal unit of Persian music, the Dastgah, has its related and typical scale, motifs. The Dastgah has a number of sub-divisions, Gusheh, each of which has an identifying range, constituent tones, that could differ somewhat from the basic Dastgah scale (this could be treated like a modulation also).[34] The repertoire of traditional pieces of Persian music is known as the Radif (row). Some 300 to 400 Gusheh – ha (Sing. Gusheh) make up a Radif, which is divided into 12 groups known as the 12 Dastgah-ha (sing. Dastgah: 'Organization'). There is disagreement between musicians about the exact number of pieces in the Radif.[35] "The Persian system is taught through the memorization of the Radif, a body of largely non metric music approximately ten hours long, which includes the twelve Dastgahs and their constituent Gusheh in prescribed order, with appropriate melodies and rhythms." After memorizing the Radif, the musicians use it as a basis for improvising and composing new music.[36]

The 12 Persian Dastgah-ha

(b = flat and p = semiflat; the tonic is underlined

Shur:	G	Ap	Bb	<u>C</u>	Dp	Eb	F	G
Abu 'Atā:	G	Ap	Bb	<u>C</u>	D	Eb	F	G
Bayāt-e Tork:	F	G	Ap	<u>Bb</u>	C	D	Eb	F
Afshāri:	F	G	Ap	Bb	<u>C</u>	D(p)	Eb	F
Dashti:	G	Ap	Bb	<u>C</u>	D(p)	Eb	F	G
Homāyun:	G	Ap	B	<u>C</u>	D	Eb	F	G
Isfahān:	G	Ap	B	<u>C</u>	D	Eb	F	G
Segāh:	<u>F</u>	G	Ap	Bb	C	Dp	Ep	G
Chahārgāh:	<u>C</u>	Dp	E	F	G	Ap	B	C
Māhur:	<u>C</u>	D	E	F	G	A	B	C
Rāstpanjgāh:	<u>F</u>	G	A	Bb	C	D	E	F
Navā:	D	Ep	F	<u>G</u>	A	Bb	C	D^1

MSP..., p. 58.

The 12 Dastgah-ha have specific names. A list is given above with their notation.[37]

Four of the 12 (Abu ata, Dashti, Bayat-e-tork and Afshari) are considered to be derivatives of Shur, and Bayat-e-esfahan is believed to be a derivative of Homayun. These derivative Dastgah-ha are popularly called the five Avazat (sing. Avaz: songs). The performance of each Dastgah begins with an introduction (Daramad), in which the melodic mode (Maqam) and the melodic pattern (maye) are presented.[38]

Let us discuss further, the modal nucleus and modal complex in Persian music. Arabic Maqam or Naghmah and Persian Gushe differ in the sense that, while Maqam and Naghmah also refer to larger modal complexes, simple or compound, the Persian term Gusheh (corner) can refer only to a unitary modal nucleus. A large complex of such modal nuclei is called 'Avaz' (voice or note).

Gushe: (Plural Gusheh-ha) This can refer to any item in one of the traditional series (radif) of musical items called Dastgah (organization, system). Some Gushe names refer to modal structure, some to fixed compositions in a particular style of performance.

Avaz: Though it refers to a composite modal complex of several unitary modal nuclei, it is also used to mean Dastgah, or a modal entity. Avaz-e-chahargah would mean either the unitary modal complex Chahargah, or a whole set of gusheh performed traditionally, with Chahargah at their head as the principal modal nucleus. The Gushe-e-Chahargah would refer to any Gusheh belonging to the Dastgah dominated by the modal nucleus Chahargah, but it would not refer to Chahargah itself.[39]

The Central Asian Systems

The melody modes of the Central Asian Region, which shares cultural and musical affinity with the countries, which are influenced by the Arab, Turkish and Persian-speaking peoples, are called Shashmakom ('six makam'). The word Makom here denotes the same idea as Dastgah in Persia *i.e.* it is made up of a number of constituent Shu'bas. In the Persio Arabic systems, Shuba is an entity, which is considered to be a branch mode of Maqam and Avaz; and on the classificatory scale is below them. In the Central Asian System, it corresponds in form and function to the modern Persian Gushe *i.e.* they are parts making up the total Makom. The Performing Style consists of the Makom having two divisions, a set of instrumental items followed by a set of vocal items. The second portion, (which is accompanied by instruments) is the vocal portion constituted by a series of Shuba. Some Shuba have an identifiable performing style, but all of them are based on a recognizable melodic mode. These Shubas which are sung in a series, may present one Makom in one portion, the same Shuba may also represent another Makom, perhaps in a different pitch. The appearance of a different melodic entity or mode in an entity being sung is called 'namud' (appearance) in Persian. For example, a Shuba in the Uzbek Makom Dugah, which is called Chargah, appears the same in configuration (though it appears a 5th higher) as the registeral climax of the first vocal item in the Makom Buzurk. Here the Shuba Chargah becomes 'namud-e-mukhayyar-e-Chargah' (appearance of an excerpt of Chargah).[40]

This can be compared with a process in the Hindustani Music system by which a Raga is developed, while being performed or presented. This process is called Avirbhav (appearing) and Tirobhav (disappearing). For *e.g.* in Raga Besant Behar, two Ragas are mixed, and the glimpse of each Raga is shown, alternately, in the process of developing the Raga.

Performing style of a Maqam, Makam (Arabic, Turkish) and Dastgah (Persian) in comparison with the Indian Raga

We find an amazing and striking similarity in the performing style or presentation, of the melodic modes of the countries of the Persio-Arabian Region (West Asia) and that of the Raga of Indian music. There are certain comparisons in concepts and functions also. The Maqam, Makam (Arabian, Turkish) or Dastgah (Pesian) is performed in different performing styles (form), taking into account certain musical concepts of modality and their functions. These are:

1. Notes and hierarchy of pitches;
2. The function of modal nuclei ('Raganga' or 'chalan'); their extension to other octaves;
3. Use of motifs (group of notes, or 'sthaya' which develop and embellish the Raga, Maqam or Dastgah);
4. The use of particular notes and their functions (like the predominant note Ghammaz in Arabic, Shahed in Persian, or Vadi in Indian music).

Scale and Pitch

"The underlying point of reference in Indian pitch nomenclature is melodic function rather than intervallic structure".[41] The basic note names associated with the syllables (as they are sung) are the same as the names of the syllables themselves, and "they were only secondarily adopted to the designation of measured intervals".[42]

In one octave of the Indian general scale only seven independent note names exist; they are Sa, Ri, Ga, Ma, Pa, Dha, Ni (Sa). In practice there are two octaves, above and below the central octave, the seven names of the notes are repeated in each octave. While as in Western Asian music, the general scale comprises two octaves, which can be extended outward; there are 14 notes in this scale. These are Iraq, Kawasht, Rast, Zirkulah, Dukah, Kurdi, Sikah, Awj, Hihuft, Mahur (or Kardan), Shahnaz, Muhayyir, Sunbulah and Buzurk. Their span consists of two octaves. In addition to these 14 separately named principal notes, "up to as many as ten auxiliary modifications (named as 'low' or 'high' plus one of the standard names)" exist within an octave span.[43]

In the Indian scale system extension to octaves above or below, replicates the names of the seven-note octave. (The central octave, is the Madhya Saptak (Octave); the lower one being the Mandra Saptak, and the higher one is the Tar Saptak) So, we can conclude, that "a basic set of Western Asian note names denotes in principle a general scale of all available pitches, while the basic set of Indian note names denotes degrees (notes) of the scale of any possible modal entity but without specifying precise pitch relationships."[44]

While a Maqam is being presented the use of the two octave spans of the scale and beyond is used to explore the possibilities of embellishing the style of presentation. Similarly, in the Indian Raga the span of seven notes of the scale (Saptak) is extended below and above to develop and embellish the Raga.

Having discussed the notion of pitch and notes in the West Asian and Hindustani Modal systems, we will now discuss certain component modal terms and concepts, which have some similarities and differences.

The following chart shows a comparative listing of some terms for the principal modal functions in Arabic, Turkish and Persian music.

	Arabic	*Persian*	*Turkish*
initial	āghāz	āqāz	agaz
	mabdā		giris
predominant	ghammāz	shāhed	gůclü
medial stop	markaz	īst	muvakkat kaliş
subfinal	zahīr		yeden
final	qurār	(forüd-e kāmel)	karar

Principal Modal Functions in Arabic Turkish and Persian Music[45]

Here it is to be noted that according to one opinion the 'final' and 'predominant' note cannot be assumed to be a tonic. Before we discuss the contents of the above chart, it would be necessary to dwell on the System Tonic, which is peculiar to Indian music, and according to one opinion, no tonic of this kind exists in West Asian music.[46]

However, according to another opinion, when the melodic modes used in Arab countries were codified and classified at the Music Congress held in Cairo in 1932, each Maqam was described in terms of a scale (which had intervallic structure), ambitus, its division into tetrachords (or pentachords) and its tonics. The tonics were perhaps introduced as a base for classification of the Maqams. The tonic has been likened to the "Qarar" in Arabic music and the starting pitch to the "Mabda" in the same system.[47]

Now, we proceed to describe the System tonic, which as we mentioned before is peculiar to Indian music. Every Indian Raga has a tonic, the note named Sa (C in Western notation), which recurs in each Raga and has only one modal position or Swarsthan (no higher or lower varieties). In terms of the Indian general scale, all Ragas have the same tonic unlike the Turkish, Arabic or Persian Maqam. The pitch frequency used by a performer for Sa is the system tonic for every item he may render. In Hindustani music it is called Sur (the note which suits the performer's voice range, and with which his octave starts). The tonic belongs to the system as a whole and not to individual modal complexes. In any performance, the Tonic system is constantly present as an unchanging drone, which is different from drones of West Asian music, which occur on occasions or sporadically and change pitch even between the same modal entity.[48]

Let us return to the modal functions outlined in the chart given, and see how they help to develop the performing style with the melody mode in the background. As we have said before each Maqam was likened to a scale (intervallic structure), with divisions into tetrachords (or pentachords). "The definition of a Maqam was later extended to include recognition of a hierarchy of pitches and melodic patterns".[49] The important point of melodic emphasis in a Maqam is the Ghammaz (Arabic), Shahed (Persian) and Guclu (Turkish), and implies recurrence. It is similar to the Vadi Swar (note) of the Indian Raga The Ghammaz (Arabic) is the most prominent note of the climactic part of the melody and it is often a 5th above the Qarar, but it may also be a 3rd or 4th above it. The term Zahir (Arabic) "is applied both to the note a step below the Qarar, functioning like a leading note to the tonic, and to a cadential phrase leading from a lower pitch up to the Qarar. The Zahir may be a semitone, a three quarter tone or a whole tone below the Qarar, its distance varying according to the structure of the Maqam."[50] The final notes Qurar (Arabic), Karar (Turkish), and Forud (Persian) stand for temporal position or finality and correspond to the 'Nyas' of the Indian Raga.

It would be relevant to mention the way a Dastgah (with its constituent Gushe) is developed in a performing style or form of Persian music. There are three or four main notes and one reference note. As the presentation develops, these main notes are emphasized, progressively. Going up the notes of the scale is like climbing a staircase. The pause is given on the notes being emphasized, dwelling on the important group of notes (modal nuclei), and then after reaching the top of the scale, the notes are retraced gradually to the starting point (aqaz).[51] This is very similar to the way the Alap is elaborated ('badhat') during the presentation of the Indian Raga.

The following figure shows how the Dastgah Segah is developed. The dot represents the reference or springboard note, 1 is the first degree (note) of the mode, 2 the second etc. The mode may also be divided into groups containing 2 to 4 notes.[52]

We shall now see the modal functions of the Indian Raga system. The following table gives the 4 most important modal functions out of the 10 characteristic ancient functions (Raga Lakshan) specified by Pandit Sarangdev in the 13th century text Sangit Ratnakar.

Progressions through the Degrees (Notes) of Segah

Dastgah Segah[53]

Gregorian	*Sanskrit*	*Persian*
initial	graha	āqāz
tenor	amsa	shāhed
final	nyāsa	forüd(-e kamel)
medial	apanyāsa	īst

4 Important Modal Functions of the Indian Raga System[54]

The modern modal functions which have taken the place of ancient ones in Indian music are: Vadi (amsa) (Sonant: Sounding out); Samvadi (consonant); Anuvadi (Assonant or auxiliary); and Vivadi (discordant note). These are different notes of the scale and are different for each Raga. They are used to develop the individual character of a Raga. The Vadi is the prominent one, the Samvadi being second in prominence. Vadi corresponds to the 'amsa' swar of the 10 laxans proposed by Sarangdeva and is similar to Shahed in Persian, Ghammaz in Arabic and Guclu in Turkish. Samvadi would be similar to the Shahed of a principal Gushe in another octave.[55] As the Raga develops, the initial notes of the scale are explored and then are retraced to the initial note. The tonic or 'Sa' is very important, as the whole Raga development revolves around the tonic 'Sa'. Step by step, each higher note is explored and each time retraced to a lower note or to 'Sa'. At every step, pauses are made on the Vadi or Samvadi to bring out the individual character of the Raga.The role of other identifying group of notes, like 'Chalan', 'Pakad', 'Raganga' which help to build the character of a Raga, will be discussed later.

It can be noticed from the above discussion, that the development of a Maqam, Dastgah and the Indian Raga have distinct similarities.

Modal Components (Nuclei) (Core Components)

We shall now talk about the structure of the Maqam and its constituent melodic units.The scale of a particular Maqam is divided into melodic units called ajnas (plural of jins, 'genre'), an idea or concept which is similar to that of tetrachord or pentachord. The following is a list, of the 17 ajnas proposed by d'Erlanger, arranged in different varieties of interval relationships like the Pythagorean diatonic, the chromatic etc..

The 17 Ajnas ('genres') or melodic units used in the modern modal system[56]

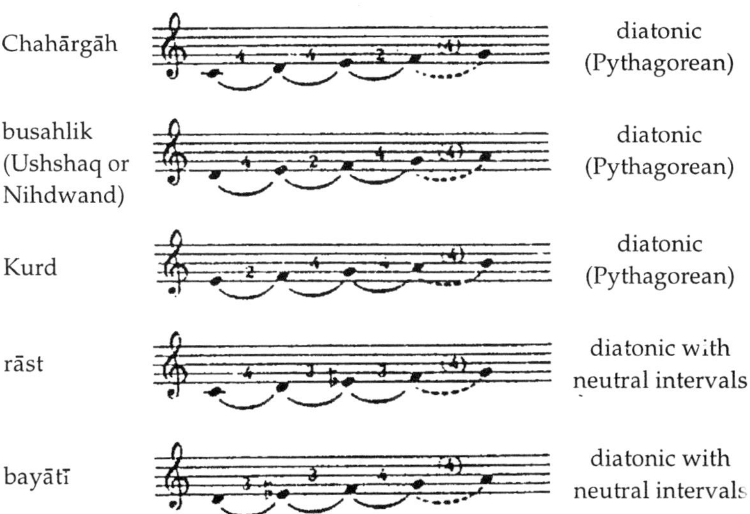

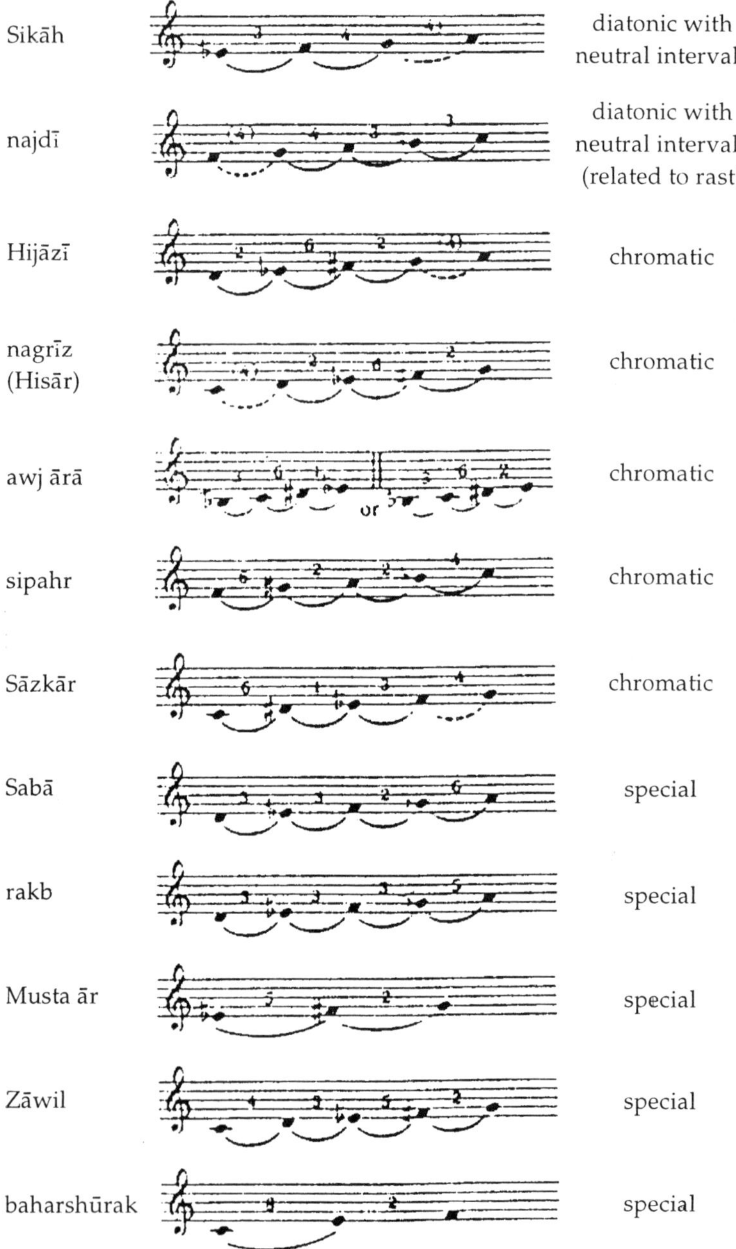
Sikāh
diatonic with neutral intervals
najdī
diatonic with neutral intervals (related to rast)
Hijāzī
chromatic
nagrīz (Hisār)
chromatic
awj ārā
or
chromatic
sipahr
chromatic
Sāzkār
chromatic
Sabā
special
rakb
special
Musta ār
special
Zāwil
special
baharshūrak
special

The sequence in which the ajnas occur is usually fixed for each Maqam and is part of the definition of that particular mode or Maqam. Some Maqamat have ajnas of the same type and others have ajnas of different types. In a third type similar ajnas are repeated at different pitch levels. A melodic process known as 'tarkib' (mixing) is characterized by the use of more than one jin at the same pitch level.[57] This process could be favourably compared to the Indian Raga presentation system. While presenting a Raga, with all the permutations and combinations of 'swar-samuh' or group of notes, sometimes a particular group of notes (sthaya) is taken from one part of the scale ('purvardh') and mixed with a group of notes from the second part of the scale ('uttarardh'); and vice versa.

These constituent units of a Maqam, called Ajnas, have been termed as modal nuclei according to some sources, and represent the core component of a mode. These modal nuclei combine together to make composite modal complexes; and the modal composite may have the same name as one of its modal units or nuclei.

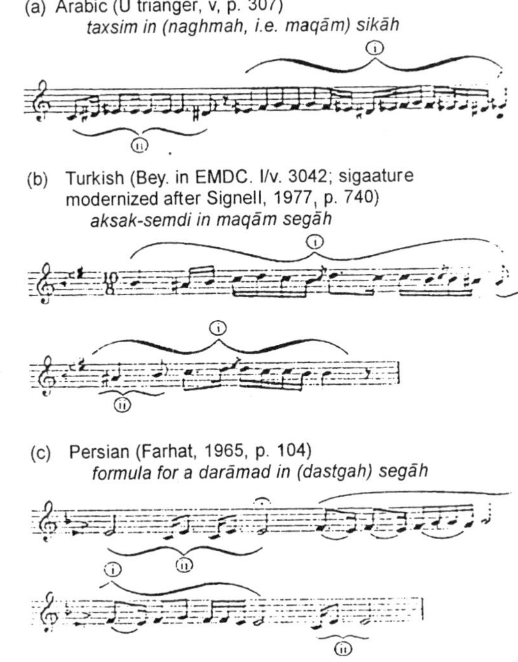

Mode Segah in Arabic, Turkish and Persian Music Systems[58]

The previous figure illustrates the modal entity Segah (Arabic Sikah), as heard in each of the three musical cultures. The modal entity is named for the note Sikah (marked *) of the general scale, which characterizes it, and with which any presentation of it must conclude. The note Segah is written as e-½ b, (Arabic), b-½ b (Turkish) and e-½ b (Persian) in the respective notation systems. As can be seen in Part (a) the note e-½ b which is called Segah is repeated in the modal units, and the modal entity is named after it. This is not the case in the Indian Raga system. No group of notes which identify a Raga (whether it is 'Mukhya Anga', 'Raganga', 'chalan' or 'Pakad' of a Raga) is named after a note of the scale.

In the Persian modal nucleus, Segah, the adjacent lower note to the final is omitted (Part c). The modal nuclei ends at Eb (Ga) and does not come back to C. This could happen in the Indian Raga Bihag, where an identifying group of notes or 'Pakad' could end without returning to the Sa; *e.g.*-'Pa Ma' (tivra), Ga Ma Ga'

Modal Complexes – Simple and Complex

The term Maqam designates any modal entity which can be recognized; it may be a nuclei modal complex or a composite of several such complexes.

Maqam Saba[59]

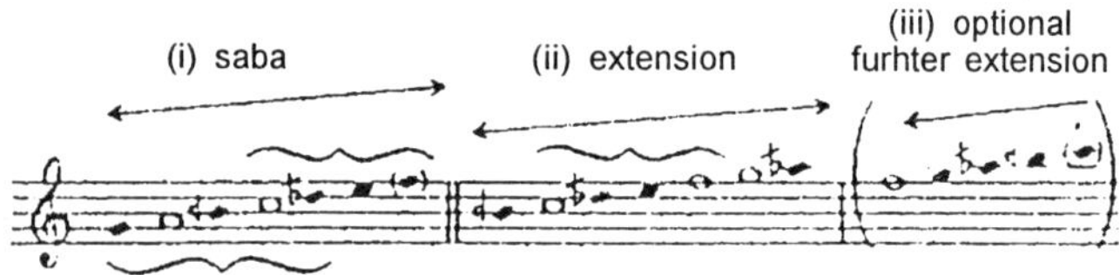

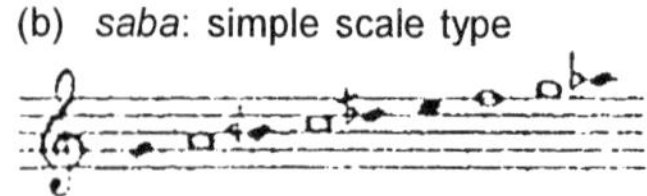

Modal Composition and Simple Scale Type of Maqam Saba [New Grove XII, 425]

The previous figure, Part (b) shows the component notes of the scale of Saba, with prominent notes singled out. In Part (a) the modal nuclei are extended to higher octaves (the nuclei in the higher octaves do not duplicate the previous set of notes). However, the single nuclei set and the composite nuclei set are called by the modal name Saba.

Here we may mention that the identifying modal nuclei as shown in Part (b) are present in Indian Ragas also and is known by the name of 'chalan', 'pakad' or 'Raganga'. The following figure shows the chalan, Mukhya Anga and Aroha Avaroha of Raga Marva.

Raga Marva[60]

Chalan, Chief Component, Ascent and Descent of Raga Marwa

It may be pointed out here, that the process shown for Maqam Saba, Part (a) (*i*) (*ii*) (*iii*), where the set of nuclei have different notes in different octaves, does not occur in Indian Ragas.

Many scholars such as D'Erlanger, Signell (1977) and Jurgen Eisner (1973) fully discussed Maqam as scale step, modal nuclei and as simple and composite Maqam. Jurgen Eisner used 20th century Arabic theorists as the basis for his proposals, using Maqam Bayyati as a sample. He showed Bayyati as modal nuclei, as well as composite Maqam, using several other modal nuclei in the course of its development.[61]

Similarities

Mr. Salvador Daniel[62] mentions certain qualities about the Modes of Arabian Music. He says that each note of the scale can be used as a starting note for a new scale; thus there will be seven different scales deriving from each scale. This theory corresponds with the Murchhna theory in the Indian Hindustani system of music, where each 'Swar' of a gram gave rise to a Murchhna. Since there were 3 'Grams' in the system, and seven notes in each 'Gram', 21 Murchhnas were produced, each giving a different melodic combination.

Maqam and It's Indian Parallels

There are three ways in which the Arabian Maqam may be considered to be comparable to the Indian Raga System. Firstly, the Maqams may be considered to be counterparts of the Indian Raga. They are sung like a Raga, and so similarities can be traced in the note patterns. Secondly, we have the comparison with the Indian Raga-Ragini system of classification. Each Maqam has got a scale, and one or more prominent notes, which decide the form it will take; the initial note (tonic) is important, on which stress or 'muqam' is given. In this way six or seven alternate combinations of notes can be derived from that Maqam. So, each Maqam gives birth to several subsidiary Maqams. The third comparison of the Arabian Maqam system is with the Indian 'that' or 'mela'; both give rise to derivative modes and are used for classification.

Mela or That – Meaning

The ordinary meaning of 'mela' is 'piecing together' or 'joining'; but the meaning of 'mela' in musical terms would be, that group of swars from which Ragas are derived. In Indian music one can say, that 'swar' is produced from 'shrutis', 'saptak' is produced from 'swar' and in turn 'mela' is produced from saptak. Any group of swars may not have the ability to produce a Raga, but 'mela' is that distinctive group of notes, which gives birth to Ragas. The concept of 'mela', from the beginning was for the purpose of Raga classification. That is why it is called the Janya Janak method. Ragas were categorized into different groups, depending on their similarity in terms of 'shudha' and 'vikrit' swars.

Mela padyati was born at the time of Matang (5th to the 8th, 9th century approx.) and popularised in the medieval times in the North and South India.

Before we mention the origin of the concept of mela in the Indian music system, we will have to take into account the views of Acharya Brihaspati, an erudite scholar and musician of the modern period, who has written exhaustively on the subject of the Muslim influence on the development of Indian music. The chapter on 'Mukam Murchhna Aur Mela' in his book Sangeet Chintamani[63] throws light on the relationship between the Arabian concept of Mukam and the Indian 'murchhna' and 'mela' concepts. According to him mela padyati was introduced into the Indian system of Raga classification by the Muslim padyati from the 11th century onwards. (Sangeet May 1969). The Arabo Persian music which was blending with the native music in the 14th century, during the time of Amir Khusrau, had a concept of classification of Ragas according to their Muqam system.

The meaning of 'muqam' is 'sthan' (place), or it is synonymous with pradesh (province). Acharya Brihaspati gives the following description of 'Mukam': A 'Mukam' consists of eight notes, instead of seven, like in a 'saptak'. Here we may mention that the 'mela' padyati also has the concept of eight notes. Therefore a 'mukam' is not a saptak (group of seven notes), but an 'ashtak' (group of eight notes). Each 'Mukam' gives rise to 2 'shubhas', making a total of 24, and each 'shubha' gives rise to 2 'gushas', making a total of 48. It is important to note here that the group of notes which constitute a "Mukam" have the distinctive ability of producing derived melodic forms, *e.g.* 'shubhas' and 'gushas'. So, the 'Mukam', was being used as a concept for classification in the Arabian Raga system.

We have to keep in mind the spirit and psyche of the period we are referring to here; when assimilation of the Persio-Arabian music was taking place with the Indian music system. According to one opinion, which is also ratified by Acharya Brihaspati, the Arabian 'Mukam' system of classification was imbibed into the Indian Raga classification system. Here, it would be befitting to point out that there is a school of thought which gives many reasons for advancing a strong opposition to the above point of view. This opinion states, among other reasons that the mela padyati already existed in India from Matanga's time *i.e.* 8th, 9th century, so there is no question of it being imported from the Arabian countries.

The Vijaynagar Kingdom was established in 1336 by Harihar and Bukk under the able guidance of Shri Vidyaranya, who became its Prime Minister. But its fortunes were being governed by the Muslim rulers of the North, where Amir Khusrau was influencing the intermingling of Arabo Indian music.

This influence spread to Vijaynagar also. Due to the non-availability of his book, 'Sangeet Saar' his opinions are spelt out in a treatise 'Sangeet Sudha' by Raghunath. Vidyaranya (1320 to 1380 A.D.) first proposed the new Mela Raga classification system in the South, on the basis of the mukam padyati of the Arabs. He collected 50 Ragas and classified them into 15 melas. According to Acharya Brihaspati, these melas were expressed with the help of the Vina. In Persian Arabian music, there are 12 notes for the purpose of getting a required Raga; the frets of the instrument, which are required to produce the notes of the particular Ragas are called 'muqam' or 'sansthan' of the Raga. This principle was adopted in the South as 'mela' from which Ragas were derived. Somnath, in Raga Vibodh (1609 A.D.) has also made it clear that 'mela' is expressed with the help of the Vina. These melas give rise to Ragas or the Ragas are classified according to them. Maqam and Sansthan are synonymous with 'that' or 'mela'. (The North Indian musicians also adopted this padyati as 'that padyati' of Raga classification). In this Muslim dominated environment, Kallinath, wrote his famous commentary on 'Sangeet Ratnakar' by Sarangdeva. According to him, the music prevalent in Vijayanagar in the middle of the 15th century was influenced by 'maqam', sansthan.

The learned secholar, Acharya Brihaspati[64] is of the opinion, that, if we do a detailed study and analysis of the Persian melodic form 'maqam' we find that a majority of them are similar to the murchhnas proposed by Bharat in the Natyashastra. However, Swami Pragnananand commenting on the subject, in his book, Music of the Nations,[65] cautions that this should be examined critically.

A List of Seven Arabo-Persion Maqams and Their Corresponding Murchhnas

1. Rast Maqam corresponds to the Pratham Shudh Murchhna of Madhyam Gram.

2. Husaini Maqam corresponds to the Fourth Shudh Murchhna of Shadajgram.
3. Hijaz Maqam corresponds to the Fourth Shudh Murchhna of Madhyam gram.
4. Rahavi Maqam corresponds to the Fourth Sakakali Murchhna of Sadajgram.
5. Iraq Maqam corresponds to the Admi Shudh Murchhna of Madhyam Gram.
6. Kochak Maqam corresponds to the Fourth Sakakali Murchhna of Madhyamgram.
7. Buzurg Maqam corresponds to the second Shudh Murchhna of Sadajgram.

Time Theory of Maqam

According to Curt Sachs,[66] the 'maqamat' have been related to the time of the day, just as are Indian Ragas. A table connecting the 'maqamat' with the time of the day and the signs of the Zodiac, are given below, as given by Curt Sachs:

Maqam	Sign of the Zodiac	Time of the Day
Rast	Ram	Sunrise
Isfahan	Bull	
Iraq	Twins	Nine O'clock
Kucek		
(Zir efkend)	Crab	
Buzurk	Lion	
Hijaz	Virgin	Midnight
Bu-silk	Balance	Afternoon
Ussaq	Scorpion	Sunset
Huseini	Archer	Night-end
Zangula	Capricorn	
Nawa	Water Carrier	Before night prayer
Rahawi	Fishes	Morning

According to Curt Sachs, Ibn Sina (980-1037A.D.), the Persian scholar, who in his book, 'Kitab-al-Shifa' and 'Alanjat' wrote extensively about Arabian theory and practice, has found comparison between musical ideas and the stars to be unsuitable, as he was against the indiscriminate clubbing of the various sciences.

Please see chart on Modal systems, characteristics and connotations (M.S.P., p. 78).

Modal Systems, Characteristics and Connotations of Persian Music

Mode	*Time*	*Colour*	*Element*	*Characteristic or Mode*	*Spiritual Connotation*
Shur	Late morning 10-12	Fire red	Fire	Meditation	Tariqat to ma'refat
Māhur	After sunset	Sky blue	Wind	Happy, easy going	Shari'at
Homāyun	From sunset to dark	Dark green	Flame	Attraction	Haqiqat
Navā	Bed time	Transparent	Combination wind and fire	Advice	Ma'refat
Segāh	From 4 until before sunset	Deep blue	Water		Tariqat
Chahārgāh	Early morning 6-8	White or yellow	Steam (water)	Excitement	Tariqat
Rāstpanjgāh	Morning 8-10	Tan	Earth	Concentration and intellect	Shari'at
Isfahan	Dawn	Light green	Light of fire	Spiritual love	Haqiqat
Abu 'Atā Dashti Afshāri Bayāt-e Kord Bayāt-e Tork	Afternoon 12-4	Bright brown Brown Burnt brown Dark grey Smoke black	Earth		Shari'at to Tariqat

These special characteristics of the Persian Modes are similar to the Indian Raga System [MSP, page 78].

Maqam vs Parad

We may explain, in short, the relationship between 'maqam', and 'Parad'. 'Parad' is a term used by a well known Sanskrit scholar, Pundarika Vithala, in his Ragamanjari (1599) as a substitute for 'Raga'. According to 'Tarjuma-i-Manakutuhala' and 'Risala-i-Ragadarpana,[67] "both denote almost the same thing, as initially a particular tonal interval (called bud), marked by its pitch point and characterised by its melodic contents, came to be known as maqam, and parad denoting the same, was mechanically devised to pinpoint that pitch in all its mathematical precision and musical potentialities". A significant fact is that Amir Khusrau lays much stress on twelve Parads and twenty four Sho'bhas while, Faqirullah gives importance only to Ragas and Raginis and their corresponding maqams and Parads in the Persio-Arabian music.

Kitab-e-Nauras

The word or term 'muqam' is also found in the manuscript 'Kitab-e-Nauras', written by Sultan Ibrahim Adil Shah-II (1580-1627 A.D.). This book was edited by Dr. Nazeer Ahmad of Aligarh Muslim University in 1956. According to Dr. N.P. Ahmad, this book is a collection of Dhrupad songs, composed by Sultan Ibrahim Adil Shah II, and the fifty nine songs were composed in seventeen ragas. These are ragas prevalent at that time in Hindustani music, the names of which are: (1) Bhupali, (2) Ramkri, (3) Bhairav, (4) Hajiz, (5) Maru, (6) Asavari, (7) Desi, (8) Purba, (9) Barari, (10) Todi, (11) Mallar, (12) Gauri, (13) Kalyan, (14) Dhanasri, (15) Kanhra, (16) Kedar, (17) Nauroz. But he refers to the 'Raga' as 'Muqam' which is an indication of the synthesis which had taken place by then, between Hindustani music and the incoming Arabo-Persian music, of that time.[68]

दर मुक़ाम मलार नौरस

झनन झनन झन मोती खाँ की तांत गाजे
तल मिरदंग भेद सों नवरस बाजे

अंतरा (बैन)

इस जग में दो कुछ लीजे
इक तम्बूरा इक कामिनी कीजे

आभोग

इबराहीम जब तूँ बूझे
तब बिहिस्त अमृत कया करूँ मुझे

There has been a spontaneous use of the word 'Muqam' as a substitute for 'Raga'. Also a point to be noted is that Hajiz and Nauroz are 'Maqams' which existed in the list of maqams given by Shafi-al-din in the Sharafian Treatise, and these were introduced to the Indian music system by Amir Khusrau in the fourteenth century.

REFERENCES

1. N.O.H.M., p. 447.
2. Harvard Dict., p. 532.
3. *Ibid.*, p. 528.
4. *Ibid.*, p. 529.
5. *Ibid.*
6. New Grove I, pp. 514-15.
7. Groves Dict. (old), Vol. 6, p. 677.
8. New Grove I, p. 515.
9. N.O.H.M., p. 428.
10. *Ibid.*
11. New Grove I, p. 515.
12. C.O.H.M., p. 195.
13. New Grove I, p. 517.
14. N.O.H.M., p. 449.
15. Music of the Nations, p. 112.
16. New Grove I, p. 518.
17. *Ibid.*
18. Harward Dict., p. 530.
19. N.O.H.M., p. 450.
20. The Genius......., p. 131.
21. Harvard Dict., p. 529.
22. The Genius....p. 131.
23. LEM, p. 37.
24. The Rise of Music......, p. 285.
25. LEM, p. 37.
26. New Grove XII, p. 423.
27. *Ibid.*, p. 424.
28. Harvard Dict., p. 530.
29. *Ibid.*
30. New Grove XII, pp. 427-28.
31. *Ibid.*, p. 428.
32. New Grove IX, p. 293.
33. New Grove XII, p. 428.
34. Harvard Dict., p. 531.
35. New Grove IX, p. 295.
36. Harvard Dict., p. 531.
37. M.S.P., p. 58.
38. New Grove IX, p. 295.
39. New Grove XII, p. 426.
40. *Ibid.*, p. 428.
41. *Ibid.*, p. 429.
42. *Ibid.*

43. *Ibid.*, p. 424.
44. *Ibid.*, p. 429.
45. *Ibid.*, p. 427.
46. *Ibid.*, p. 430.
47. New Grove I, p. 522.
48. New Grove XII, p. 430.
49. New Grove I, p. 522.
50. New Grove I, pp. 522-23.
51. M.S.P., p. 58.
52. *Ibid.*, pp. 58-59.
53. *Ibid.*
54. New Grove XII, p. 434.
55. *Ibid.*
56. New Grove I, p. 523.
57. *Ibid.*
58. New Grove XII, p. 424.
59. *Ibid.*, p. 425.
60. *Ibid.*, p. 430.
61. *Ibid.*, p. 426.
62. Music of the Nations, p. 113.
63. Sangeet Chintamani, Brihaspati, pp. 211-28.
64. Sangeet Chintamani (1st part), pp. 212-19.
65. Music of the Nations, p. 116.
66. The Rise of Music, p. 286 .
67. Tarjuma-I-Manakutuhala...., p. LIII.
68. Hind. Music, pp. 80-83.

3

Raga: The Hindustani Melodic Mode

HISTORY OF DEVELOPMENT OF RAGAS IN HINDUSTANI MUSIC

The meaning of the word Raga, as used in different ancient texts on music, in various contexts is quite different from the meaning accepted now. It has been used in various ways by Bharat in the Natyashastra and by Kalidas in his epic plays, but in the context of music it is associated with the root word 'ranja' which means 'to colour' 'to tinge', 'to please'. According to R.R. Ayyangar's[1] commentary on Sarangdeva's 'Sangita Ratnakar', the definition of a Raga, according to Sarangdeva, (quoting Bharata and Matang) should be as under: 'A succession of pleasing sounds, the product of creative imagination and aesthetic flair, sparkling with melodic beauty and captivating the minds of listeners – that is a Raga'.

The essence of a Raga, according to Sarangdeva, is brought out in the following sloka:

"यों ऽ सौ ध्वनिविशेषस्तु स्वर वर्ण विभूषितः
रञ्जको जनचित्तानां स रागः कथितो बुधैः।"[२]

That is, a Raga is a specific and special composition of sounds, which is adorned with note patterns of ascending and descending order, and it pleases the minds and hearts of a listener. The fact that a Raga also embodies the ten or thirteen 'lakshanas of jatis' has been suggested by Kallinath, in his commentary on Sangita Ratnakar, which would change the above definition thus:

"यों ऽ सौ ध्वनिविशेषस्तु स्वरवर्ण विभूषितः
तथा च जातीनाम् ग्रहांशादि दस ;(त्र्योदश) लक्षणैःलक्षितः।
रञ्जको जनचित्तानां स रागः कथितो बुधैः।"

'Literally, a Raga is something that colours or tinges the mind with some definite feeling – a wave of passion, or emotion',[3] is how O.C. Gangoly portrays the effect of a Raga on a listener.

What is the origin of Ragas and how did they evolve? In the dictionary of Karnataka music, it has been said that the word 'Raga' came into use during the time of Kalidas. Many scholars like Matang (700 A.D. to 800 A.D.) and Nanyadev have mentioned about Kashyap's Raga descriptions. Kashyap was a musician scholar and his time is estimated to be 500 A.D. According to Matang's 'Brihaddeshi', Kashyap's definition of a Raga is as under:

"चतुर्णामापि वर्णानांयोगा रागः + शोभन (?)
सर्वो द्रुष्यते येन तेन रागा इति स्मृता।"

From this it is presumed that a Raga had got a definite form in the 4th, 5th century.

In Bharata's Natyashastra (approx. 2nd cent. A.D. to 4th, 5th cent. A.D.), Raga definition is not there, and there is no chapter on Ragas; however Matang's Brihaddeshi mentions about the use of 5 gram Ragas in the presentation of drama. Bharata classifies melodies under the name of Jatis, under two modes or scales (gramas), the sadja grama and madhyam grama. Bharata's jatis give the genus out of which the Ragas have been derived. The Jatis being similar to Ragas and having the same object, Ragas gradually took the place of Jatis.

In the historical evolution of Ragas, Matang's Brihaddeshi (approx. 8th, 9th century) is a very important landmark, because the word 'Raga', as is understood in subsequent texts on music, is first mentioned here.[4]

"स्वर वर्ण विशेषेण ध्वनिभेदेन वा पुनः।
रज्यते येनयः कश्चित् स रागः सम्मत सताम्।"

'A Raga is called by the learned, that kind of sound composition, which is adorned with musical notes in some peculiarly stationary, or ascending, or descending, or moving values (varna), which have the effect of colouring the hearts of men', is the explanation given by O.C. Gangoly.[5]

Both Dattila (a music scholar, a contemporary of Matang) and Matang mention the presence of 18 Jatis. According to Matang,

Jatis generate the Gram Ragas, by making use of the tonic initial, the prominent or Ansa note. Matang defines: 'the Jatis as being borne out of the initial notes and srutis (microtones). Hence they are called jatis, from which is borne the consciousness of flavour that is Jati. By reason of the birth of all kinds of melodies, jatis are so called'. Matang has categorised 32 Gram Ragas under 5 types of melodies, he called Gitis. These are Shudha, Bhinna, Gaur, Raga and Sadharana gitis. These gram ragas were borne from jatis and the factors which determined their characteristics were the ten 'Lakshanas' which were compulsory for the rendition of Jatis. The Raga Gitis are fourth in Matang's list, which are described as follows: "Attractive note compositions with beautiful and illuminating graces are known as Raga Gitis. Where the four varnas (probably the four characters of values of duration, ascent, descent, and movement) are met with in a graceful combination that is known as Raga". The eight varieties under the category of Raga Gitis, are Takka, Sauvira, Malava-pancama, Khadava, Vottaraga, Hindolaka and Takka Kaushika. These are the earliest Ragas known by name. Matang clearly describes Deshi Sangeet as that which is sung in different provinces by the common people as well as the rulers, and there's no binding by strict rules, and Marg, as that which follows some rules. The Grama Ragas (Marg Sangeet) gave rise to Bhinn, Bhasha, Vibhasha (Deshi Raga). According to Sunanda Pathak,[6] Deshi Ragas could also be taken to mean Deshi Sangeet.

Matang represents an early stage in the development of Raga. There's a considerable gap between the next treatise of historical value. In 1131 A.D. Someswara, who was King of the powerful Chalukya kingdom in the West, wrote 'Mansollas', which is the last of the books written before the influence of the Muslims changed the course of Indian music. Here also Marg and Deshi have been mentioned, and the origin of Ragas is given as Jatis, and the Ragas gave rise to Bhashas, Vibhashas and Antara Bhashikas (Deshi Ragas). The names and descriptions of certain Ragas like Sri Raga, Malava-Kaushik, Hindola, different varieties of Todi gives us an idea of the fact that a century before Sarangdeva's Sangita Ratnakar (1210-1247 A.D.,) many of the Ragas mentioned there had already come into existence.

The most exhaustive and authoritative summary given on Ragas is by Sarangdeva, whose treatise, Sangita Ratnakara, is a monumental work of the medieval period. He lived in the Court of the Yadava dynasty at Devagiri (Daulatabad), which was a centre of cultural and intellectual activity of the South and North India. By Sarangdeva's time the use of ancient concepts like 'gram', 'murchhna', the idea of emergence of Ragas from Jatis, was disappearing. The Jatis were rigid in their observance of the 13 Lakshanas. The concept of 'tivra' swar was introduced during this time. He gives a list of 34 Ragas of earlier times and enumerates 264 Ragas which were popular during his time. Sarangdeva describes the characteristics of Gram Ragas and their sub-divisions, Upraga, Raga, Bhasha, Vibhasha, Antar Bhasha and traces their origin to Jatis, and also mentions the 'Lakshans' like Grah, Ahms, Nyas etc. Gamak and Alankars used in Raga gayan are also described.

At this time North Indian music adopted a new 'Swar Gram' or scale, while as South India continued to adopt the old 'Swar Gram' or scale. This gave rise to the split into two Padyatis: the Hindustani Sangeet Padyati and Karnataka Sangeet Padyati. When Pandit Sarangdeva was writing his treatise in Devagiri, Sultan Allahuddin Khilji's invasion of the South, very greatly influenced the music scenario of the South as well as the North.

Major radical changes in music theory and practice were witnessed from the 13th to the 18th century.

FUSION OF INDIAN MUSIC WITH THE INCOMING PERSIAN AND ARABIAN MUSIC

The first half of the fourteenth century marks the most significant stage in the development of Indian music. The blending of Persian and Arabian music with the Hindustani music then prevailing, further increased the difference between the Karnataka Sangeet Padyati of the South and the Hindustani Sangeet Padyati of the North. In the South, ancient terms were continued but in the North, 'tivra' 'tivratara' and 'komal', new terms were introduced.

The music from Persia was accepted, absorbed and mixed with the indigenous Raga system, according to their structural similarities. During the rule of the Khilji dynasty, due to political stability, cultural development was given an impetus, and during this phase a natural outcome was the amalgamation of the Persian-Arabian music with the Hindustani music. Sultan Allahuddin

Khilji (1296-1315 A.D.)., who was himself a lover of music, had in his court, scholar, musician and poet, Amir Khusrau who was knowledgeable in Persian Arabic music. He understood and appreciated the principles of Hindustani music and contributed towards the development of Indian melodies. According to O.C. Gangoly,[7] "By a judicious combination of Persian airs (Maqams) and Indian Ragas, Amir Khusro introduced many derivative melodies, hitherto unknown to the Indian Raga system". He made interesting combinations of Persian and Hindustani Ragas and invented new Sankeerna Ragas like Raga Mazir, Sazgiri, Eman, Ushhak, Muwafiq, Ghanam, Zilaf, Farghana, Sarparda, Bakharaz, Manam; To some Ragas he has given new names: Qawl, Tarana, Khyal, Naqsh, Niger, Baseet, Talana, Suhla.

Indraprastha Mata

'Indraprastha' was the ancient name of Delhi, and according to some scholars the blending of the Persian Arabian music with the contemporary Indian music of that time came to be known as the 'Indraprastha' Mata. Under this many Indian Ragas were classified by Maqam Padyati (principle). There were some Ragas which had old names, but due to changes in note patterns, they had shifted from one 'mela' or 'that' to another. For example, Raga Vasant and Shri shifted from Kafi 'Mela' or 'That' to Poorvi. This new tradition of Indian music was called Kavval Bachhon ki parampara and in due course this was known as the 'Indraprastha Mata'.

Development of Dhrupad and Khayal

When Raja Mansingh Tomar sat on the throne of Gwalior in 1486, the Muslim influence was prevailing on all aspects of music. He thought of popularising the traditional Sanskrit form of composition called 'Prabandh' being sung at that time. The Dhrupad form of gayan emerged, at this time, in the popular local language, Brijbhasha. The subject matter of these compositions was worship of God, and they were well received by the music lovers of that period. The emergence of Dhrupad is to be viewed from the perspective of Abul Fazl, who called it 'mass's favourite and elite's own choice'. Inspite of the tremendous impetus music had received at the Courts, the popularity of folk music or local music was also increasing. A significant treatise, 'Manakutuhala' was written at this time. There was an assembly of the best known musicians and connoisseurs of that period in Raja Mansingh's court which included Sikander Lodi, Nayak Bakshu, Nayak Bhannu, Nayak Pandvi of Telengana, Mahmood, Lohang, Karna, Sultan Hussain Shah of Bengal, and the prevalent trends on music were discussed and analyzed. This was recorded in a book called Manakutuhala in the name of Raja Mansingh Tomar. According to 'Ain-i-Akbari', significant innovations in music were taking place and we find new trends in the development of music at this time. At the time Manakutuhala was written Vaishnav-Bhakti lead to the emergence of a special song form known as Bisnupad. Dhrupad emerged as a form popular in the Court and among the common man. Nayak Bakshu played a key role in developing Dhrupad into a developed form, at the court of Mansingh Tomar of Gwalior.

Faqirullah says that the language of the Gwalior region, enriched by the Radha Krishna theme and further vitalised by the recently popularised Bishnupada, was a Desavali dialect known as Desi-bhasa or Prakrit bhasa or Brij Bhasa. This could be the emergence of the Khayal.

In 1599, when Pundarika Vithala wrote his Raga Manjari, he refers to Persian airs, 'Parads', which were embellished with 'Gamakas', which term was used in place of Taans, in music parlance. Since Taans were a compulsory part of Khayal and not Dhrupad, it could be surmised that the form known as Khayal had already made its emergence in the musical repertoire of the period. The emergence of Khayal is characterised by the blending of Arabic word, Persian style and Indian thought, which gave it a definite character.[8] During the reign of Akbar and Jehangir at Agra and then during Shahjahan's reign at Delhi, the assemblage of artists included Gwaliaries, whose dialect was Gwaliari. They met with an equally developed Dehlavi, with Persian as their language. Against the Dhrupad, nurtured in the court of Gwalior and Delhi, the Qawwali, Ghazal and Lok gita were encouraged by the Sufi saints. In this spirit of intermingling, there was a well synthesized language called Hindustani which developed and the growth of Khayal received an impetus in this atmosphere.

Much of the classicism of music in modern India emerged

because of the way the Dhrupada gave way to Khayal during the medieval period.

Navras

In Bijapur Sultan Ibrahim Adil Shah II (ruled 1580-1627 A.D.) wrote 'Navras', which is a collection of Dhrupad compositions. In 'Navras' Ragas have been identified with Maqam. These were Bhupali, Ramkri, Bhairav, Hajiz, Maru, Asavari, Deshi, Poorba, Barari, Todi, Malhar, Gauri, Kalyan, Dhanashri, Kanhra, Kedar and Navroz.

Swar Mela-Kalanidhi

After Sarangdeva, the great landmark in the South is provided by a short but an eminently scientific treatise entitled 'Swar Mela Kalanidhi' (1550 A.D.) written by Ramamatya, of the Vijayanagar court. The most important contribution was the formulation of a scientific principle of classification of the ragas, on the basis of the common elements of their characteristic note structures.

The old Janya-Janak system of Raga classification, dating back to Yastik (which corresponds to the Raga Ragini Putra system of the North) is replaced by Ramamatya with the Mela Padyati. At Ramamatya's time Ragas were derived from 'Shadja Gram', the old Gram Murchhna Jati Padyati had disappeared. He takes the Mukhari mela as the Sudha Scale and gives it precedence. Ramamatya took note of the old principles and combined them with the changes and new derivations, so that they became acceptable, to the new requirements, *e.g.* Sarangdeva talked of 12 'vikrit' swaras, while, Ramamatya mooted 7 vikrit swaras.

Mela or That

The origin of the Mela That Padyati is attributed to Vidyaranya, who laid the foundation of the Vijayanagar empire, around 1337. He is considered to be the Aristocles of his time; he found 50 Ragas which were classified on the basis of 'Maqam Padyati', under 15 melas.[9] According to N.K. Bose, [10] in the Northern school, Mela or That was introduced at different times by Lochana, Vithala, and Ahobala; there were a total of 26 melas. In the Karnataka padyati authors like Ramamatya, Pundarika Vithala, Somnath, Venketeshwar and Tulajendra, classified Ragas into 30 melas.

Pundarika Vithala

Pundarika Vithala, a scholar who lived during Akbar's reign (1556-1605), wrote four treatises, on music, and accepted the 'mukhari' mela of the south as Shudha saptak; however he has described Ragas both under North Indian Hindustani Sangeet Padyati and South Indian Karnataka Padyati, in his books.

Pandit Lochan

When Pandit Lochan wrote "Raga Tarangini' (15th cent. approx.) Shudh that Kafi was accepted, and the term 'Maqam' was used as a synonym of 'Sansthan' or 'mela'. According to him two padyatis of Raga classification *i.e.* That Classification and 'Stree Purush' classification were used. Along with Dhrupad, Khayal form of singing had also come into practice.

Abul Fazl wrote the 'Ain-e-Akbari (around 1574 A.D.), which reflects the cultural scene of those times, and in which Raga-Ragini classification has been mentioned. Dhrupad form of Raga gayan has been mentioned as Deshi Sangeet and in different provinces different forms were prevalent, Chutkula in Jaunpur, Qawl, Tarana in Delhi, Vishnupad, in Mathura etc.

Swami Haridas, a saint scholar, and Tansen, his pupil, a prominent musician – composer, who popularised the Dhrupad form of singing and invented Ragas like Miya-ki-Todi, Miya Ki Sarang, Miya Ki Malhar, lived during Akbar's time.

Vyankatmakhi

In the latter part of the 17th century Vyankatmakhi wrote 'Chaturdandi Prakashika' in which he has followed the South Indian Karnataka Sangeet Padyati. He has constructed 72 melas, based on Mathematics, and out of these chose 19 for Raga classification. This was an important milestone in Raga classification and formed the basis for the present Raga that classification prevalent in Hindustani music today.

Hridayanarayana Dev (1660 A.D.)., wrote two books, in which the pattern of Raga descriptions is slightly different from the pattern adopted in the past. Instead of giving only the swars which are present and absent, the actual swars are mentioned hereby starting a new trend, which was also adopted by Bhatkhande. He has also mentioned the 'Aroh-Avroh' pattern of ragas, which is similar to the descriptions in present times.

Pandit Ahobal

At the end of the 17th century, Pandit Ahobal wrote 'Sangeet Parijat'. Accepting the Mela That Classification, Ahobal introduced in his Raga descriptions, the concept of 'Udgrahak Taan', for the initial group of notes with which a raga begins. This was a definite step in the evolution of Raga development. Most authors mention the same swar as grah, ahmsa and nyas, except Ahobal who gives different swars for Ahms and nyas, thereby reflecting a progressive musical sense.

Pandit Srinivas

In the latter part of the 18th century, Srinivas wrote Raga Tatva-Vibodh, in which he clearly accepts the 'That' padyati. He describes a Raga as having 4 parts – udgraha, sthai, sanchari, and muktai. At the time of singing a Raga, 'murchhna' was the first part of Raga alaap. 'Mela' decides the swars to be used in the Raga, the aroha-avroha is decided by the 'murchhna' and the Raga name is decided by the 'murchhna'. After this the alaap or udgraha is sung. Gradually 'murchhna' and 'mela' lost its relevance and there was no stricture about the first part of the Raga or udgraha. A raga could begin with the Madhya sadj note.

Muhammad Reza

In 1813, Muhammad Reza wrote 'Nagmat-e-Asifi', in which he has expressed his dissatisfaction with the Raga-Ragini-Putra classification of Ragas, according to Bharat, Hanuman, Kallinath and Someshwar. He proposed his own Raga-classification on the basis that the Raga and Raginis derived from them should have common 'swar' combinations or 'avyav'. In this treatise, for the first time Bilawal has been accepted as the Shudh Saptak. This is the foundation of our present Hindustani Sangeet.

In Modern Hindustani Raga presentation, the ancient 'jati lakshans' are not applied, but are reflected in corresponding modern terms. Previously each Raga had a special Swar as the Grah, Ahms, Nyas; now every Raga begins with 'Sa' or 'Ni' and also ends with 'Sa'. The 'ahms' swar is the vadi swar, which predominates in the Raga presentation. In the beginning of the 19th century, there was a spurt in the development of music, due to the efforts of two great stalwarts, Pandit Vishnu Narayan Bhatkhande and Pandit Vishnu Digambar Paluskar. In 1921 Pandit Bhatkhande composed 'Sri-mal laksya Sangitam' and 'Abhinava-raga-manjari', in which he accepts the Bilawal Mela as the fundamental scale, or Sudh 'That', and classifies Ragas under 10 thats. By this time 7 Shudh and 5 Vikrit swars were being used in Hindustani Sangeet Padyati.

HISTORY OF RAGA CLASSIFICATION

As we have said before, the Arabian Maqam system corresponds to the Raga Ragini classification system and the Mela That classification system of Indian music. We propose to give in short a historical background of Raga classification in Indian music. It would help us to understand the two systems better.

In order to study any concept minutely, it has to be classified before an analysis is possible. This is a natural process. As the process of Raga development was taking place in different periods of history, in order to meet the changing requirements, various scholars classified Ragas in different ways.

According to Sunanda Pathak, Raga Classification can be divided into three main periods:

I. Ancient Period
   1. Gram Murchhna Jati Classification
   2. Raga Classification System (according to Sarangdeva)
   3. Shudh, Chhayalag, Sankirna Classification

II. Medieval Period
   1. Raga-Ragini Classification system
   2. Mela That Classification System

III. Modern Period
   1. Ragang Classification system
   2. Mela That Classification system[11]

I. Ancient Period

1. Gram Murchhna Jati Classification System

Jatis were the musical forms, which were the forerunner of Ragas. During Bharat's Natyashastra, a monumental treatise written around the 2nd to 4th century A.D., 18 jatis were classified into two modes or scales or grams – the shadj gram and the madhyam gram. Matang classified 32 Gram Ragas under 5 types of melodic forms, he called Gitis, in his 'Brihaddeshi' written in the 8th century A.D. These gitis were mainly Shudha, Bhinna, Gaur, Raga and Sadharana gitis. These gram ragas were derived from jatis.

2. Classification System According to Sarangdeva

Sarangdeva's 'Sangeet Ratnakar' (13th century – here, we may note the fact that some historians treat the medieval period to start from the 9th century and some from the 13th century) belongs to a period in the history of Indian music, when there was a confluence of the ancient and the medieval periods. On the one hand there existed Bharat's Gram Murchhna and the Jatis deriving from them; on the other hand the medieval Raga-Ragini classification system had come into vogue. The number of Ragas during Sarangdeva's time had increased, which included the old ones related to Jatis. Sarangdeva proposed a classification of Ragas, prevalent during his time into the following categories:

(1) Gram Raga; (2) Raga; (3) Upraga; (4) Bhasha; (5) Vibhasha; (6) Antarbhasha; (7) Raganga; (8) Bhashang; (9) Upang and (10) Kriyang.

Categories like Ragang, Bhashang, Kriyang and Upang were described by him in the broad category of Deshi sangeet; in each of these there were two categories, 'Poorva Prasidha' and 'Adhuna Prasidha'.

3. Shudha, Chhayalag and Sankeerna Classification System

This includes 3 categories under which Ragas were grouped

(*a*) Shudha Raga – These were Ragas under which no trace or glimpse of any other Raga existed. *e.g.*, Bhairav.

(*b*) Chhayalag Raga: These were Ragas in which traces or glimpses of other Ragas existed *e.g.* in Raga Shudha Kalyan we get traces of Kalyan.

(*c*) Sankirna or Mishra Raga: These were Ragas in which two or more ragas were mixed. e.g. Raga Bhairav and Raga Bahar were mixed to make Raga Bhairav Bahar. In Raga Khat (also called Sat or Shat) there is a mixture of 6 Ragas, *i.e.* Suha, Kanhra, Sarang, Desi, Gandhari, and Sughrai. This type of Mishra Raga has been mentioned profusely by Faqirullah, in his Raga Darpana when he talks of the synthesis of Arabo-Persian music with the Indian Raga system.

II. Medieval Period

In the medieval period, Raga-Ragini classification as well as Mela That classification was in vogue.

1. Raga-Ragini Classification

At Matanga's time itself, in the 5th to 8th century A.D., the concept of 'Stree purusha' and 'janya-janak' relationship between Ragas was evident. Naradmuni in Sangita Makarand (approx 8th century) proposed 6 Ragas and 36 Raginis. The Male Female Neuter classification of Ragas was first put forward by Sudha Kalash in 'Sangitopanitshar' in the 14th century, in which 6 Ragas gave birth to 36 Raginis. In Sangeet Darpana (1625 A.D.) Pandit Damodar classified Ragas according to 4 opinions or 'Mata', the Bharat Mata, Shiv Mata, Hanumanmat and Kallinath Math, each of them describing the emergence of Raginis from Ragas. Other 'Matas' being used for the purpose of classification were Someshwar Mata, Ragarnava Mata and Indraprastha Mata. According to Dr N P Ahmad,[12] during Raja Mansingh's period (1486-1516 A.D.) in Gwalior 'the Raga-Ragini system for classifying Ragas was very much in vogue, whereas the That system was not utilized'. Pundarika Vithala, in the 16th century introduced the Raga-Ragini Putra classification in which he attributed male attributes to Ragas and female attributes to Raginis.

It is to be noted that Nanyadeva (1097-1133 A.D.) does not mention the concept of female Ragas nor does Sarangdeva after him (13th century).

2. 'Mela' or "That' Raga Classification System

At this time scholars stopped deriving Ragas from Gram Murchhna and Jatis and also classifying the Ragas according to Raga-Ragini and Putra Classification. The "Mela" or 'That' system of Raga classification was born, and its proponent was Vidyaranya (1320-1380 A.D.) the author of 'Sangitsar'. Around 1337 Pandit Vidyaranya founded the Vijayanagar Empire, and is credited with devising the Mela System of Raga classification, based on the Arabian theory of Maqam modal system. His theory comprised of the concept of Ragas being derived from Melas; the Ragas which had common 'shudh' and 'vikrit' 'swars' were grouped into one category or group called 'Mela' and the Raga which was very well known in the group was chosen to give a name to that "Mela".

The reason for the development of Mela is Raga. Mela is produced from Saptak, Saptaka is produced from Swar and Swar is produced from Shrutis. Mela was conceived for the purpose of Raga classification. That is why it is called 'Janya Janak' method.

Ramamatya (1550 A.D.) in 'Swar Mela Kalanidhi' made the most important contribution towards the development of Mela-That classification. He accepted the Mukhari Mela as the sudha scale and gave it precedence over others. In the Mela-Padyati introduced by him, there were 20 Melas.[13]

Pundarika Vithala, during Akbar's reign (1556-1605A.D.) accepted the Mela Padyati of Raga classification. In the middle of the 17th century Vyankatmakhi constructed 72 melas on the basis of mathematical principles, 19 of which were actually adopted for Raga Classification.

III. Modern Period

In Modern times, two forms of Raga classification are in vogue:

1. The Raganga Classification System
2. The Mela – That (Sansthan) Classification System

1. Raganga Classification System

In 1813, Mohammad Reza, a nobleman of Patna wrote Naghmat-e-Asifi, in which he expressed his dissatisfaction with the absurd and meaningless Raga-Ragini-Putra classification system prevalent at that time. Dr. N.P. Ahmad[14] says, 'he boldly criticized all the four Matas (viz. Bharat Mata, Kallinath Mata, Hanumana Mata and Someshwara Mata)...and pronounced them as entirely out of date...and then laid down his own mata'. According to him there should be some similarity or common feature between the Raga and its Raginis. He proposed a list of 6 main and 30 derived Raginis. His main Raginis were Bhairav, Malkauns, Hindol, Shree, Megh and Nat.

Another Raganga system was proposed by Narayan Moreshwar Khare of Ahmedabad in the late 20th century. This was to counter the limitations of the That Padyati of Raga classification, in which, with the number of Ragas increasing with the progress of time, it was not possible to categorize all of them in the limited gamut of 10 Thats. Pandit Khare said there were some special and distinctive group of swars or 'Vishisht swar sandarbh' on which any Raga is based. Many of these group of swars get their special identity by special arrangement of their 'Aroh-Avroha' or Vadi-Samvadi, or relationship or Samvad between two or three swars in a group. Ragas which contain these 'distinctive group of notes' or, 'vishisht swar sandarbh' should be treated as independent Ragas; other Ragas which contain glimpses of these special group of notes contained in the independent Raga, should be called Raganga or Ragas derived from the main Raga. Pandit Khare proposed 26 such groups of independent Ragas with their derivatives. For *e.g.* 'ma re pa' group of notes or Raganga characterise Raga Malhar, and any Raga which contains these swars or Anga of Malhar, would be sung with Malhar anga.[15]

Pandit Bhatkhande defined Raganga as a group of particular notes or 'Angas', which are the main feature of the body of a Raga, and any Raga classification which is done on the basis of these 'Angas', is known as the Raganga classification. The angas help in the formation of mixed Ragas (Sankeerna Ragas). In the medieval times, this classification was made popular by Lochan, Bhavabhatt, Ahobal, Faqirullah (Raga Darpana). Bhavbhatt has given 'Bhed' of Nat, Karnat, Kalyan, Velavali, Todi, Gauri, Gaur, Varati etc. Sultan Husain Sharqi of Jaunpur has given types of Raga Shyam, which information is given in Faqirullah's Raga Darpana. Pandit Bhatkhande has given 5 Angas of Kafi that – Kafi, Dhanashree, Kanhra, Sarang and Malhar.

2. The Mela That Classification System

Ramamatya, Lochan, Somnath, Pandit Vyankatmakhi all propounded the 'Mela' Raga classification theory. Vyankatmakhi based his theory on mathematical principles and constructed 72 Melas, which were widely accepted in the Karnataka Sangeet Padyati. Out of these 19 melas are in practice today. In modern times Pandit Bhatkhande was influenced by the Mela classification theory of Vyankatmakhi and classified all the prevalent Hindustani Ragas into 10 Thats which were the Hindustani counterpart of the Karnataka Mela system.

REFERENCES

1. *Sangeeta Ratnakara of 'Nissanka'* Sarangdeva by R.R. Ayyangar, Wilco Publishing House, B'bay, p. 72.
2. *Sangita Ratnakara of Sarangdeva*, Ed. by Pandit S. Sastri, Adyar Library and Research Centre, p. 2.
3. *Ragas and Raginis*, O.C. Gangoly, Munshiram Manoharlal Publishers Pvt. Ltd., p. 1.
4. Matang, '*Brihaddeshi*' (Trivandrum edition) p. 81.
5. *Ragas and Raginis*, O.C. Gangoly, Munshiram Manoharlal Publishers Pvt. Ltd., p. 2.
6. *Hindustani Sangeet Me Raga Ki Utpatti Evam Vikas*, Dr. Sunanda Pathak, Radha Publications, New Delhi, p. 37.
7. *Ragas and Raginis*, O.C. Gangoly, Munshiram Manoharlal Publishers Pvt. Ltd., p. 38.
8. *Tarjuma-i-Manakutuhala and Risala-i-Ragadarpana*, p. 32.
9. *Sangeet*, February, 1966, p. 7.
10. *Melodic Types of Hindustan*, N.K. Bose Jaico Publishing House (1968), pp. 403-04.
11. *Hindustani Sangeet Me Raga Ki Utpatti Evam Vikas*, Sunanda Pathak, Radha Publications, New Delhi, 1989, p. 214.
12. *Hindustani Music*, Dr. N.P. Ahmad, Manohar Publisher, Delhi, p. 32.
13. *Ragas and Raginis*, O.C. Gangoly, p. 52.
14. *Hindustani Music*, Dr. N.P. Ahmad, p. 57.
15. *Raga Vigyan*, Pt. Vinayakarao Patwardhan, an article, 'Raganga Padyati' by Pt. N.M. Khare, Sangeet Gaurava Granthmala, Pune, 1958, Part VI.

4

Blending of the Melodic Mode of the Persio-Arabian Region and the Hindustani Raga

Our objective in this chapter is to present a comparative study of the melody modes of the Persio-Arabian Region and Ragas of Hindustani Music. In order to do so it was important to discuss their historical development, which we have done in the previous chapters. As the Muslim rulers established and consolidated their hold over most parts of India, there was bound to be a cultural exchange also between the Persian Arabian influences being brought in and the music being practiced indigenously. At this point, it is in order to emphasize a very important point, something we have mentioned before, that there is an opinion that Indian music has influenced music of the other nations, from the time of the Greek philosopher, Pythagoras (580 B.C. to 500 B.C.). He is said to have visited India and imbibed knowledge of subjects like Music, Ayurveda, etc., and when he went back, these theories and practices influenced Greek music. "Some scholars are of the opinion that it was Pythagoras who had added to the growth of Greek music with the materials of music from India. Prof. O' Leary and other savants have proved that Pythagoras came to India, and learnt the art of music."[1] Swami Prajnananand[2] further quotes Prof. Lane to fortify his viewpoint, 'that they (Arabs) formed the system of music which has prevailed among them for centuries partly from Greek, and partly from Persian and Indian treatises." It is a well known fact that Greek music has influenced the music of Persia and Arabia, till about the 11th century AD; and when Muslims invaded India in the 10th and 11th centuries beginning with Mahmud Ghaznavi, and gradually consolidated their presence, their music and art also greatly influenced the prevalent theories and practices of India. So, the knowledge taken from here by Pythagoras was again brought back by the Persio Arab musicians who started a process of intermingling of the two cultures.

Here, we quote an excerpt by Swami Prajnanananda, to highlight the point that we have made above. "We find that during the reign of the Mughal Emperors, Humayun and Akbar, India was influenced by Persia in the domains of music, and architecture. It is also found that Amir Khusrau introduced some Persian modes and tunes in the system of Indian music, during the reign of Alauddin-Khilji in the fourteenth century. However, it is found in history that not only countries like Persia, Arabia and Greece are indebted to India, but India is also indebted to other ancient civilized countries for different materials of culture and civilization in different times".[3] The foreign melodies gradually got amalgamated as Ragas and Raginis of the Indian system, as mentioned before in the chapter on 'History and Development of Ragas of Hindustani Music'. Here, it would be in order to recapitulate in short the history of the development of the melody mode of the Persio-Arabian Region. The Maqam or Arabian mode was modal in character, as we see in the chapter on Maqam. According to Pelican History of Music,[4] Ibn Misjah (d.c. 715) may be regarded as the father of Arabian classical music, and perhaps the first theorist to codify its theory. During this period, there existed eight 'finger modes' (asab) for the lute. Music theory, at this time was influenced by Greeks, a process which continued till the 11th century. Gradually these developed and got more systematized into eighteen modes (four primary, eight subsidiary and then six additional modes). In the 13th century, Shafi-al-Din (d. 1294 AD), who was one of the foremost musicians of the Persio-Arab world, introduced a new music theory based on the old 'Khorasanian Pandore'. The melodic modes, popular at that time, got absorbed in the new modes proposed by Shafi-al-Din. The proposed 12 principal modes were called 'Maqam', each of them had two Ragas deriving from them called Shubhas, which were 24 in number. Each 'Shubha' had further 2 Raginis under them called Gusvas, which were 48 in number.

Swami Prajnanananda[5] is of the opinion that the system of the Maqams and their derivatives of Arabian music correspond to 'that' or 'mela' and the Raga and their Angas of Indian music. The Larousse

Encyclopaedia[6] also confirms this view of the similarity of the nature of the music of the Perso-Arabian countries and India. Though 400 years before, at the time of Arab invasion of Sindh, many musicians had settled there; however mutual social and cultural exchanges started from the 11th century, when Sultan Mahmud Ghaznavi (d.1030 A.D.) invaded India. It was this system of the melodic modes, called 'Maqam' and their subsidiary 'Shubhas' and 'Gusvas' of the Persio Arabian music that was imported by the Muslim settlers in India, as is stated by Maulvi Abdul Halim Sharer.[7]

With the founding of the Khilji dynasty, an important era commenced in the area of the blending of the two music systems of the Persio-Arabian Region and India. The foremost among the personalities credited with bringing about this harmonious blending of the two music cultures was Mir Amir Khusrau, who lived during the reign of Sultan Allahuddin Khilji (1296-1315 A.D.). The Sultan himself was a great connoisseur and patron of music. As a result of the political stability that existed during the Khilji dynasty, the development of the fine arts was given an impetus and a natural outcome was the amalgamation of the Persio-Arabian music with the Indian counterpart.

Here, an important fact to bear in mind is that, when we attempt to relate certain Ragas with their counterparts in Arabian music, *i.e.* the Maqams, we must remember that the melodic structure and form of the Ragas, as well as the Maqams that existed then in the medieval period, may have been very different from the form that exists now in the modern times.

CONTRIBUTION OF MUSICIANS TOWARDS THE BLENDING OF RAGA AND MAQAM

We will now take a look at the contributions of some prominent musicians (and their writings) who have been associated with the intermingling of the two music systems, that of the Persio-Arabian Region and the Indian. We would also have to take cognizance of certain musical treatises of historical importance, where in mention has been made of the cultural exchanges that were taking place at that period and the resultant new forms and melodies that were coming into existence. This period may be ascribed to be approximately from the 13th century A.D. to the 17th Century A.D.

Here we may mention that these mutual exchanges could be described in two ways:

1. By way of identifying individual Arabian Maqams with their corresponding Indian Ragas.
2. By way of describing the composition of new Mishra Ragas and their component elements as a result of the interest that the Muslim settlers were taking in the existing native music.

We get a very vivid picture of the mutual exchanges that we are attempting to describe from Faqirullah's Raga Darpana (1662) in Persian and from Tarjuma-i-Manakutuhala and Risala-i-Ragadarpana[8] which is an English translation of the above. According to Dr. N.P. Ahmad,[9] "Raga Darpana is basically a translation and commentary on the earlier book Man Kautuhal, which was written during the period of Raja Mansingh Tomar of Gwalior (1486-1516 AD)." Faqirullah has given details in the first chapter about the book Man Kautuhal, and his own description may be summarized as follows:

"To those who are fond of music Faqirullah says that he found an old manuscript, "Man Kautuhal". This book was written during the rule of Raja Mansingh, who was the King of Gwalior and was a great patron of music. He had a vast knowledge of this art. He composed Dhrupad style of music. He discussed and debated the subject of music with some renowned musicians of his time. Following are some of the names of such musicians: Nayak Bhannu, Nayak Bakshoo, Nayak Pandvi of Telangana, Mahmood, Lohang, Karna.

When above experts were assembled in Gwalior, the King felt it was very rare for so many Nayaks to assemble together. He, therefore, considered it desirable that the views of different musicians about the various Ragas be discussed and the same may be recorded in writing so that posterity may be benefitted from such writings. Consequently, all the performers and scholars of music discussed the various Ragas, Raginis and their Putras, and compiled a book on music, in the name of Raja Mansingh. This book was named 'Man Kautuhal'. Since such a book could be considered a reliable and authoritative source, I have chosen to translate it. I have prepared a brief version of Man Kautuhal and named it Raag Darpana (Mirror of Melody). Raga Darpana would eliminate the need for going through Bharat Sangeet, Sangeet Darpana and Sangeet Ratnakar."

In the following paragraphs, we make an attempt to put forth the observations of Faqirullah on the subject under discussion, as he reported on the existing trends of the times.

After giving an exhaustive list of mixed Indian Ragas, which were popular at that time, and identifying their component Indian Ragas, Faqirullah in Raga Darpana, goes on to say that he has mentioned all the Ragas till now based on information gathered from 'Man Kautuhal' and that hereafter he would continue his narration with the information gathered from the contributions made by Mir Amir Khusrau, Sheikh Bahauddin Zakaria Multani and Husain Sharqi.[10]

MANSINGH AUR MANAKUTUHALA

According to Mansingh Aur Manakutuhala (1954)[11] which is a Hindi translation of Faqirullah's Raga Darpana, Amir Khusrau chose 12 Ragas out of the Ragas (here the word 'Raga' has been used loosely for both 'Maqam' and 'Raga') that were in use, at that period, and named them according to the names of 12 'tals'. He combined Barari, Malari and Husaini to compose a Raga called Diwali. He added Panjgah Maeer Raga to Todi Raga and called it 'Movar'. The name of Raga Poorvi has been changed to Ganam and Shahnaz Maqam has been combined with the Indian Shatrag to make Zailf Raga. In Persian music Shatrag has got another name-Gizal. Apart from Shatrag, there is no other Raga which is the same in Persian and Indian music. Amir Khusrau feels that according to the trends prevailing in his time, there was no difference between 'Marg' and 'Deshi' music. Shatrag has the same form in Persian as well as Indian music, whether it be 'Marg' style, or 'Deshi' style.

There was some Raga called 'Fargana' which was sung by the 'Kavvals' of Afghanistan. Apparently Fargana was a place in Persia, after which this Raga was named. The 'alap'of this Raga was combined with Raga Sarang of the Indian system to make a new Raga Usshaq.

According to Shri Dwivedi, author of Mansingh Aur Manakutuhala[12], Gaud Bilawal and Gaur Sarang were mixed to make the very popular Raga Sarpardah, about which Amir Khusrau is said to have remarked; "I sang this Raga and I called it Sarpardah". This Raga is taught and sung like an aprachilit Raga even today. (Aprachilit Raga is one which is not commonly sung by all musicians). Further there is mention of Raga Farodast, which was produced by mixing some melodies with Kanhra Raga and of Aimani Raga, produced by mixing the Persian Maqam Nairez with the Indian Raga Yaman.

The Raga Sazgiri came into existence by mixing Purvi, Vibhas, Gaur, Gunkali with the Persian Maqam Iraq. The Indian raga Kalyan was intermingled with the Persian maqam Nairez and given the new name of Shanam. Faqirullah points out that some Ragas like "Sazgiri, Bhakarz, and Ushshaq were actually created by a process of combination of two Ragas" or more and singled out for attention by Mir Amir Khusrau; while as some others were given less attention and merely given new names, after minor alterations. For example, Raga Aiman and Raga Vasant were combined to make Raga Aiman-Vasant.

TARJUMA-I-MANAKUTUHALA AND RISALA-I-RAGADARPANA

According to Tarjuma-i-Manakutuhala and Risala-i-Ragadarpana a translation in English of Faqirullah's Raga Darpana, we get a similar picture as the one given in Mansingh Aur Manakutuhala of the intermingling of the Persian and Indian Ragas, as described by Faqirullah with slight changes in names and spellings. Below, we give a description of the composite Ragas, along with the notes and commentaries available in the above mentioned book.

Mir (Amir Khusrau) – God's grace be upon him did prefer to choose twelve Ragas, out of the known ones, and assigned to them suitable names. Those (twelve) were composed as: In Bairari and Malasri, he mixed Dogah and Husaini, naming the resultant melody Muwafiq. Others also call it Vilavali. According to notes to the translation in Tarjuma-i-Manakutuhala....,[13] there is a tono-melodic relationship between Husaini and Dugah. Husaini is a major Maqam, and its first derivative or Shobah has got two 'naghmas' or melodies, and is therefore called Dugah (two melodies). In the Persio-Arabian system, each Maqam has got two "Shobas" 'one rising from its lower tetrachord (pasti) another from its upper tetrachord (bulandi). 'Pasti' and 'bulandi' to be understood as 'purvanga' and 'uttaranga' of the Indian terminology'.[14] Muwafiq, literally meaning accordant (agreeing) was composed as a Maqam, which would be the opposite of Mukhalif, an accepted Persian Maqam. Mention may be made here of the three words Vilāvali, Vilavāli and Vilāvala, being used here for the same melodic structure, even though the structural similarity between Muwafiq and Vilavali may be doubtful, just as

Husaini and Bilavala of the present day do not have any structural similarity. Bilavala could be considered to be a phonetic variant of Vilavala.

Khusrau mixed Todi with Panjgah, a derivative or Goshah of Muhayyir, and named it Muhayyir. In the Groves Dictionary of Music and Musicians, Vol. I (old)(pgs. 179 to 186), 'Muhaiyar-al-Husain' is the name given to an 'awazat'. The notes to the translation in Tarjuma-i-Manakutuhala describe Mohayyir as a Shobah of Husaini, and Panjgah that of Rast: 'sounding on the upper and lower tertrachords, respectively'. Amir Khusrau is supposed to have been very enamoured of Mohayyir, mentioning it often in his prose and poems.

Purvi, the Indian Raga, has been renamed as Ganm by Khusrau. This was a name given by himself as there is no mention of this name in the works of authors prior to him. The word 'Ganm' refers to a tribe. Its co-root Maqam was the Arabic Ghanam 'meaning booty plundered in war'.[15] The Persian Maqam Shahnaz was intermingled with 'Khat-raga' (presumably also found in the Arabian maqam system) and called it Zilaf. According to the elaboration given in the notes to the translation in Tarjuma...,[16] Zilaf, a popular central Asian melody may have contributed towards the emergence of Zila of the Zila-Pilu combine, presumably of the Indian Raga system. In the Persian system Khat-raga is the counterpart of 'Gazal'. 'Ghazal', is more often read as Ozzal, but Amir Khusrau has phonetically associated it with ghazal; therefore the former reading seems intended. Khat Raga or Shat Raga is supposed to have the same form in both the Marga and Desi system of music of the Indian variety; and according to Faqirullah the Arabian music also had a melody of similar form and name. Khat Raga is a combination of six ragas, the legendary Raga Deepak being one of them, and therefore it derives the name of Shat or Khat.[17]

Like Zilaf and Bakharz, the Persian 'Maqam', Farghana is supposed to have originated in Central Asia, according to Amir Khusrau, and 'all made India their homeland.'[18] However, Farghana is not found as a 'maqam' or even its derivative, shobah or gosha, so when we refer to Farghana as a maqam, it is 'used rather loosely'[19] and it has been actually referred to in Persio-Arabian music as a lahn or Awaz i.e an upcoming regional tune introduced in India by one of the ethnic groups coming here in the wake of the Turks.[20] Khusrau combined Farghana with 'Sarang' and Basant of India and Nawa of Persia, (which is an important Maqam even listed by Shafi-al-din in the 13th century) and called the resultant Raga as Ushshaq. Ushshaq is also an important Persian Maqam named by Shafi-al-din in his Risala-al-Sharifya. Here we may add a note that Nawa has got as its derivative, 'the even colorful Navruz practiced in South India as Nurocika.'[21]

Another important principal Maqam Rast from Shafi-al-din's list of Maqams of the 13th century was introduced by Khusrau into the mainstream of the Indian Raga system, when he combined it with Gauda Bilavala and Goud Saranga, to create a beautiful melody Sarpardah. Literally speaking Rast means 'leading straight to' (as against going zig-zag). Amir Khursau based his Sarpardah on it, which eventually lead to the shaping of Bilawala as a major scale. According to the opinion of some experts Rast and Bilawala had 'all its notes straight'.[22]

Technically the characteristics of the melodic scale of Rast and Bilawal 'constituted of unmodified notes'.[23] Sarpardah, as its name signifies is a leading parad (a melody corresponding to Maqam in the Persio-Arabian system, and that which has got imbibed into the Indian system) which is almost the same as a basic scale. Mohammad Reza wrote Naghmat-e-Asifi[24] (in 1813 A.D.), and declared Bilawal to be the Sudh scale of the Indian music system, as well as its Sudh 'that', a theory practiced even now as an equivalent of 'C' major of western music. This may well have had its roots in history, when 'Sarpardah' Raga or 'parad', was developed by Amir Khursau (1251-1325 A.D) and identified by Faqirullah in Raga Darpana (1633-66 A.D.). From the time of Amir Khusrau to Faqirullah, Rast and Sarpardah have been accepted as being similar to each other.

Farqirullah quotes poet Amir Khusrau's verse as under:

در گونڈ، بلدول و گور سارنگ، و از مقاماتِ

فرسِ راست را ملحق سرپرده نام نهاده

چنانچه خود (امیر خسرو) می فرمایند:

گاه ترنم به نوائی کرخاست

جانبِ سرپرده شد از راه راست

"And sometimes in melody-weaving the voice, as it rose, was led towards Sarpardah by the way of Rast (the pun being on the 'straight path' and the smooth run of notes)". Further, Faqirullah in Raga Darpana, talks about the references to 'Rast' made by the poet, in his historical masnavi 'Qiranussadain', wherein he intimately remarks: "Rast appeals straight to the heart as the sharpness of its notes flies straight as an arrow.....".

"And the same Sarpardah, in due course, brought Bilavala within its fold, this is proved also by Pundarika's contemporary reporting (soon after 1599 A.D.) to the effect "सरपरदोऽथबिलावले"... Thus from Rast to Sarpardah and from Sarpardah compounded together with Bilawala, to the present day Sudha scale has its own history ranging from 13th to 17th, 18th centuries".[25] Here another point of historical importance, about the development of Indian music is highlighted, that the adoption of Bilawal scale as Sudha scale of modern times was not made consequent upon copying of the European major scale.

Having talked about Rast, Sarpardah and Bilavala, in the above paragraphs, now we proceed further, with the description of other combinations of Persian and Indian airs.

Khusrau produced the Raga Farodast, by mixing Raga Kanhra with a Persian 'ahanga'. The full form of Farodast is 'Farud-dasht', 'procedurely denoting the finale, or closing phrases of an orchestral performance',[26] in particular Naubah band music. Farodast was derived from this by Amir Khusrau. He produced Yamini through an admixture of Aiman and Nay-rez. Aiman appears to be only a corruption of Yemen. The new Raga Sazgiri was created by combining the Persian Maqam, Iraq, with the Indian Ragas, Purbi Bibhasa, Gaura and Gunakali.

"Saz-giri, on the face of it, looks like an innovation meant to make it resemble its kr-dhatu words Deva-giri, Guna Kri etc. But, whether it was a virgin contribution of Amir Khusrau, may be viewed in the light of the fact that the noted art-historian Ustad Said Nafisi of Iran, cites it among the 148 most popular melodies of the Sasanian period, which pre-dates Amir Khusrau (ref. Tarikh: Tamaddun-J-Sassani P.13)."[27] Whether or not Sazgiri was originally composed by Khusrau may be left to doubt, but we have evidence that he refers to it in his poem Qiranussadain. In this he says that the melody Sazgiri, as sung in Iraq, sounded like the melody 'Iraq', as sung in that land. Faqirullah has singled out this Raga for indepth study.[28]

According to further information gathered from the Notes to the translation in Tarjuma-i-Manakutuhala....,[29] we gather that the Arabo-Iranian Maqam Iraq as it was being taught in 1978 in the 'College of Traditional Music' in Baghdad, resembled the melodic structure of the Indian Raga Kafi, as well as that of the first tone or mode of the diatonic scale Phrygian. The ten-note scale, of the Maqam Iraq starting from mandra dha, Alif (A) is reproduced below.

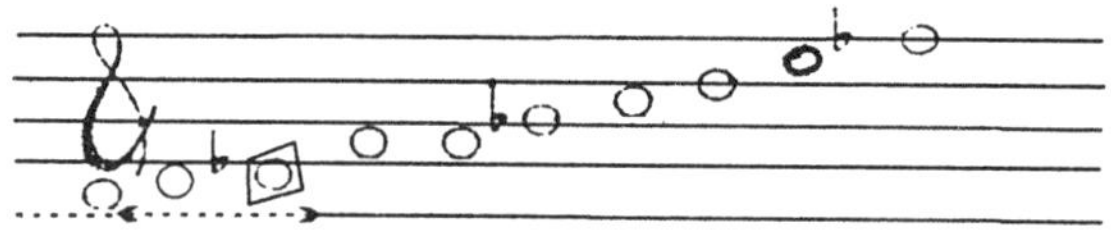

Notation of the Maqam Iraq
[Ref. Tarjuma-i-Manakutuhala,
Notes to the Translation, page 273 (128)]

Bakharz was a Turkish melody, brought to India during Khusrau's time. Khusrau intermingled it with Deskara. The Raga Sanam was a mixed raga composed by Amir Khusrau by combining Kalyan with Nay-rez. Sanam is an Arabic term for 'idol' and 'Ney-rez' is a Persian word meaning flute-tune.

Khusrau has singled out Sazgiri, Bakharz, Ushshaq and Muwafiq, for singular attention and these along with their Indian counterparts could be taken up for detailed analysis and study.[30] Thakur Nawabali, in his Marifun Naghmat, has elaborately described some Iranian ragas like Yemin, Nawa, Zilaf, Sarpardah, Sazgiri and Husaini, which have survived in the Indian system till modern times. In the case of other Maqams and Ragas, Khusrau did go only so far as to allot to them the congenial company of some maqam or ahanga and making them adopt a fanciful name.

Pundarika Vithala

The fact that the Raga and the Maqam were merging with each other, is also brought out by the fact that the illustrious Sanskrit writer, Pundarika Vithala (1599 A.D.) in his treatise 'Raga Manjari', acknowledged this turn of events in the musical history of India, and is the first Sanskrit writer to relate the Persian melodies with the Indian. An erudite scholar of the period, he came to Akbar's court after the fall of Asirgarh (1599 AD). He wrote for Raja Mansingh Kachwa, perhaps in Fatehpur Sikri itself. In Raga Manjari, he says:

अन्येपि पारसीकेया रागाः परद नामकाः।
सम्पूर्णाः सर्वगमकाः काकल्यानि तरिताः सदा।।

'Besides these (the indigenous) are the Persian ragas called parad. All of these are sampurna, full of gamakas, and sharpened kakali notes, invariably employed'. The 'Parads' referred to above have been equated with ragas as follows:

"Rahavi with Devagandhar, Nishapur with Kanhara, Mahur with Sarang; Zangula (Vulgo Zangla) with Vangala; Ahanga with Desi, Ghara with Malhara; Shahnaz with Kedara; Iraq with Dhanashri; Husaini with Jaijavanti, Busalik with Malava, Yaman with Kalyan; Sarpardah with Vilavala, Bakharz with Deshkara, Hijaz with Asavari; and Ushshaq with Devagiri (Ragamanjari Sls 2-14).[31]

Faqirullah

After Pundarika Vithala (1599), Faqirullah is the only one among the reliable music scholars to have touched upon the subject of Indianization of the incoming Muslim musical influences. He reported his observations during the period 1662-66 in his Raga Darpana approx. sixty years after Pundarika Vithala; and by this time many of the Persian airs had merged with the Indian system. For example, Pundarika Vithala had included Raga Yaman among the 'Parsikeya ragah', while as Faqirullah makes it fraternize with Gunakali and Kalyan in giving shape to Bhopali.[32] The other ragas which were imbibed, as reported by Faqirullah, were as under:

"Purbi, Gauri and Shyama melodically mingled correspond with Farodast" (Persian Farudasht): p. 45.

(Khusrau (1251-1325 AD) had combined Raga Kanhra with a Persian ahanga to make Raga Farodast).

'Bringing in Shahnaz, a Persian maqam, Khatraga was given the name of Zilaf (p. 59) (this intermingling is the same as in the time of Khusrau)'.

'Farghanah, one of the Persian maqams, when mixed with Sarang, Nawa and Basanta, made consonant with each other came to be called Ushshaq' (p. 61) (This combination is the same as in the time of Khusrau).

'(From Indian melodies) Gaunda, Bilavala and Gaura-Sarang, and from Persian maqams Rast, when mingled with one another, yield

Sarpardah' (p.61) (Khusrau is reported to have made the same combination).

In Aiman an admixture of Nayrez yields Yamani'(p. 61).

'Purbi, Bibhasa, Gaura, Gunakali (the Indian ragas) and Iraq, the Persian maqam, made to mix with each other, lead to what has been named as Sagziri' (p. 63).

'In Desakara, Bakharz, a Persian maqam mixed, came to be called Bakharz' (p. 63). 'In Kalyan, an intermingling of Nayrez gave the one named as Sanam' (p. 63). 'Turk Todi (Skt. Turuska Todi) has Dogah (shoba) of Husaini as its components' (p. 71).[33] All the above combinations reported by Faqirullah to have existed during his time, bear resemblance to the ones reported to have been composed by Khusrau in the early 14th century.

Faqirullah, the author of Raga Darpana (1662) was himself knowledgeable in the music of both the Indian and Arabian systems and in the second part of the treatises, he has mentioned about his knowledge of 11 naghmas, which have similarity with Indian ragas, which would have been popular during his time. According to 'Tarjuma-i-Manakutuhala and Risala-i-Ragadarapana[34] these are as under:

- Uzzal and Khat (Sata) ragas are the same
- Mukhalif is accordant with Ramakali
- Nay-rez sounds so akin to Kalyana
- Ashiran and Badahansa are very close to one another.
- Dugah and Sudh-Todi exercise extreme proximity
- Nawa and Saranga have closest resemblance.
- Rast and Nata exhibit direct accord.
- Arban and Purya Dhanashree are very much alike.
- Majawat and the Persian Naghmah in which Barwah is these days sung and is popularly and commonly called Barwa; and some know it as Thumri are all closely related to each other. Shah-naz and Sri-Raga which the people of Punjab so fondly sing have a sort of relationship. Meghlub and Basanta are mutually related.

Hazarat Bahauddin Zakariya Multani (1862 A.D.)

Hazarat Zakariya belonged to the Suhrawardi Silsilah, in the category of a Sufi-sheikh. Musicians from Persia, Central Asia and

Arabia used to visit his Khanqah at Multan. He was a gifted musician, knowledgeable in the Indian as well as the Arabian music systems, and is said to have exercised his influence far and wide. There are quite a few ragas alive to this day, which are from his creations.[35]

Tohfat-ul-Hind

Another significant treatise on music presumably during Akbar's reign, or may be after it, was Tohfat-ul-Hind. According to Dr. N.P. Ahmad[36] the name of the author given in Riew's catalogue is Mirza Khan. "According to another opinion, during Akbar's time, one of the grandsons of Abdur-Rahim Khan – e-Khanan was named Mirza Khan, who was alive in 1055 A.H. (1645-46 A.D)".

In the chapter on Raga Adhyay, a list of Ragas is given which were invented by Amir Khusrau. They are reproduced below,[37] and are more or less the same as reported by Faqirullah in Raga Darpana, except for the difference found in the origin of Raga Muhaiyar. As reported in Tohfat-ul-Hind, this Raga is based on Raga Gara and a Persian Muqam, or according to another opinion a combination of Todi and Usshaq. While as in Raga Darpana, Faqirullah describes Muhayyir as a mixture of Todi with 'Panjgah' a derivative or goshah of Muhayyir. Again in Tohfat-ul-Hind, Yaman is a combination of Hindol and a Persian Maqam, while as in Raga Darpana, it is reported to have been composed by mixing Aiman (corruption of Yaman) with Nairez.

Ragas innovated by Amir Khusrau are the following:

1. Muhaiyar: This Raga is based on Raga Gara and a Persian Muqam. According to another opinion, it is a combination of Todi and Ushshaq.
2. Sazgiri: It is a combination of Purvi, Gauri, Gunkali and a Persian Muqam.
3. Yaman: It is a combination of Hindol and a Persian Muqam.
4. Usshaq: For making the Raga, a Persian Muqam is combined with Sarang and Basant.
5. Muafiq: It is also called Devali. It is an outcome of the combination of Todi, Malshri, Dogah and Husseini.
6. Ghanam: It has been composed through some alterations in Raga Purvi.

7. Farghan: It is also called Farghana. It is a combination of Gunkali and Gaura.
8. Sarparda: It is also called Sarparda and it has been constructed by combining Gaud Sarang with a Persian Muqam.
9. Bakharz: It is a combination of Deshkar and a Persian Muqam.
10. Farodast: It is a combination of Raag Kanhra, Purvi, Gauri, Shyam and a Persian Maqam.
11. Sanam: It is a combination of Kalyan and a Persian Muqam. Some people identify it as Nairez.

COMMENTS OF MODERN AUTHORS ON THE BLENDING OF MAQAM AND RAGA

Let us now consider the commentaries of some 19th century musicians, who reported on the process of assimilation of the incoming influences into the Indian music system. The spirit of intermingling, of adjustment and exchange, continued to pervade the atmosphere long after the first set of mixed Ragas were composed by Amir Khusrau. Many scholars, who were knowledgeable in the Indian as well as the Arabo-Persian music systems, have given their commentaries on their blending.

MUSIC OF INDIA – 1793 A.D.

It would be befitting here, to mention the views of William Jones and N.A. Williard (Music of India – 1793 A.D.), who have given a detailed account of the Maqams, Shobahs and Goshas of the music of the Persio-Arabian Region, which according to them, had got assimilated with the indigenous music. They have also mentioned about the similarity found between the Raga-Ragini-Putra classification System and the Maqams and their derivatives.

MADAN-UL-MUSIQI

Mohammad Karam Imam, who belonged to the period of Nawab Wazid Ali Shah of Avadh, in the middle of the 19th century, has written a treatise 'Madan-ul-Musiqi' in which he has talked about Amir Khusrau's contribution towards the synthesis of the Persio Arabian Maqams which were gradually introduced into the Indian raga system prevalent at the time.[38] This process, incidentally had started from the 11th century onwards. In the 6th chapter (pg. 141) he has described various types of Gauris, two of which are said to have counterparts in the Arabian Maqam system. The types of Gauri Ragas mentioned by him are as under:

1. Godani Gauri
2. Chaiti Gauri
3. Asa Gauri
4. Lata Gauri
5. Bhatiyal Gauri
6. Manohar Gauri and
7. Prasthani Gauri

Out of these two types, the Prasthani Gauri and the Manohar Gauri have similarity with the Maqam Iraq and Maqam Usshaq, respectively. Both these maqams are to be found among the 12 primary Maqams of the Arabian scholar Shafi-al-din . Here we may mention that Amir Khusrau is considered to have likened Iraq with Sazgiri,[39] while as currently it is being taught in Baghdad in "The College of Traditional Music," in a note pattern similar to that of Kafi. According to Tohfat-ul-Hind[40] Amir Khusrau mixed Purvi, Gauri, Gunkali with the Persian maqam 'Iraq' and called it Sazgiri. Again, if we go further and find out the composition of the Raga Sazgiri, as it is sung now, we find it is produced by mixing Puriya with Purvi.[41] It is to be noted that tracing the form and nature of the Persian and Indian ragas which were blended, to the present times, would be an exercise, which could be taken up separately, and would be beyond the scope of the present work.

Mohammad Karam Imam, in his book Madan-ul-Musiqi, also talks of many varieties of Bhairav, and one of them was a Raga innovated by Hazrat Mir Ali, who combined a Persian maqam with Sind Kafi. Muwafiq has been described as a mixture of Malashri, Barari, Husaini and Sanam (p. 151), while as in Raga Darpana, Muwafiq is said to be a blend of Barari, Malashri with two maqams of Arabian origin, Dogah and Husaini. Muwafiq is also called Vilavali and it has been called 'Dewali' by the authors of Tohfat-ul-Hind and Mansingh aur Manakutuhala'.[42]

Mohammad Karam Imam has also talked of many Ustads like Hazrat Bahauddin Zakariya Multani (1862 A.D.), Sultan Hasan

Sharqi of Jaunpur (1460 A.D.) and Faqirullah, who were gifted musicians, connoisseurs and composers of their times. They greatly contributed towards the development of Indian and Persio Arabian music and their mutual blending. Other combined ragas reported by him are as under:

Mujir:	Combination of Multani and one more Raga.
Gauri:	It is reported to be similar to Poorvi.
Zilaf:	Combination of Parsee maqam Shahnaz and Khat. (Similar to Faqirullah in Raga Darpana and the author of 'Mansingh Aur Manakutuhala'. Khat raga is reported to be sung in a similar way in both the Margi and Desi styles of music)
Ushshaq:	Combination of Basant and Sarang
Sarparda	Bilawal and Gaud Sarang were mixed with the maqam Rast.
Farodast:	Combination of Kanhra and another raga
Yaman:	Combination of Aiman and Nairez
Ghazal:	Combination of Poorvi and Vibhas and Gaura
Sanam:	Combination of Kalyana and Nairez
Sazgiri:	This has been mentioned as Khorasan.

MOUSIQUI HAZRAT AMIR KHUSRAU

Now, we turn to the memory of the late Ustad Chand Khan, doyen of the Delhi Gharana of Hindustani Music, about whom Dr. Krishna Bisht and Dr V.K. Rangra, in their book Ustad Chand Khan[43] have said; (he) "was not only one of the foremost vocalists of his time, he was also an excellent teacher…another facet of his life was his interest in musical literature." His third book 'Mousiqui Hazarat Amir Khusrau' (published in 1978), "gives the history of Indian music since Vedic times linking it with the history of music in Arabia, and finally their fusion."[44] Apart from mentioning the Ragas innovated by Amir Khusrau, as a result of the blending of Indian and Arabian music, various talas invented by Amir Khusrau are also tabulated. Some varieties of musical forms originating from Arabian Music like Tarana, Naqsh, Gul, Qaul, Qalbana are also explained.

According to Ustad Chand Khan, Amir Khusrau was well versed in Arabian Ragas or Maqams, as well as their prevalent

Hindustani counterparts. The following are the list of Ragas, innovated by Amir Khusrau (according to Ustad Chand Khan), and their component Ragas.[45]

1. Sazgiri: Combination of Poorvi, Gaura, Gunakali, Gara, Kafi, Desh
2. Mujir or Mujeh:
3. Tawafiq: Combination of Zilaf, Husaini and Sarang
4. Ushshaq: Combination of Sarang, Basant and Nawa
5. Ghanam: Combination of Poorvi, Yaman and Hindol.
6. Neshapur: Combination of Yaman, Hindol and Azam
7. Muwafiq: Combination of Todi, Malashri and Dogah
8. Zilaf: Combination of Shahnaz, Khat and Husaini
9. Ghazal: Combination of Dhanashri, Khat and Kafi
10. Oj: Combination of Gunakali, Iraq and Malashri
11. Gara: Combination of Kafi, Nauroz and Ghazaal.
12. Bakharz: Combination of Deshkar, Farghana and Nawa.

Ustad Chand Khan is of the opinion that the Raga classification system prevalent in the maqam 'padyati' or system (with each maqam having shobas and goshas or subsidiary ragas deriving from them), was similar to the Raga classification system found during that period in the Indian Raga system (where Raginis, Putras or Bhariyas were emanating from the Main or 'Mool' raga).

The second important factor pointed out by Ustad Chand Khan is that the Indian Ragas combined by Amir Khusrau to make the resultant mishra ragas, were very different from each other, i..e. their individual characteristics were dissimilar. So it is difficult to understand how mutually different ragas could have combined to form a resultant mishra raga. Further, the nature and form of the ragas prevailing then might have been very different to the structure of the ragas as we know them now. So, the fusion or the blending of Maqam with Ragas and the composition of Mishra ragas, leaves many questions unanswered.

Mention of Persian Ragas by Pandit V.N. Bhatkhande

Pandit V.N. Bhatkande, the music scholar and theoretician of the Modern period, had felt the need to study books by Persian authors to get an idea of the fusion between Persian and Indian Ragas. He had himself referred to Sanskrit, English and Persian scholars and given descriptions of the Persian Ragas which were imbibed into the mainstream of Indian music. Ragas created by Amir Khusrau as a result of the blending of the two cultures have been profusely mentioned by him in his four part Sangeet Shastra. According to Pt. Bhatkhande, Raga Sazgiri had been mentioned by Mr. Bannerjee to be similar to Bhairav, Raga Zilaf has been mentioned as having a definite Persian origin. A detailed study of these and other ragas could be taken up in future research projects.

REFERENCES

1. *Music of the Nations*, p. 129.
2. *Ibid.*, p. 109.
3. *Ibid.*, p. 130.
4. P.H.M., p. 123.
5. *Music of the Nations*, p. 112.
6. L.E.M., p. 37.
7. Maulvi Abdul Halim Sharer, *Sangeeta*, September 1933 (An article, Hindustani Music).
8. Tarjuma-I-Manakutuhala... .
9. Hind. Music, pp. 20-21.
10. *Mansingh Aur Manakutuhala*, p. 75.
11. *Ibid.*
12. *Ibid.*, p. 76.
13. *Tarjuma-i-Manakutuhala*, p. 271.
14. *Ibid.*
15. *Ibid.*, p. 272.
16. *Ibid.*
17. *Ibid.*
18. *Ibid.*
19. *Ibid.*
20. *Ibid.*
21. *Ibid.*
22. *Ibid.*
23. *Ibid.*
24. Hind. Music, p. 57.
25. *Tarjuma-i-Manakutuhala...*, Introduction, pp. LII and LIII.
26. *Tarjuma-i-Manakutuhala...*, Notes to the translation (No. 69, No. 125), pp. 268, 272-73.
27. *Ibid.*, (No. 127), p. 273.
28. *Ibid.*, (Nos. 128, 131), p. 273.
29. *Ibid.*, (No. 128), p. 273.

30. *Ibid.*, (No. 131), p. 273.
31. *Tarjuma-i-Manakutuhala...*, Introduction, p. xxv.
32. *Ibid.*
33. *Ibid.*, pp. xxv, xxvi.
34. *Tarjuma-i-Manakutuhala...*, p. 227.
35. *Tarjuma-i-Manakutuhala...*, Notes to the translation (No. 106), p. 271.
36. Hind. Music, p. 34.
37. *Ibid.*, p. 53.
38. *Madan-ul-Musiqi*, pp. 156-57.
39. *Tarjuma-i-Manakutuhala...*, Notes to the translation (No. 128), p. 273.
40. Hind. Music, p. 53.
41. Mariffunnagmat (Pt. I) p. 300.
42. *Mansingh aur Manakutuhala*, p. 75.
43. Ustad Chand Khan, Preface.
44. *Ibid.*, p. 35.
45. *Mousiqui-e-Hazrat Amir Khusrau*, p. 201.

5

Iqa-Rhythmic Melodic Mode of the Persio-Arabian Region-Comparison with the Tala of Hindustani Music

CONCEPT AND HISTORY OF IQA

In the music of the Arabian countries the modal concept of melodies has a parallel in their rhythmic patterns, which are also modal in character. Such rhythms, together with the modal melodies and their embellishments, comprise the three essential characteristics of Arabian music from early times. As we have mentioned before, the music of the Persio-Arabian Region (or West Asia) was influenced prominently by three cultures, Arab, Persian and Turkish. Iqa is the metric unit of the Arabian and Persian music. The word Iqa, used for rhythm and its patterns, was systematized by the third quarter of the seventh century.[1] It is similar to the Western rhythm measure but closer to the Indian Tala system. In Turkish music 40 or 50 rhythmic cycles, called Usul are used.[2] Al-Kindi and Al-Farabi also called the seven or eight principal rhythmic modes, used by the Mesopotamians and Syrian Arabs, by the term Usul (9th, 10th century).[3] This aspect of music is well preserved in Turkey. As we mentioned in the chapter on History of Music of the Persio-Arabian Region, till the 16th century, there was considerable amount of fusion between the music of the Arab and Persian speaking people, and the melodic and rhythmic modes, would have had a common structure.

However, due to political considerations, the music in Persia developed along different lines and subsequently, though rhythmic sophistication continues, the Iqa system has virtually disappeared in Iran (former Persia). "Rhythmic variety extends from strictly metric with rhythmic ostinato through free rhythm with metric elements to the thoroughly non-metric. Improvisatory techniques stress development of short motifs through variation, extension, contraction and melodic sequence."[4]

Dr. H.G. Farmer says that ..... "the Persians have been claimed as the inventors of Iqa or rhythm by Iban Khirdadbih".[5] According to another opinion, there was an healthy exchange between Arabia and Persia in the field of art and culture, and the Persians adopted the rythmic modes of the Arabs, Iqa, 'although it was not until the time of Harun (786-809 A.D.) that they took the Ramal mode.....'[6]. The 'Ramal' mode was a rhythmic pattern added later on by Ibn Muhriz.

The Systematists, following Safi Al-Din defined the rhythmic cycles in two ways; one was to divide a cycle into the same number of sections as there were units, and a symbol was given to indicate the units sounded; the other was to divide the rhythmic cycle into feet of two to four time units, and giving the syllables ta, na (each equivalent to one time unit) and tan, nan (each equivalent to two time units) to different units. Ta and tan were initial in a foot, na was medial and nan final. It was assumed that the initial time unit was always sounded, the final one was not sounded most of the time and the sounding of the medial unit was optional.[7]

The following is an extract from Safi-al-Din's Kitab-al-adwar, showing the rhythmic cycles. These are representative examples of each rhythm mode, as variants also existed.

Rhythmic Cycles – Shafi Al-Din (13th century)[8]

thaqīl awwal	Oo. Oo.Ooo.O.Ooo.	(3+3+4+2–4)
thaqīl thānī	Oo.Oo.O.Oo.Oo.O.	(3+3+2+3–3–2)
khafīf al-thaqīl	O.OxO.OxO.OxO.Ox	(2+2+2+2–2–2+2+2)
thaqīl al-ramal	Ooo.Ooo.O.O.O.O.O.O.Ooo.	(4+4+2–2–2–2+2+2+4)
ramal	O.O.O.O.O.O.	(2+2+2+2–2–2)
khafīf al-ramal	O.Oo.O.Oo	(2+3+2+3)
hazaj	Ooo.Oo.Oo.O.	(4+3+3+2)
tākhifī	O...O.O...O...O...O.O...	(4+2+4+4+2–4)

O = initial time unit of foot (always sounded); o = medial time unit (optionally sounded): . = final time unit (not sounded); x = final time unit (sounded).

After Shafi-al-Din, al Ladhiqi was able to describe 18 cycles, which were in common use and another 9, which were rare. The longer cycles had symmetrical time units (compounds of feet of 2,4 and 8 time units); the shorter ones having asymmetrical combinations of units (compounds of feet of 2 and 3 time units). Examples of the latter are Rawan – 2 + 3 + 4; Samai – 3 + 3 – 4.[9]

The Iqaat (singular Iqa) are metric modes employed in various metric compositions, to influence the nature of phrasing and the patterns of accentuation of a musical composition. These modes are rendered on percussion instruments within the ensemble, including the Tablah (a vase shaped hand drum) and the Riqq (a small tambourine). Each Iqa has a specific name and pattern of beats ranging in number from two to twenty four or more.

Following is a list of the beat patterns of Iqaat most commonly heard in the contemporary music of Egypt and the Levant.[10]

List of Beat Patterns of Iqaat-Egypt and Levant

Wahdah Saghirah 4/8

Wahdah Kabirah 8/8

Wahdah Taqasim 8/4

Ayyub 4/8

Wahdah wa Nisf 8/8

Baladi 8/8

Sa'idi 8/8

Masmudi 8/4

Sama'i Thaqil 10/8

Sama'i Darij 6/8

Ithnayn'Ala Thamaniyah 2/8

Sittah'Ala Thamaniyah 6/8

The Genius..., p. 132.

Following is a list of eight rhythmic modes described by Al Kindi (d.c. 874):[11]

Eight Rythmic Modes Described by Al Kindi

1. *Al-thaqīl al-awwal*
2. *Al-thaqīl al-thānī*
3. *Al-makhūrī*
4. *Khafīf al-thaqīl*
5. *Al-ramal*
6. *Khafīf al-ramal*
7. *Khafīf al-khafīf*
8. *Al-hazaj*

NOHM..., p. 448.

Each of these modes is given above in its cycle (daur) or theme, which is repeated at one's liberty. Each of these rhythmic modes could have variations also; several of these branch modes or variations are called Anwa. In Ikhwan al-Safa, twenty two different arrangements of these rhythmic modes have been given. Al Farabi (d.850 A.D.) and some other Arabian theorists have described these modes, some of which are supposed to have become very popular. These rhythmic modes were an inherent constituent of all measured music, (al naghm al mauzun). Each consisted of a distinct cycle (daur) of beats and rests which was repeated throughout a performance. Al-Kindi (d.c.874), who was a scholar of Arabian music has forwarded the idea of comparing Arabian modes with the rhythmic modes of the Jews. The following excerpt gives us an idea of these Jewish modes.[12] (Similar to the list of modes mentioned above.)

The eight rhythmic modes of the music of the Jews were:

1. first Mode = Al-Thaqil al-awwal, which was comprised of three consecutive beats followed by a quiescent beat. According to Al-Farabi and Al-Khwarizhu, this first mode consisted of adwar of three consecutive beats, but they have not mentioned about the quiescent beat. The alphabetic signs or notations of the beats and rests were: ta ha ta ha ta ha ha ha, etc. *i.e.* ta = a beat and ha = a rest.

2. Second Mode = Al-Thaqil al-thani, which comprised three consecutive beats, a quiescent beat and a movement beat.
3. Third Mode = Al Makhuri, comprised two consecutive beats without the time of a beat between them, followed by a solitary beat which was characterised by a rest following or its equivalent.
4. Fourth Mode=Khafif al-thaqil, comprised three consecutive beats, without the time of a beat between them, but with the time of a beat between every three beats.
5. Fifth Mode = Al-Ramal comprised a solitary beat, with its characteristic rest following and two consecutive beats.The notation of the two light beats = tau..tau, tau, and tauna tau tau.
6. Sixth Mode = Khafif al-ramal, comprised three movement beats, as defined by Al-Kindi and Sa'adyah.
7. Seventh Mode=Khafif al-Khafif, comprised two consecutive beats, and between every two beats and two beats of the time of a beat as mentioned by Al-Kindi. But it is interesting to note that Ibu Khurdadhbih, Al-Farabi and Al-Khwarizmi have not mentioned about this mode.
8. Eighth Mode=Al-Hazal, fundamentally this eighth mode belonged to a conjunct rhythm i.e a rhythm, in which the time values of the beats are of equal duration.

Al-Kindi's (c.801-873) definition of the rhythmic cycles was imprecise and probably was related to early Abbasid practice than to Umayyad practice. However, during this time (8th, 9th century) identifying the rhythmic mode of a song was apparently more important than naming its melodic mode. The rhythmic cycles were divided into two sets – Heavy and light (like the melodic modes) and may have referred to different performing styles.[13]

During this time, for the Arabs, rhythm was associated with the sister science of Prosody (metre: Science of versification). Ibn Sina and Al-Farabi dealt with the subject of rhythm in detail, but their descriptions and explanations were very abstract. Ibn Zaila (d.1048), a pupil of Ibn Sina put forward the various patterns of beats that could occur, and indicated that the rhythm cycles were flexible internally.[14]

Rhythmic Cycles (8th-9th centuries)[15]

'heavy' slow		*'light' fast*	
thaqīl awwal	O O O	kahfīf al-thaqīl	O O O .
thaqīl thani	O O O . O	mākhūrī	O O . O .
ramal	O . O O .	khafīf al-ramal	O O O
		Khafīf al-khafif	O O .
		hazaj	O O . .

O – sounded beat; . – unsounded beat

Shafi-al-Din relied on Al-Farabi for most of his definitions on Rhythm but his explanations were independent, clear and unambiguous.

The rhythmic modes evolved and changed after Al-Kindi. The following is an example of the Mujjanab Al-Ramal mode (the rhythm notation is shown on a single stave line under the melody notation). The Ramal Mode has 12 beats.[16]

An Example of the Mujjanab Al-ramal Mode

These rhythmic modes were performed on a tambourine (daira) with jingling metal plates (sunuj) or bells (jalajil) in the frame, a drum (tabl), or tiny kettledrums (nuqairat). Two or more tones were obtained on these instruments, one of them low and strong and the other high and weak. In addition to these the plectrum (mizrab) by which the strings of the lute were pulsated, also okayed this rhythm when it was convenient.[17]

During the 13th century A.D. when Safi-al-Din's new theory of music called 'the Systematists' was influencing Arabian music, the system of the melodic and rhythmic modes became more elaborate and found the pattern, which, in outline is retained to this day.

The pattern of rhythm described during this period is given later in the section on the Structure of the rhythmic mode, Iqa.

Later on Qutb al-Din added a further five cycles, including one called Turki. By the late 15th century, further additions to the system had taken place; al-Ladhiqi lists and describes 18 cycles of rhythm which were common, and lists 9 rarer ones. Some of these are extremely complex having a large number of units; e.g. thaqil-48, darb al-fatah-88, chahar darb-96. The structural details of these complex rhythmic modes are given later, in this chapter.[18]

Composition and Structure of the Rhythmic Mode, Iqa

Let us now attempt to understand the composition of the rhythmic mode, Iqa. Each Iqa (or Wazn) has a unique pattern of beats numbering from 6 to 38. Although, theoretically about 100 Iqaat are said to exist; in actual practice, a much smaller number is used and in modern times even Western metres are used.[19] Basically these rhythmic cycles are measures of musical compositions, with their component units representing units of measurement of time of a particular melodic piece. It always becomes necessary, when attempting such descriptions to compare its components with a corresponding rhythm pattern of some other musical system. The pattern of Iqaat may also be explained with reference to Western theory of music. Each of these measures "had a basic cycle (daur) and variant species (anwa). The basic cycles varied in complexity: thus that of Khafif-al-ramal is simple and equivalent to a western 6/8-bar of quavers (two groups of three), while that of Khafif-al-thaqil is like an asymmetrical bar of 10/8 made up of 3+2+3+2 quaver beats where the last beat of each of these four groups is a quaver rest."[20]

Each cycle of the rhythmic mode is made up of "a determined succession of qualitatively differentiated beats or accents (naqqarat, plural of naqqara), which is repeated throughout the entire piece or section of it." The cycle is made up of principal beats (naqarat asliyya) divided into ajza (parts), each of the ajza being made up of one to five smaller units. The beats are called by the following names: dum (strong beat); tak (weak beat); mah (a beat stronger than dum and usually following it); Ka, Kah or Ke and ta (beats weaker than tak).[21]

From the above we surmise that the cycle of an Iqa consists of alternated rests and beats, which are recognized by their sound and timbre. In the Egyptian tradition, the dumm, is produced by hitting closer to "the Central position of the drum or tambourine head", and emits a deep sound. The takk is a high pitched crisp sound made by beating or tapping near the rim of the instrument. For the purpose of notation, the dumm is represented by a note with a downward stem, and the 'takk' by a note with an upward stem. Although the theoretical presentation and description is simple, the practical interpretation can be highly complex and presents a variety of possibilities. The above method of playing on a percussion instrument is used by contemporary percussionists. While performing, the percussionists remain within the principal framework decided upon, but usually "improvise further rhythmic sub-divisions and create numerous variants using a vast vocabulary of timbral effects".[22]

CYCLES OF AN IQA

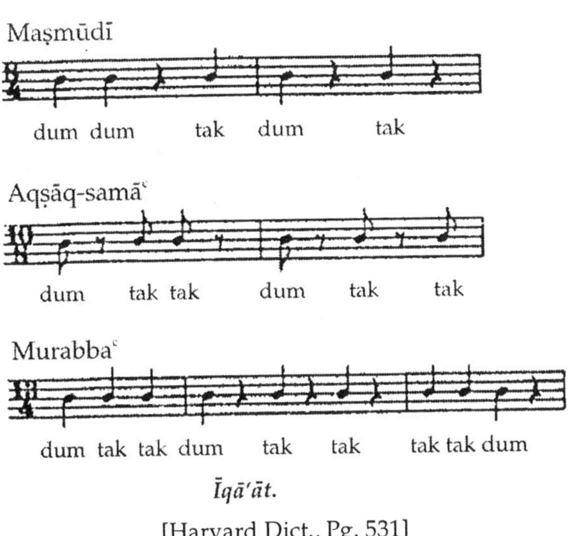

Īqā'āt.

[Harvard Dict., Pg. 531]

TALA OF HINDUSTANI MUSIC

The rhythmic modes used in Persio-Arabic music may be compared with similar types existing throughout the East. In the Indian Raga-Tala system also, rhythm or 'laya' and the concept of measurement of rhythm, Tala, is a must for any melodic composition. 'Swar' *i.e.* tone, laya, *i.e.* rhythm, and 'pada' *i.e.* words or literature, are the three important musical concepts without which most musical forms cannot be composed.

The word Tala, implies beating or striking together. It could be done by handclapping, striking together of cymbals or playing on percussion instruments like the Tabla, Pakhawaj, Dholak etc.. The natural sound emanating from the top surface of the percussion instrument, which is made of leather, forms the 'bol' or 'theka' (Syllables) of the Tala, like 'dha', 'dhin', 'tin', 'ta'. These 'thekas' may be played on the instrument, or spoken with the accompaniment of handclapping. Similar to the Arabian rhythm, Iqa, a deep or high pitched sound is produced, depending on whether the surface of the instrument is hit nearer the centre, or nearer the rim, respectively.

Each cyclic measure (avartan) of the Hindustani Tala consists of divisions called 'vibhag', having a number of beats called 'matra'. The first beat of each division may be called a 'tali' (also called 'bhari') or 'khali'. While indicating the beats of a Tala by handclapping, the 'tali' is shown by a clap and the 'khali' by a rest or waive of the hand; the other 'matras' being counted on finger joints. While playing the Tala on the percussion instrument, more emphasis is given on the 'tali' than on the 'khali'; generally deep sounding 'thekas' like 'dha' 'dhin' are used for playing the 'tali' and light sounding 'thekhas' like 'ta', 'tin' are used for playing the 'khali'. The first 'tali' of each cycle or 'avartan' of a tala is called the 'sam', with which any melodic composition begins or ends. We may note, here, that the technique of playing the percussion instrument in the Hindustani Tala system, consisting of an alteration of beats and rests, which are recognizable by their sound or timbre, finds a parallel in the rhythm cycle of an Iqa, the Persio-Arabian metric system. Another notable similarity between the two rhythmic systems lies in the way the cycle of an Iqa or Tala is presented in a programme; in both the cases, within the structured framework of the cycle, there is a possibility of creating a variety of rhythmic sub-divisions with different timbral sounds.

The cycles of a few common Talas of Hindustani Music are given ahead. Most of these Talas are associated with a particular Form or Style of Presentation of Hindustani Music; Ektal is for Khayal; Cautal for Dhrupad, Dhamar for Hori, Dhamar; Dadra, Kaharva and Dipchandi for Thumri and other light classical forms.

Cycles of a few Talas of Hindustani Music (Each 'bol' or 'theka' represents one 'matra')[23]

tīntāl	:	$^{+}$dhā dhin dhin dhā/^{2}dhā dhin dhin dhā
		^{0}Dhā tin tin tā/^{3}tā dhin dhin dhā
Ektāl	:	$^{+}$dhīn dhīn/^{0}dhāge tirakiṭa/^{2}tū nā
		^{0}kat tā/^{3}dhāge tirakiṭa/^{4}dhī nā
cautāl	:	$^{+}$dhā dhā/^{0}dhīn tā/^{2}kiṭa dhā/^{0}dhīn tā
		^{3}tiṭa kata/^{4}gadi gina
dhamār	:	$^{+}$ka dhi ṭa dhi ṭa/^{2}dhā –
		^{0}ga ti ṭa/^{3}ti ṭa tā –
jhūmrā	:	$^{+}$dhin dhā tirakiṭa/^{2}dhin dhin dhāge tirakiṭa
		^{0}tin tā tirakiṭa/^{3}dhin dhin dhāge tirakiṭa
rūpak	:	^{0}tin – traka/^{2}dhin–/^{3}dhā ge
jhaptāl	:	$^{+}$dhī nā/^{2}dhī dhī nā/^{0}ti nā/^{3}dhī dhī nā
dādrā	:	$^{+}$dhā dhī nā/^{0}dhā tū nā
kaharvā	:	$^{+}$dhā ge nā ti/^{0}nā ka dhin –
dīpcandi	:	$^{+}$dhā dhīn –/^{2}dhā dhā dhīn –
		^{0}tā tīn–/^{3}dhā dhā dhīn –

$^{+}$ indicates *sam*, the first *matra*, except in *rupak*, which begins with a *khali vibhag*.
^{0} indicates a *khali vibhag*. Arabic numbers indicate *tali* vibhags other than *sam*.

In contemporary music practised in the late 20th century, in Kuwait and Bahrain, pearl fishermen utilize percussion instruments including a clay pot 'comparable in construction and playing technique to the ghatam of South India.'[24]

REFERENCES

1. NOHM, p. 451.
2. Harvard Dict., pp. 530-31.
3. NOHM, p. 451.
4. Harvard Dict., p. 531.
5. Music of the Nations, p. 128.
6. *Ibid*.
7. New Grove I, p. 519.
8. *Ibid*., p. 520.

9. *Ibid.*
10. The Genius..., p. 132.
11. NOHM, p. 448.
12. Music of the Nations, pp. 115-16.
13. New Grove I, p. 516.
14. *Ibid.*, p. 517.
15. *Ibid.*
16. NOHM, p. 455.
17. *Ibid.*
18. New Grove I, p. 520.
19. Harvard Dict., p. 530.
20. PHM, p. 124.
21. New Grove I, p. 523.
22. The Genius..., p. 132.
23. Harvard Dict., p. 782.
24. The Genius ..., p. 135.

6

Instruments

In this chapter we will be describing as well as making a comparative study of the instruments of the music of the Persio-Arabian Region and Hindustani music. In this process our aim would be to find out their similarities and differences; and also whether they influenced each other in the evolutionary process.

Two opinions have to be borne in mind when we compare the Indian instruments with the Arabic or Persian instruments. One point of view believes that the instruments evolved within India from earlier known instruments; second, that they were imported with the invasions which took place during various historical periods. In the case of most Indian instruments, there is a strong opinion that they evolved from or are modifications of our own ancient instruments. Here we may mention the viewpoint proposed by Allyn Miner on the subject of change and synthesis brought about by the continuous invasions of the northern parts of India after the 11th century, and specially after the establishment of the Delhi Sultanate in the 12th century by the Turkish Moslems. For six centuries 'the art, literature, religion and customs of Turkish, Persian and Central Asian cultures came to India with the artists and scholars of the Muslim courts. Historical records hint that for some time the Persian music of the courts thrived without any influence of India's musical culture (cf. Askari 1972:102). Eventually, however, the presence of Indians in the courts became a force for change and synthesis.'[1] Allyn Miner tells us, that this process began significantly at the time of Amir Khusrau and came to an end under the great Mughals by the 16th and 17th centuries.

Iconographic Evidence

The study of the development of instruments has been greatly helped by iconogrpahic evidence, *i.e.* the presence of sculptures, in temples and Buddhist places of worship. For example, in tracing the history of stringed instruments, we find that bow harps and short necked lutes were being used from the 2nd century B.C. to the 8th century A.D., the period when Buddhism dominated South Asia. The Burmese saung-gank and Chinese p'i-p'a developed from these. The iconographic remains of the period from 7th century A.D. to the 13th century A.D. reveal that these bow harps and short-necked lutes were replaced by stick zithers, with one or more strings. Some of them are seen to have bowl shaped resonators also. These are the ancestors of the modern Bin or Vina of Hindustani Classical music.

Another important point of view that would be kept in mind as we proceed in this chapter is, that in the evolutionary process, as migrations took place and there was intermingling of cultures, instruments travelled from place to place. In this context we must remember that a few Indian instruments also owe a debt to many other areas and countries other than Persia & Arabia, in their development.

Here, it would be pertinent to give the example of the lute, to show how similarities have been found in instruments of different countries. According to Curt Sachs, this could have resulted from movement of instruments along with the invasions. The lute corresponds to the Indian Vina and the Koto or Chin in China. It existed between 206 B.C. and 220 A.D. in the orchestra of the Chinese Haw Dynasty. The Veena is depicted in the Gandhara statuettes in 100 A.D. The classical Arabic name Ud is given to the same instrument in Asian countries and Egypt. In North African countries, west of Egypt, the Greek word Qitara has been adopted. This was taken into Arabic before 1000 A.D. along with other terms of the Ancient Greeks. The philosopher Ibn Sina (Avicenna) who was born in Persia in 980 A.D. used the Persian term Barbat. According to one writer, the Persian King Shahpur I (241 to 273 A.D.) invented the instrument.

History of India Which Allowed the Cultural Intermingling

While comparing the Arabian and Persian instruments with their Indian counterparts it would be pertinent to mention the historical events which resulted in the intermingling of the cultures of the two regions. The history of the sub-continent of India bears evidence of major migrations, which took place through the passes and valleys in the North West mountains of the sub-continent. There were major inroads and excursions from Alexander the Great in 327-324 B.C. to Nadir Shah in 1739 A.D.. By the 10th, 11th century, groups from Afghanistan, Turkestan introduced Islam to India;[2] and the Sultanate of Delhi had established a predominantly Muslim rule throughout the Indo-Gangetic plain, by the 13th and 14th centuries. The Sultans of the Tughlak Dynasty tried to conquer the South in the 14th century, but the majority of South India was ruled by Hindu Kings during the Vijaynagar period (mid 14th to 16th centuries). Some parts of South India like Tanjore and Travancore never came under Muslim rule. This was the reason that the southern parts of India were not influenced by Arabo-Persian music as much as the North.[3]

Here, we may mention an example of the resulting influence of the mingling of cultures and races. A similarity is found in the husky vocal quality and a strong slow quaver of the voice between singers from Kashmir and Persia. 'The plucked Sehtar and the mallet struck Santur are both played with the rapid repeated note riz characteristic of Western Asian string instrument technique.'[4]

In the case of Arabo-Persian instruments, it is surprising that not much account has been accorded to instruments in the descriptions given by theorists of the Arabo-Persian region. In the post Safi-al-din (died 1294 A.D.) period, Abd-al-Qadir (died 1435 A.D) in his treatises has described the various Arabian instruments as a general survey. Some of the instruments described are of Chinese and Indian origin. An European organ adopted by the Arabs or Persians in their art music is also mentioned. This reflects the ease with which instruments travel and also 'the musical debt of the surrounding cultures to the Islamic Middle East'.[5]

The continued penetration of Islamic faith and culture and Arabo-Persian influence, into the sub-continent of India resulted in a strong distinct intermingling in music and especially in Hindu instrument making. The outer shapes of most instruments coming from the Arabo-Persian areas were preserved and according to Curt Sachs, the foreign names in many cases were kept intact or adapted to local idioms. Terms such as Sitar and Rabab were not changed, and others, such as Sanskrit Sanayi and Tamburi can be traced to Persian instrument names like Surnaya and Tambur. The Marathi Sarod comes from the Persian Sarud.[6]

Definition and Classification

According to the Groves Dictionary of Music, instruments are 'the tools by means of which we manipulate the raw materials of music. The instruments share a relationship with one another'.[7] There are some factors which all instruments have in common, as there are other factors, which overlap these common principles and cause the instruments to sound unlike each other.

According to Suneera Kasliwal, a classification proposed by Hornbostel-Sachs in 1914, on the basis of accoustic principles is as follows: (1) idiophones, (2) aerophones, (3) membraphones and (4) chordophones. In the West this classification is considered to be the most scientific till date.[8]

In the account given in the New Grove Dictionary of Music and Musicians Vol.I, on Arabian Music, Folk, Instrumental (pp. 535-538), the instruments described fall under the above four primary categories. In Western countries, there is a view that, while classifying instruments into three categories *i.e.* string, wind and percussion, membraphones and idiophones may be considered in the percussion category.

This classification has been accepted in India for more than two thousand years. Bharat uses the term Atodya for all the musical instruments and classifies them in four major classes *i.e.* tata (chordophones), avanadha (membraphones), ghana (idiophones) and sushira (aerophones) (quote Bharat Natyashastra 28/1).

> Tatam chaivavanaddham cha ghanam sushirmeva cha/
> Chaturvidham tu vigyeyamatodhyam lakshanvitam//

Bharat further clarifies that while tata and avanadha were considered primary because they produced swara and tala, ghana and sushira were subsidiary. Melody comes from tata and sushira while ghana keeps the metre and avanadha adds vigour, explains Bharat.[9]

Curt Sachs says that instruments are products of human imagination, which in its creativeness has no boundaries. He says, 'But a completely logical classification is an impossibility because instruments are the artificial contrivances of man. They do not lend themselves to a consistent system as do plants and animals.'[10]

Sources

The Arabian civilization, can be traced back to the third millennium B.C., but it lost its wealth, power and culture; when with the rise of the Roman Empire the old trade routes between the Mediterranean and the Orient were abandoned. However, new centres of trade and prosperity grew in the first few centuries A.D.; they were Al-Hijaz (Arabia) and Al-Hira (ancient Babylon). In these towns and surrounding areas migrating Arabs mingled with all the nationalities of the Persio-Arabian Region and their musical life had 'an international, interoriental character, which, much too carelessly, we call Arabian'.[11]

In the beginning of the 7th century A.D. Islam unified the region from the Malayan Archipelago to Spain, and a homogeneous culture emerged, where instruments were exchanged between nationalities of this region.

The Kurdish spike fiddle was found in Egypt, the old Semitic frame drum was found in Arabia as well as Spain, the Persian Oboe found in Borneo as well as in Morocco. These oriental instruments travelled to Islamic empires as well as Europe.[12]

The Persio Arab theorists have not given much attention to the description of instruments used in Art music of the Arabs. Al Kindi (c.792-874) provided information on the lute, Al-Farabi (d.950 A.D.) was concerned with the scales that could be produced rather than the structure. Safi-al-din and after him theorists of the Systematist school paid even less attention to instruments. An anonymous treatise, Kanz-al-tuhaf, and treatises of 'Abd-al-Qadir list a number of instruments with details of construction. Some of these were Chinese and Indian and even an European organ has been described. This shows how instruments travelled and the debt of the Islamic Middle East to its surrounding cultures.[13]

One of the sources for obtaining information about Indian instruments are the iconographic remains from the 2nd century B.C. to the 13th century A.D. These, for example trace the history of the Indian Vina to its stick zither ancestor, which in turn developed from bow-harps and short necked lutes.

Once the Muslim influence in the political and cultural areas was established in the Indo-Gangetic plain, by the 13th century, a number of chronicles of Muslim historians were written. A Persian treatise on Indian music called Lahjat-I-Sikander Shahi (1489-1517A.D.) dedicated to the Afghan King Sikander Lodi, was the first of many similar Persian treatises which depended on Sanskrit works on the subject, like Sangita Ratnakar (13th Century), Sangita Samaya Sar and Brihaddeshi (8th, 9th century)[14]. The 'Ghunyat al-Munya of the 14th Century is a prominent Persian treatise on Indian Music. One of the sources of obtaining valuable information on Indian instruments are the ancient texts: Vedic literature (approx.1000 B.C.), Natyashastra written by Bharat (4th, 5th century A.D.), Matang's treatise Brihaddeshi (8th, 9th Century) and Sarangdeva's Sangita Ratnakar (13th century).[15] Apart from this general literature, epigraphical records, sculptures, reliefs and paintings in Hindu, Buddhist and Jain rock temples and caves also provide evidence of the existence of instruments. The excavations of the Indus civilization (2000 B.C.) at Harappa and Mohenjo-Daro in Punjab and Sind provide evidence of the first instruments. The oldest reliefs at Bharahat in Central India (2nd cent B.C.) give musical scenes.

According to Suneera Kasliwal, each of these sources, including the oral tradition, have their limitations in presenting a clear picture of the instruments, and one has to make up for this lacuna by one's own conjectures and interpretations.[16]

The most important source of information about Indian musical instruments and their chronology is found at Borobudur in Java. Here Indian settlers (800 A.D.) had built a gigantic temple, the walls of which were carved with reliefs. These give us an idea of the life and culture of the Hindus before Islam. Among these reliefs, 20 of them depict musical scenes, which includes all the instruments popular at that time. [17]

STRINGED INSTRUMENTS

Instruments made of stretched strings of grass, animal gut or metal wire are known as stringed instruments or chordophones or tata vadya. There are many varieties of these instruments and many methods of playing them. For example they may be struck with sticks, plucked with bare fingers or a plectrum, or a bow could be used to play the instrument.[18] According to B.C. Deva, these "instruments might have grown out of many kinds of tools and contraptions." Some of the possible sources suggested by him are a hunting bow, ground harps and bamboo zithers. The bamboo zither is known as the Gintang in Assam and the Ronza gontam in Andhra and is considered to be the mother of all zithers.[19]

According to B.C. Deva, stringed instruments could be broadly classified into three major classes. One group is the drone instrument used as an accompaniment and does not play melody. Examples of this instrument which is also called Sruti Veena, are Gopi yantra, Ek tara, Do tara and the foremost of them all, the Tanpura. The second group called the polychords, include the harps, lyres, dulcimers and others where, one string is used for one tone. The third group, called the monochords consist of one or more strings, and each of these strings is used to play a melody or tune, independently of the other strings. Examples of these are the Sitar, Sarod, which may also be used as solo instruments. Monochords may be fretless, fretted, with a short or long 'neck' or 'danda', or stem. They may also be plucked or bowed.[20].

B.C. Deva talks about two types of polychords. One type is "bow shaped or arched, with a resonator and an arm danda." Examples of these are the Veena-with or without suffixes and prefixes-, lyres and harps.[21] The second type of polychord is box type. In India we have the santoor and swarmandal as examples. Here a wooden chest acts as both a rest for the strings and a resonator. In the West it is known as a Dulcimer.[22]

According to B.C. Deva, after the drone, the polychord, the third variety of stringed instrument is the monochord or the fingerboard instrument.[23] These may be of the zither variety or the lute variety. Examples of the lute variety are the Kacchapi, the rabab, sarod, sitar and the Karnataka Veena (the Tanjore Veena); those of the zither variety are the fretless Eka Tantri, Alapini and Vichitra Veena, and the fretted Kinnari and Rudra Veena. The instruments which create melody or raga, belong to the swara Veena category, and can be used as solo instruments.

Here it would be pertinent to mention that zither like instruments are typically Indian, while the lute variety of instruments can trace their ancestry to Arabo-Persian countries.

Another classification proposed for making the study of the hundreds of varieties of string instruments, easier and more scientific, is the Hornbostel – Sachs classification introduced in 1914. This categorises the chordophones in four basic types: Zithers, lutes, lyres and harps.[24]

Zithers: A zither has no neck or yoke; the strings are stretched between the two ends of a body, whether this body is in the usual sense a resonator itself, or whether it requires an attached resonator. They can be subdivided into stick zithers, tube zithers, board zithers and long zithers. Rudra Veena and Vichitra Veena come into the stick zither category while the Santoor comes under the board zither category.

Lute: A lute is composed of a body and a neck. The neck serves both as a handle and as a means of stretching the strings beyond the body. In most cases the strings are stopped. If played with a bow, it is a bowed lute or fiddle such as the Sarangi and its varieties. The sub-categories of lutes are short necked lutes and long necked lutes. In the short necked lutes, the neck is an extension or elongation of the body. The long necked lutes are those in which the neck or stick or stem is longer than the body. The Sitar and Tanpura fall in this category.

Lyre: A lyre has a body, with a yoke replacing the neck. The yoke consists of two arms projecting upward, and a cross bar connects the upper ends of the two arms. The strings are stretched over the soundboard and are attached and fastened to the crossbar at the top. Lyres can be either plucked or bowed and can be of two types: box lyre and bowl lyre.

Here it would be pertinent to mention that no lyre types of instruments are found either in Indian or Arabo Persian music.

Harp: The Harp is the only instrument in which the strings are vertical to the soundboard. The strings are attached to the soundboard, but run vertically away from it. All harps are plucked and the strings are unfretted and numerous. The varieties in this instrument are arched harps, angular harps, vertical harps and horizontal harps. In ancient India, the Mattakokila Veena of Bharat was a harp with 21 strings. B.C. Deva elaborates on an ancient south Indian instrument called Yazh, which belonged to this category.[25]

In order to understand the Indian stringed instruments further, we'll have to go into another classification, which divides them into two categories: the plucked instruments and the bowed instruments. The first group includes the Sitar, Sarod, Rudra Veena,

Tanjauri Veena, Vichitra Veena, Gottu Vàdyam, Tanpura etc.; whereas the bowed group includes instruments like the Sarangi. The plucked instruments may be fretted and non-fretted. The Sitar, the Rudra Veena, the Tanjore Veena are fretted; the Tambura as the drone instrument, the Sarod and Gottu Vadyam are non-fretted. Similarly bowed instruments can also be fretted, like the Dilruba and Esraj; while the non fretted bowed instrument is the Sarangi. The Violin is an important bowed instrument accepted as an Indian classical instrument. An ancestor of the various types of Sarangis is the ancient bowed instrument, Ravanhatta, which is still used by folk singers of Rajasthan and Gujarat.[26]

There are innumerable stringed musical instruments in the Persio-Arabian Region and India. As the subject is very vast and extensive, a few of them have been taken up for detailed discussion and comparison.

UD (LUTE)

The 'Ud (Lute) is considered to be the noblest instrument of art music, based on mathematical principles, and is related to cosmological theories and speculation. According to some opinions it corresponds in the Near East to the Veena in India and the Koto or Ch' in in the Far East.[27]

In the first few centuries after the advent of Islam there was social and cultural interaction between the Arabian tradition and Persia (Iran) and Iraq. Arabian musicians such as Ibn Misjah and Ibn Muhriz (both dc 715) travelled through Iraq and Iran and absorbed and assimilated new elements without compromising their own essential characteristics. As part of this instrumental innovation, the Persian wooden bellied variety of short necked lute ('Ud) was introduced as an accompaniment to vocal music.[28]

According to the New Oxford History of Music, the credit for the invention of the 'Ud (Lute) may be given to Tubal b. Lamak. During the Sasanid Period (224-642 A.D.) Shahpur I (d.272) is said to have introduced the Lute into his land.

According to another source of information, Ibn Suraij (d.c.726) was the first to introduce the Persian Lute into Mecca (c.685), during the flourishing reign of the Umayyad Caliphs (661-750 A.D.). This was an important event since its accordatura (tuning) (taswiyya) and frets (dasatin) 'were the means of widening the gamut and generally consolidating Arabian Music'.[29]

According to Carl Engel, the Arabs had become acquainted with Persian Music, even before they conquered it in 641 A.D. She informs us that an Arab musician of the name of Nadr Bew el-Hares Ben Kelde is recorded as having been sent to the Persian King Khosroo Purviz, in the 6th century, for imbibing the art of performing on the lute and also learn Persian music. It is said that on his return he brought the lute to Arab lands.[30]

It may be pertinent here to mention that in the Gandhara style Statuettes of India (about 100 A.D.), a similar lute like instrument has been depicted.

Whatever the period in history the lute travelled to the Arabian Region and other countries from Persia; we have evidence that it was of Persian origin and in pre-Islamic days was called the Barbat. The Arabs took it with its Arabic name, 'Ud, and according to one opinion, introduced it to Europe, through Spain, which was under Arabian rule from 8th to 15 century. Here it became the famous Lute, so popular during the Renaissance. However, for reasons, which are not clear, the 'Ud has lost its place among the popular instruments of Iran (Persia, formerly), though it is commonly used in other parts of the Middle East. (Handout of Iran Culture House, New Delhi).

According to Curt Sachs, the lute got its modern form in Andalusia, Spain, where oriental and occidental tendencies combined, to give the oriental lute 'a distinct neck, an almond shaped body and a central sound hole, with a rose'. From Spain, the lute reached Egypt and later it got imbibed in Europe, as one of its most prestigious instruments. Here the name of the instrument also underwent a change, from 'Ud to Lute, and as such it held a position of importance for three centuries.[31]

The principle meaning of the word 'Ud, by which the instrument is known in Asiatic countries is 'flexible stick', and not 'wood' as is generally supposed.[32] The precursor of the 'Ud was the Persian Barbat, although there existed earlier lute types with parchment bellies. When the parchment was replaced by wood, the instrument came to be known as 'Ud (wood).[33] It is safe to assert that the musical bow was a predecessor of the earliest lute, but this would refer to the long necked lute, in which the handle was derived from a 'flexible stick'. Later, the name 'Ud' was also given to the short necked lute, which was not directly connected to the musical bow.

The earlier lutes had the following main features: the wooden body was bulging with a thin wooden soundboard. It also had the frontal stringholder, the lateral pegs and the double gut (or silk) strings. These lute designs were later represented in Persian miniature paintings, but did not resemble the modern Arabian lute. 'The wide pear shaped body tapered towards the peg box not forming a distinct neck, and two crescent-shaped soundholes were cut on either side of the soundboard instead of the large central sound hole'. The instrument had four pairs of strings, called from the lowest to the highest – bamm, matlat, matna, zir. Bamm means 'high' and corresponds to the Greek 'hypate'.

The four strings were symbols of the elements, the phases of the moon, the directions, the seasons, the weeks of a month, the divisions of a day, of the body, of human life and the four humors. A fifth pair of string above the zir was introduced as early as in the 9th century to complete the range of two octaves.[34] The present five pairs of strings are tuned to d' e' a' d'g'. The strings are made of nylon or gut and metal wound silk, and plucked with an eagle's feather or plastic.[35]

According to the New Oxford History of Music, the instrument with four strings was tuned to G-c-f-b_b; (pa, sa, ma, ni) (ni is 'Komal') and by the ninth century when a fifth string was added, this corresponded to the note e, (ga). The strings were made of silk, neatly twisted.[36] The five double courses of strings are tuned to G', A', D, G, C (Pa, Dha, Re, Pa, Sa). The first course may also be tuned to F'.[37] The neck of the instrument was provided with frets of string which were tuned according to the system of seventeen intervals in the compass of an octave.[38]

There is an important point to be made here about the lute; the lutes either of older times or of today, do not have frets, inspite of the theoretical use of the word 'dasatin', plural of Persian 'dast' or 'hand', which is a word to indicate frets. Perhaps, in theory, the reference to frets indicated the position of the stopping fingers. A quill plectrum 'zahma' is used to pull the strings. The lute plays melody; chords are not known. Sometimes a drone may be played as an accompaniment to melody.[39]

It is surprising that not much attention has been given to instruments in the accounts given by theorists of the Persio-Arabian

Region. Al Kindi (d.c.874) has provided information regarding dimensions and construction of the Ud, and it was one of the instruments associated with the art music of that time. Al Farabi (10th cent.) has mentioned in his Kitab-al-musiqi-al-Kabir about the plucked string instrument, Ud.[40] Al Kindi's treatment of scale, like that of later writers was expressed in terms of fretting on the Ud.

The Ud may be played solo or in an ensemble. It has a warm timbre, low tessitura, and micro tonal flexibility. An instrument typical of Egypt and the Levant, it is known as Amir al tarab or the 'prince of enchantment'. 'Intricate visual ornamentation is typical of the Ud, especially in the rosette design and the wood inlay'.[41]

We have been discussing, in earlier pages, about musical instruments of the 'Ud (lute) variety, which had their origin in the Persio-Arabian Region or the Middle East. With the conquests and invasions by races and people from these regions, into the sub-continent of India from the 11th century to the 16th century, an entire set of cultural practices, along with language, religion were introduced into the mainstream of Indian life. One of the areas in which changes were brought about were musical instruments. The 'Ud(Lute) variety of instruments influenced the development or evolution of many Indian instruments like the Sitar, Sarod, some varieties of Veena, Sarangi Sarinda, Tanpura etc.

Here, we may mention that lutes may be long necked lutes or short necked lutes. The short Lute had a neck shorter than the body. It originated from an instrument with a wooden body which 'tapered upward to form a neck and a fingerboard, not, as with the long lute, a stick with a small resonance shell at its under end'. Here the long lute refers to a long necked lute, where the 'stick' is the 'danda' or long neck. According to Curt Sachs, the musical difference between the two lies in that, in short lutes the melodic scale in principle, is formed by all strings consecutively, whereas in long lutes it is obtained from one string only by stopping the strings, while the others accompany. One exception here would be the Tanpura, where each string produces a different note.[42]

According to B.C. Deva, lutes 'are those stringed instruments in which the fingerboard is an extension of the resonator. On the other hand, it will be recalled, that in zithers the resonator was placed below the dandi. It was also seen that the Ek tar was one of the possible origins of the lute type wherein the gourd might have been replaced by a wooden bowl. Examples of this direction of evolution were the two kinds of Tambooras. These instruments are, however, drones and are not employed for playing any tunes or Ragas for which purpose other lutes were fashioned'. In the Musical Instruments, B.C. Deva recognizes two types of lutes; the shortnecked variety and the long necked one. In the short necked lute the bowl projects into a curved neck, which is further extended into a short fingerboard. The long necked variety of lute consists of a resonator with a neck which continues into a long stick or danda (fingerboard). What is being emphasized here is that necks are almost the same size in both a short necked and a long necked lute. The difference lies in the length of the fingerboard; hence the adjective short necked should be replaced by short fingerboard; and the long necked by long fingerboard.[43]

EVOLUTION OF THE SAROD FROM THE LUTE AND RABAB

Gandharan Lute – Short Lute

In the first few centuries after Christ, a small area in Kashmir, called Gandhar was under strong Greek influence. Indian art was influenced by this, and several statuettes and reliefs carved in this style belonging to about 100 A.D. have been found, representing players on a short lute. According to Curt Sachs, this lute is the "venerable ancestor of the Islamic, the Sino-Japanese and the European lute families." [44] However it is important to note the fact that an instrument of this type had an early existence in India predating the Muslim excursions. These Gandharan lutes were also called barbed lutes, perhaps due to a 'unique and prominent protrusion at the base of the neck'. Allyn Miner is of the opinion that the Gandharan Lute and the later Indian Rabab cannot be historically linked.[45]

Curt Sachs informs us that the oldest short Lutes are depicted on Persian figurines of the 8th century B.C. excavated from the Tell at Susa, in Iran (formerly Persia). The body is very small and narrow, measuring about 2 feet in length and 8 inches in width. The figurine is too small to decipher the details. No trace of short lutes has been found between this earliest evidence and the Gandhara statuettes, some eight hundred years later. The Gandhara lute has a pear shaped body, tapering towards the short neck. It has a frontal string holder, lateral pegs and either four or five strings. These features are similar to the 'Ud or Lute, we discussed earlier, which originated in the Persio-Arabian Region and travelled to Europe.

Here we must point out that while as the Gandhara Lute is similar in all features to the Arabian Lute, it is different in one way that it has a barb. Instead of a continuous taper towards the neck, in its outline, the contour is broken on either side by a barb. The barb has survived in many forms of instruments of the Lute family, which travelled to the sub-continent of India. In a modern lute called the Rabab or Sarod, the hollow under the barb is so exaggerated that it forms a deep channel and makes a kind of waist in the outline of the front, which forms a groove in the side of the body. All these 'waisted lutes' (and some Indo-Persian long necked lutes) are abnormally deep; instead of being softly rounded at the rear, they have a ridge so that they look 'chicken-breasted'. In the Mafatih al-'ulum, the Arabian encyclopaedia of the 10th century A.D., there is a passage which says that a certain Persian lute was called Barbat, for 'its resemblance to the breast of the duck'.[46] Here, we must point out that, according to another source, we have stated that the Lute was called the Barbat in Pre-Islamic times.

Lute to Rabab

According to Curt Sachs, the lute that existed before the 10th century in the Persio-Arabian Region had evolved from the Gandhara Lute. It's pegbox was bent backwards in a sickle shape and had lateral pegs. The string holder was not frontal but on the lower end of the body, and a skin served as the soundboard. Islamic conquests and migrations carried this lute from Persia, south to Madagascar. It came to be known by a Turkish name called Gambus, Kabosa or Qupuz.[47]

As such, the instrument retained the pear shaped body tapering towards the pegbox, the front was covered with skin and it had lateral pegs. The number of strings was reduced to one or two, and the sickle shaped peg box was cut off, and only a stub remained. The Spaniards called this instrument a Moorish Guitar. This in turn developed into a Lute. Having acquired a bow in the 10th century, as a bowed instrument it was called a Rabab; the plucked instrument existing alongside. In the 16th century, this instrument was known as the Mandola or Mandora.[48]

RABAB

According to the Genius of Arab Civilization, the most important and popular instrument found in the Persio-Arabian Region or the Arab-influenced world, is the Bedouin Rababah. Played with a bow made of horsehair, the instrument consists of a quadrilateral sound box covered with skin, and a single string made from horsehair. "Capable of a wide range of dynamic accents and ornaments, this instrument is the essential melody instrument of the nomadic Bedouins". It is known as Rabab al-Shair when it has one string (Rabab of the poet). Curt Sachs also describes this instrument in the category of Spike Fiddles. The Spike Fiddle is mentioned by Al-Farabi, a Turk theorist, who wrote in Arabic.(T.H.M.I. p. 255). It is played by poet-musicians to accompany their epic songs. It is used to play interludes between vocal singing, and the interludes are more subject to variation than the vocal part. One variety of Rabab, with two strings, called Rabab al-mughanni (Rabab of the singer) is played by poor street singers and beggars.[49] Here we may note that the Rababs described above are bowed and may also be called fiddles. The Rabab shown on pg.137 of the Genius of Arab Civilization is similar to many folk regional instruments of India; e.g., Ektara (Maharashtra) and the Tumbi (Punjab), (described by B.C. Deva in his Mus. Instr., pages 138-140) except that the Rabab has two strings and is bowed, and the Ektara is plucked by finger or plectrum and has one string. A typical Ektara of the Kashmir region is a chordophone, which has a bamboo piece inserted through a gourd covered with a skin. A single steel string is stretched over the bamboo stick and tied to a wooden tuning peg at the upper end of the stick. It is used as a drone instrument.

Dr. H.G. Farmer, the scholar who wrote extensively on Arabian music, mentions that the Rabab has been referred to in Arabic texts of the 10th century, as a bowed instrument. The same instrument, variously called Rubab, Rebab, Rabob was very popular throughout West, Central, South and Southeast Asia. According to Allyn Miner, in the Arab world and Southeast Asia the Rabab has evolved into a bowed instrument of the spike fiddle variety.[50]

The instrument mentioned by Al-Farabi was possibly a pear shaped instrument, with one to four strings. A variety of this instrument which was boat shaped, a survivor 'of the sound chest of the old barbiton', was probably the Rabab of Muslim Spain praised by Yahya b.Hudhail (d.995 A.D.) and Ibn Hazm (d.1064 A.D.).[51] The term Rabab is a generic term denoting bowed instruments in general and meaning 'a stringed instrument played by a bow'.

The question now arises whether the Rabab was a descendent of an ancient Indian instrument of the short necked lute variety like the Kacchapi Vina, or an instrument which was adapted from a Persian Rabab imported from the Persio-Arabian Region. There are various view points put forward by various authors. According to one opinion, the 'immediate ancestor of the Rabab in India is clearly the Persian instrument of the same name'. In the Mughal Courts, after the 16th century, there was Persian influence in the court life and Indian paintings of the early Mughal period show a Rabab quite frequently and uniformly, which Allyn Miner refers to as the Persian Rabab.[52]

These Persian Rababs have a tapering collar between body and neck, which has an angular shape. The collar during this early period was not as prominent as it would become later. The long peg box is bent back at an angle. The skin covered body is round or oblong. It may be that the Persian Rabab was modified and assimilated into the Indian aesthetic tastes of that period which were dominated by the Dhrupad style of music. There is evidence in late Mughal provincial and Pahadi miniature paintings of a Rabab, which is unique to India, and is referred to by Allyn Miner as the Dhrupad or Indian Rabab.[53]

Since Mughal paintings of the 17th century show this Rabab, and this period approximately relates to the period of the great musician Tansen in Akbar's Court, who was associated with Dhrupad singing, Tansen's contribution in adapting and innovating on this instrument appears a possibility. This Rabab is 'characterized by a large round skin-covered body and a distinctive and pronounced turned back collar around the base of the neck'.[54] The neck tapers toward the end to a peg box which is often a distinctively ornamented, rounded or scroll shaped box positioned behind the upper neck.

The invention of some sort of Rabab is associated with Guru Nanak (1469-1538 A.D.), the first of the Sikh Gurus, whose disciple

Mardana was a Rabab player and musician. The Dhrupad Rabab remained on the Indian music scene for about 200 years after Tansen. It nearly disappeared from the scene by the late 19th century, although a few famous musicians continued playing it into the 20th century, like Allauddin Khan, disciple of Rampur's Wazir Khan.[55]

It is necessary to mention here about a Rabab originating in Afghanistan, and establishing itself in northwestern India, by the mid 18th century. In Afghanistan, this Rabab exists today as a prominent instrument. It is also found in Pakistan and Kashmir. The Afghani Rabab was a short necked lute with a deep narrow body and a sharply indented waist. Carved out of a single piece of wood, the body tapers into a hollow neck. As the waist divides the hollow sounding body into two sections, the instrument is sometimes sub-classified as a 'double chested lute'. At the upper end of the wooden fingerboard of the Afghani Rabab two to four tied frets of gut are present. According to oral traditions like those from Karamatullah Khan, the veteran Sarod player, the Afghani or Kabli Rabab may have entered India, as a marching instrument, played by soldier – musicians of the early Mughal armies, say around 1650 A.D.. Groups from Afghanistan, mainly Rohillas and Pathans settled down in Centres near and eastward of Delhi in an area called Rohilkhand (end of 18th century). Its capital Rampur developed as the centre for Rabab playing. Gradually these Rababiyas merged with the mainstream Hindustani Court musicians[56], and according to some opinions, were responsible for the evolution of the Sarod.

According to another viewpoint regarding the origin of the Rabab and Sarod, it is believed that the Rabab developed from the Kachhapi Veena mentioned in Bharat's Natyashastra (2nd century A.D. to 4th century A.D.). Among the 3 categories of string instruments mentioned by Bharat, *i.e.* the vakra, kurmi and alabu, the vakra was a hard type chordophone, kurmi was a lute type chordophone and alabu was a zither like chordophone. We shall take up the Kurmi category for discussion. The word Kachhapi and Kurmi both suggest that this instrument resembled a tortoise (Kurma), with a flat round body and a small fingerboard resembling the neck of a tortoise. This has been depicted in murals, sculptures and paintings in Amaravati, Nagarjunakonda, Ajanta and Pawaya (Madhya Pradesh), from the 2nd century B.C. to the

6th century A.D. This lute type instrument has been identified as the Chitra Veena by B.C. Deva and Prof. L.M.Mishra. Sharan Rani a renowned Sarod player refers to the instrument as being the predecessor to the Rabab and Sarod.[57]

SAROD

The Sarod is one of the most celebrated instruments of Hindustani music today. The word Sarod or Sarud means music or singing in Persian. Its mention occurs as early as 1830 A.D.[58] According to B.C. Deva, the origin of the instrument could perhaps be traced to an instrument of 'unusually wide compass known as the Sharud.' In his opinion it was invented by Ibn al-Awas, a person hailing from the Central Asian Region of Samarkand, in the year 913 A.D. The Indian Sarod could have been a descendent of the Central Asian instrument, Ud or Lute. The similarity lies not only in appearance and construction but in the ending of the word Sarode which is like Ud.[59]

According to various written and oral evidences, the Sarod is a descendent of the many varieties of Rabab that were being played in the Indian sub-continent in the early and middle nineteenth century. The Sarod was the 'outcome of the combination of the structural characteristics of the Seniya Rabab, Afghani Rabab and the Sursingar'. However there is more similarity with the Seniya Rabab, in its tuning and technical aspects, so perhaps a view could be taken that it was an indigenous instrument.[60] However according to Mohammad Karam Imam's Ma'dan al-Musiqi (1854 A.D.), there appears evidence that the Sarod was a descendant of the Afghani Rabab. An Afghani Rababiya, Ghulam Ali Khan and his brother Murad Ali Khan are the earliest musicians associated with the Sarod and are credited for creating the instrument by bringing about some changes in the Rabab. Ghulam Ali Khan was the grandson of a Rabab player from Afghanistan, Bandagi Khan, and must have lived in the first half of the 19th century. He was associated with the music scene in the courts of Reva, Lucknow and Gwalior. Hafiz Ali Khan and son Amjad Ali Khan (the well known Sarod player of today), are descendants of Ghulam Ali.

It is not clear when the name Sarod was applied to the Rabab. There are two structural differences which 'distinguish the modern Sarod from the Afghani Rabab; the replacement of the gut strings with steel strings and the covering of the fingerboard with a metal plate.' These changes were brought about by Karamatullah Khan's father Na'mat-ullah Khan (1816-1911), when he was living in Nawab Wajid Ali Shah's Court in exile in Calcutta from 1858 to 1869.[61] These are documented in Karamatullah Khan's book Israr-i-Karamat urf Naghmat-i-Niyamat and Risala Sitar (1908).[62]

In Karam Imam's (Ma'dan-ul-Musiqi-1854) description of the Sarod being played at Lucknow, it is mentioned as a larger version of the Afghani Rabab, still with gut strings and wooden fingerboard.

As mentioned earlier, the changes brought about by Na'matullah Khan included changing the fingerboard with a brass plate, replacing the gut strings with steel ones; and he also removed two gut frets that had been on the Rabab.[63] Karamatullah Khan's Sarod is larger than that of his father's instrument. 'It has a more rounded face, a smaller rounded waist, a larger and deeper body and a fish shaped peg box bent to the back. It has six main strings, one chikari and fifteen tarab strings'. These features resemble those of the modern Sarod.[64]

The 20th century legendary musician Allauddin Khan, a student of Wazir Khan and Ahmed Ali, along with his brother, Ayet Ali Khan (himself a musician and expert instrument maker) introduced the modifications which made Sarod a fully developed instrument. It became more suited to the Dhrupad style prevalent at that time. After these changes, the soundbox (drum) became more circular and larger; the number of sympathetic strings was increased from nine to fifteen; one more chikari string was added; for the four drone strings added an extra jawari was fixed at the top of the fingerboard. This new model had improved tonal quality, better sustenance of sound (Sans), better volume and was equipped with an improved reverberating quality. Previously the instrument was suitable only for fast passages, but now it was equipped for playing the elaborate alapchari of the been style.[65]

The body of the Sarod is made of a single block of wood, which may be teak, tun or sagwan. The body is divided into three parts: the peg box, the fingerboard and the resonator. The Sarod is played by a plectrum called 'Jawa', made of coconut shell held in the right hand. The left hand is used to play the strings with either the fingertips or nails.[66]

There are mainly two types of Sarods; the Sarod with eight strings having an extra resonator fixed in the bottom of the peg box, which is longer than the other type, is played by Ali Akbar Khan, son of Allauddin Khan, and his disciples; the sarod with six strings, which has a smaller oval shaped body than the sarod with eight strings, is played by Amjad Ali Khan, the son and desciple of Hafiz Ali Khan.[67]

LONG NECKED LUTES OF THE PERSIO-ARABIAN REGION

Here, we give descriptions of some long necked Lutes, which are in popular use, in folk traditions as well as in concert ensembles presenting classical forms of music, in the Persio-Arabian Region.

Buzuq-Long Necked Fretted Lute

One instrument played in both folk and urban contexts in the Levant (erstwhile Syria and Palestine) and Iraq is a long necked fretted Lute with metal strings commonly called Buzuq. Generally, this instrument is played by gypsies, who are constantly travelling from place to place. The Buzuq is equipped with a carved sound box and resembles the Turkish Saz from which it appears to have been derived. Modern varieties of this instrument are also equipped with mechanical pegs.[68]

The Tar-Long Necked Fretted Lute

In Iran, string instruments, especially plucked lutes are often used to accompany vocal music. The Tar, a long necked fretted lute with a total of five or six strings (two strings being duplicated) has a double belly covered with a membrane of sheepskin or the skin of a calf foetus. It is used as an accompaniment to music generally derived from courtly traditions as well as contemporary classical tradition. The Tar was introduced into Iran only in the 18th century. In Azerbaijan (in erstwhile Soviet Republic) and northern Khurasan, an instrument called Tar-e-qafqazi or Tar-e-torki was being played, and this had additional five drone strings, which resonate sympathetically, but are also plucked as open strings.[69] The Tar and the Setar have a common range, but their difference lies in the Tar having an interconnected double sound box, because of which it has a deeper and fuller tone. The tar has movable frets and is played with a small metallic plectrum.

In Saudi Arabia, the Tar is considered to be part of the inherited classical music tradition and is incorporated skilfully in the folklore music and dance groups.

The Setar-Long Necked Lute

The Setar is an instrument of contemporary classical tradition in Iran. This long necked lute type of instrument is related to the ancient Tanbur. It has four strings and a small half pear shaped sound box. It is played with the strumming action of the right index finger nail. The Setar has moveable frets and a range of two octaves and a 5th.

The Dutar-Long Necked Lute

The Dutar is a long necked lute with two strings used in the folk music traditions of Iran and neighbouring areas. There are many legends concerning the origins and the long history of the Saz and the Dutar. It was supposed to have been invented by various people like Galen, Solomen and Kei Qobad, among others. The type of this instrument found in the region of Khvaf and Bakharz produces a fuller tone than the type found in Turkey, which is smaller. There is a near Eastern theoretical tradition and belief that silk strings and a sound chest made out of mulberry wood produce a harmonious resonance by virtue of the common material from which they are produced.[70]

Tanbur-Long Necked Lute

The Tanbur used in religious ceremonies by members of various dervish orders in Kordestan, resembles the Sitar of courtly tradition but has a larger belly and only two (occasionally three) strings. This is one of the ancient instruments in use in regional folk music, and is a long necked lute which has travelled to countries as far apart as India and Yugoslavia.[71]

The relationship of these long necked lutes of the Persio-Arabian Region with similar stringed instruments of Hindustani and Carnatak music has been discussed in the relevant context, while describing the Indian Sitar and Tanpura etc.

VINA

The general term for any string instrument in Sanskrit music literature has always been the term Veena. Scholars are of the opinion that the word Vina may have been derived from the root Vana, which means to sound. The instrument is associated with Goddess Saraswati, who is visualised as holding a Veena in her hands and is revered as Veenapani or Veenapustaka Dharini. There is mention of Veena in Aitareya – Brahmana, as Daivi and Manushi Veena. In the Ramayana, Lava and Kush recited the story of Rama to the accompaniment of the Veena. Ravana was a great Veena player.[72]

In a general sense, the name Veena refers to any musical instrument, producing sound by vibrations of a string. The Rig Veda refers to the Veena, but not in name. In the Yajur Veda, Veena was played during sacrificial rites to obtain fourfold blessings of Dharma, Artha, Kama and Moksha.[73] According to Curt Sachs, the Rig Veda (1500-1000 B.C.) mentions 4 instruments, Aghati, Bakura, Gargara and Vana. The Gargara is a stringed instrument and it is supposed to resemble a horizontal arched harp. This is the only stringed instrument depicted on Indian reliefs before the Christian era.[74] The term Vina as mentioned in the Yajur Veda (V530) is supposed to be the same instrument as Gargara of the Rigveda. The Dravidian civilization (around 2,000 B.C.), the precursor of the Aryan civilization (1700-1400 B.C.) in India can trace its origin to Egypt and Mesopotamia, with which India was linked by sea commerce in the 3rd millennium B.C. There may have been Mesopotamian or Egyptian influence on Indian instruments, as for example the word Vina may have been derived from the Egyptian word 'Vin' and it referred to a Harp. This Harp like instrument, which was called Vina in the ancient days disappeared from the scene about a thousand years ago, and after that the word Vina was used for a stick zither. A point may be stressed here, that though the 'Vina' is considered to be one of the earliest instruments of India, this term earlier referred to a

'Harp'and only later got associated with the stick – zither instrument.[75]

In describing the variety of stringed instruments, we have mentioned that these can be of three types; the drone instruments, the polychords and the monochords. In this context it is interesting at this point, to mention another view point made by B.C. Deva, while tracing the history of the Vina from a polychord of harp variety to a monochord of the lute and zither variety. In Musical Instruments, B.C. Deva tells us that the polychords of the Harp and Veena variety were dominant on the Indian scene from the pre historic times till about the 10th century A.D.. After that they vanish from the scene, except the Santoor and the Swarmandal. The monochord or fingerboard instruments like the Kachhapi Veena, the Rabab, the Sarod, Sitar, Karnataka Veena, which are of the lute variety; and the Kinnari Veena, the Rudra Veena, which are of the zither family, appeared and took over from the harp like polychords, dominating the music scene till today. B.C. Deva says that this was a great landmark in the evolution of our instruments. 'An entire music and musicology are left behind, a system based on harps is given up and a new one founded on fingerboard : Vinas…'.[76]

The primitive form of the stick zither found in the reliefs in the temple at Mavalipuram, in the 7th century A.D., consists of a stick with a half calabash attached near one end to serve as a resonator, with two strings stretched along the stick. After 1000 A.D., half a calabash was provided at the opposite end also. Around 1400 A.D., the modern form of the stick zither with a whole calabash at either end came into existence.[77]

According to Curt Sachs, the Vina or Mahati Vina (large Vina, Hindustani Bin), as it is known today is a form of stick zither. It has a round stick and two big gourds suspended from the two ends. There are four or five wire strings plucked with a wire plectrum. Two additional steel strings are placed outside the melody strings and played with the small fingers of either hand, or with the right thumb. The frets are movable and project from the stick like vertebrae in a backbone. These are about 20 in number, and can be shifted easily to tune the instrument to various scales or Ragas.[78]

The varieties of broad necked lutes found in India are many and include the various types of Vinas – the Kacchapi Vina, with a big gourd and six strings, the Sauktika Vina, with a nacre body tapering to the head of an ibis; the Kinnari Vina, with an ostrich egg for a body; the Prasarini Vina, with an additional neck and fingerboard alongside the first one; and the Kaca Vina, with a glass finger board. These broad necked lutes are the Indian variety of the southwest Asiatic Tanbur-Sitar family.[79]

As we have said before, instruments of various countries as they evolved, found similarities with each other, may be because they travelled with migrants, invaders or trade travellers. According to the History of Musical instruments, the Arabian lute can be said to be parallel to the Vina in India. They have a similarity to the Koto or Ch'in in the Far East.[80]

According to the New Groves Dictionary, we are informed that bow Harps and the short necked ovoid Lutes were found in abundance in the iconographic remains of the 2nd century B.C. to 8th century A.D. The two principle types of Vinas, the Vipanci and Citra Vina described in the Natya Shastra are similar to the bow Harps and ovoid Lutes, respectively, found in the iconographic remains mentioned above. From the 7th century A.D. to the 13th century A.D., these two string instruments disappeared from sculpture and were replaced by stick zithers with one or more strings. They often had bowl shaped resonators or supports. These stick zithers are the direct ancestors of the modern Bin of Hindustani classical music. The Natya Shastra also describes playing techniques for the Vina. Since some of these techniques are for an instrument with open strings to be played with both hands, it could be surmised that this instrument could be of the nature of a harp.[81]

After the Afghan and Turkish conquest, lute types reappeared in South Asia. They were not the ancient ovoid lutes, but rather long necked and short necked lutes of many varieties. There was an interaction between the lute types which had come with the invaders and the indigenous stick zithers, and led to the development of classical string instruments of later years. Both had the essential principle of changing pitch by shortening or lengthening a vibrating string. The basic principle of the ancient bow harp Vina, as distinct from the above, was the presence of a separate string for each pitch.

It has been noticed that South Indian Vina is more similar to the Western Asian long necked lutes. While the high frets of the stick zither Vina is present in the South Indian Vina, the supporting gourd at the end of the stick, opposite the tuning pegs has been replaced, with a wooden bowl to which the stick is attached. Thus the stick is converted into the long neck, inherited from the long necked lute of Perso-Arabian descent. On the other hand the North Indian Hindustani Bin (stick zither) preserves not only the high frets but also the ancient form of a stick supported by two gourds. It is possible that the South Indian Vina is a descendant of the medieval South Asian stick zither and the Western Asian long necked lute.

An important point could be mentioned here, that the stringed instrument which corresponded to a harp in ancient India, had open strings (and was of the polychord variety). Its disappearance in the middle ages and the appearance of instruments with stopped strings like zithers, lutes and fiddles, also introduced flexible intonations and pitches to the music produced (monochord variety). According to Curt Sachs, this introduction of shaded melody could also be attributed to the coming to India of the Islamic culture between 1000 and 1600 A.D., as shaded melody and rhythmic patterns were typical to Persian and Arabian music as well. However this is not to undermine the presence already in ancient and medieval Indian music, of shading graces and other adornments in melody, called 'gamaks'.[82]

Rudra Veena

Having discussed in the previous pages, the relationship between the Veena and its predecessor instruments, we now give the historical background of two types of Vina, the Rudra Veena and the Tanjauri Veena found in Indian Classical music.

In the Natya Shastra Bharat gives elaborate descriptions of string instruments. There are three types of Veenas; the mukhya, meaning the main one; the anga, meaning secondary; and the pratyanga, meaning subsidiary. Bharat does not give the name of the main Veena, but Kallinath (15th century) describes a polychord called Swarmandal which according to him was the Mattakokila Veena, (the main Veena of Bharat), a type of harp, being used as a drone, in addition to the Tambur, Veena and Flute.[83] The Mattakokila Veena had 21 strings.

The secondary or the Anga Veenas are Chitra and Vipanchi; and the subsidiary or Pratyanga Veenas are Kacchapi and Ghoshak.

Till the 6th century A.D. string instruments were not fretted. Matang (8th, 9th century A.D.) introduced frets in the Veena, and called it Kinnari, after the community to which he belonged, the Kinnari Jati. During the same period, the subsidiary Veena of Bharat, called Ghosha or Ghochika also attained recognition as the Ektantri Vina, which was fretless, and hence could be used to give the minutest Sruti (micro tone). Till Sharangdev's time (13th century A.D.) Ektantri Veena was the reigning instrument, after which the fretted Kinnari came into prominence. This had two strings and three gourd resonators. Abul Fazl (Akbar's time-16th century A.D.) and Rana Kumbha (Sangeet Raj – approx. 1440 A.D.) also mention this Veena; it is mentioned in the texts till the 18th century. Rudra Veena is a developed and modified version of the Kinnari veena; it has the frets arranged in such a way that all 12 swaras in an octave can be played, which was not possible in the Kinnari. The Rudra Veena would have been named around the 15th century; but it attained its final shape in the beginning of the Mughal period (16th century).

Both the Ektantri Veena and the Kinnari Veena are descendants of the stick-zither Veena, which was South Asian in character and not borrowed from the Arabo-Persian influences that came into the sub-continent of India.[84]

The Rudra Veena consists of a stem or a fingerboard, about three and a half feet long and has two broad gourds fixed in the stem, which is now made of teak wood. About twenty two wooden immovable frets are fixed on the stem, and thin sharp-edged plates of brass are fixed on top of the frets, called 'sara'. There are seven strings in all: four main playing strings over the fingerboard, passing through two bridges and being tied up to the respective pegs, and three drone strings passing on the sides.[85]

The Tanjauri Veena

According to one opinion, the fretted Kinnari was changed and modified to the Rudra Veena in the North and to the Tanjauri Veena in the South. Having adopted the lute type of body instead of the second gourd at one end of the stem, a surmise is made that the South Indian Vina developed from the long necked lute, which was brought to the sub-continent of India, by Arabo Persian influence. However, there may have been an indigenous predecessor to the South Indian Veena. Allyn Miner tells us that long lutes appeared in South India in the tenth century, in temple sculpture, in the Chalukyan period at Pattadakol and at Chidambaram in the 12th century. This indicates the existence of these long lutes in the music life of that time. It is possible that the long lutes of the temple sculptures re-emerged as the Karnataka Vina later.[86]

B.C. Deva opines that the present Tanjauri Veena is an evolved version of a regional folk instrument called Nanduruni. According to him there are no links between the primitive Arabo-Persian lutes and the modern Veena. The Central Asian Tambur also cannot be connected to the Vina, though both are lutes, with necks and long fretted stems. So, the conclusion, according to B.C. Deva is that the South Indian Vina developed from the regional instrument Nanduruni.[87]

NORTH INDIAN AND SOUTH INDIAN VINA [THMI, p. 225]

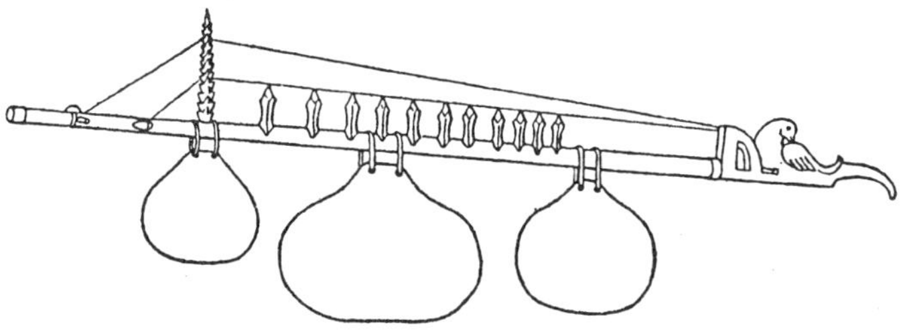

South Indian stick zither *kinnari*

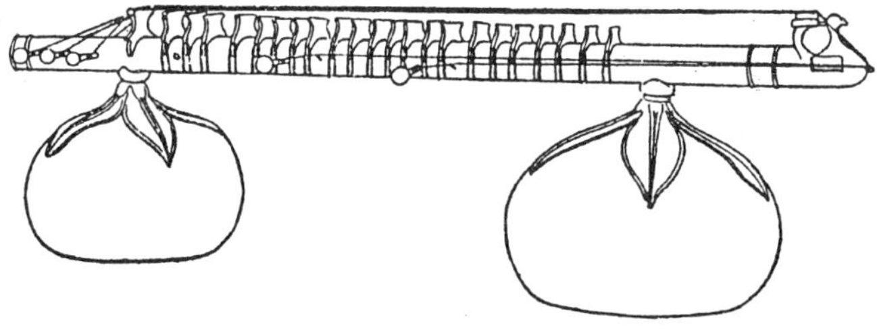

North Indian vina

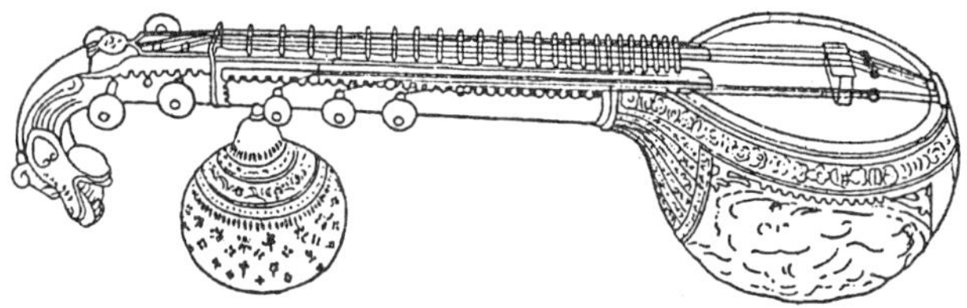

South Indian Vina.

TAMBURA-TANPURA

The Tanpura in Hindustani Music and Tambura in Carnatak music, is a drone instrument. It provides a drone *i.e.* adhar swar, which gives a background which is melodic, but does not produce melody.

According to one opinion, the Tambura is associated with the Tumburu Veena mentioned in the Mahabharat, which was named after Rishi Tumburu, who was a semi divine Gandharva such as Narad, and Bharata in our ancient scriptures. There is a possibility that this instrument travelled to other countries from India in ancient times, with travellers engaged in trade, religious missionaries or cultural ambassadors. Subsequently, it appeared or reappeared on Indian soil in the 11th century during the invasion of Mohammad Ghaznavi. This opinion would substantiate the theory that the instrument was not imported.

Another theory about the name of the instrument is that the Tumbura, Tumbur or Tumburi Veena was named after its vital part tumba or gourd, which acts as a resonator. The use of this tumba in a Tambur, however, was introduced about four centuries ago, as the Persian Tambur originally possessed a wooden body and the gourd was not used in its construction.[88]

A commonly accepted theory about the origin of the Tanpura is that its ancestor was the Tambur, a fretted long lute, which arrived with the occupation of Punjab by the Ghaznavids from present day Afghanistan.[89]

The Long Lute or Arabian Tanbur

Henry G Farmer informs us that according to a manuscript in his possession, the Tanbur came 'from the Sabaeans who measured the earth, and so it was called the 'measured' lute or Tambur al-mizani'.

This instrument was probably identical with the lute that afterwards was called 'Tambur from Baghdad'. The length of its two strings was divided into forty equal parts, which may have corresponded to an ancient Mesopotamian standard measure. The long lute is interesting because its scale was metrical, not a musical one. However this 'pagan' or pre-Islamic tuning was given up as early as Al-Farabi's (d.950 A.D.) time. Al-Farabi was one of the foremost of Arab theorists.[90]

According to a History of Arabian Music (1929), by H.G. Farmer, the string instrument Tanbur is similar to a Pandore.[91] The long lute or Arabian Tanbur, has a full metallic timbre. It has a small, pear shaped body with a long neck, which does not have a peg box. The frets are made of gut, the strings are thin and made of wire and the plectron of tortoise shell. In outer appearance it resembles the ancient lutes of Babylonia and Egypt. Its history has a Turkish origin also, because the position of the pegs testify to mixed Arabo Persian and Turkish antecedents. They are shaped like the letter T, and are inserted, some from the front and some from the side. The side pegs reflect Arabo Persian descent of lateral pegs, and the front pegs are taken from Turkish instruments. Accepting the Turkish influence in the long lute the Arabs call it Tanbur Kabir turki or 'large Turkish lute'. The Persians use the term Tar or 'string' for the instrument, combined with a numerical prefix indicating the number of strings used, *i.e.* the Dutar has two strings, the Setar three, the Cartar four and the Panctar, five strings.[92] It is incidental that these terms sound quite Indian.

As we have said before, H.G. Farmer finds mention of Tambur, the fretted long lute in Arabian manuscripts, dating back to the 8th century. It was known as the instrument of Baghdad, and by the mid 10th century, the Tambur had become a commonly used instrument throughout the Middle East. It is supposed to have arrived in India at the time of the invasion of North West India by Mahmud Ghazni of modern Afghanistan. According to Allyn Miner, one of the first Indo-Persian poets, Masud-i-Sa'ad-i-Salman mentions about the presence of the Tambur in the court at Lahore, as one of the many Arabian and Persian instruments being used there. In 1200 A.D., Hasan Nizami, one of the earliest Persian chroniclers mentions the use of the instrument.[93] Amir Khusrau, a prominent Court musician in the Court of Allauddin Khilji (13th century), describes the Tambur in detail. It has been mentioned in accounts of the Court of Sikander Lodi (15th century); in Ain-i-Akbari in the 16th century and depicted in a miniature of the Jehangir period (17th century).

Ibrahim Adil Shah (1580-1627 A.D.) of the Deccan Court of Bijapur patronized Muslim Court culture, including music, and himself was an expert Tambur player. He was fascinated with the music and religion of his Hindu subjects and a collection of his songs (he was also a composer of Dhrupads) the 'Kitab-i-Nauras' exists. Allyn Miner says that his style of music blended elements of Persian and Indian forms and melodies. He also says that the instrument became Indianized around this time and was called the Tamburha or Tambura.[94]

The Tambur depicted in the earliest miniature paintings gives a consistent description of the instrument of this time. It consisted of a small pear shaped body with a flat face and a long, narrow tapering neck. The tuning pegs, four in number were in lateral positions on the sides of the peg box, at the end of the neck. The bridge was thin, and the guts were wrapped round the neck. The instrument was made entirely of wood. Amir Khusrau describes the Tambur, as having two strings of silk and two of metal.

Faqirullah (1665 A.D.) in his 'Raga Darpana', mentions that the Tambur had two strings of metal and two of gut, or five strings made of iron or copper. This would be a period relating to early 16th century as Raga Darpana was partly a translation of Manakutuhala a treatise written during the regime of Raja Mansingh Tomar of Gwalior (1486-1516 A.D.).[95] The point to be noted about the Tambur being used in this period was that the bridge of the instrument was very thin like the violin and guitar, and the flat bridge of Tanpura, as it is known today, was a later adaptation, taken from the Veena. This gives the instrument its reverberating sound. According to Allyn Miner, the flat surface bridge – a factor unique to Indian string instruments, dating back to an early period – was an adaptation of the Persian tambur to its Indian environment. It now became a drone instrument to be used as an accompaniment to vocal music.[96] Allyn Miner further tells us that the drone Tanpura which was widely depicted in paintings of the 17th century, was of a larger size, which made it different from its predecessor the melody Tambur.

References made about the music scene in the Court of the Mughal Emperor at Delhi, in the Muraqqa-i-Delhi (1738 A.D.), reveal that the Tambur and Tambura, existed as two separate instruments.[97]

The Sangeet Parijat (1650 A.D.), an Indian treatise of music of great relevance and importance mentions two types of Tamburas, one nibadha (fretted) and the other anibadha (fretless). The former may be referring to the sitar; the latter definitely refers to the development of the Indian Tambura as a drone instrument. Both the instruments were made of wood. The use of the gourd or pumpkin, an adaptation from the Veena, was a later development.[98]

The instrument known as the Tanpura today developed through various influences. Firstly, it borrowed from its predecessor, the Persian Tambur. Secondly, there was a need for the development of a drone instrument for classical music. It's development also received an impetus by the presence of many drone instruments like the Ektara, the Gopiyantra, Kinnari etc., in the folk music of that time, especially the devotional bhakti cult music of the 14th, 15th century. With the mingling of classical music and the music of the common bards, the early drone instrument evolved. As this new instrument was similar to the Persian Tambur being used in the Courts at Delhi, in basic appearance and structure, it was named after it. It was different from the Persian Tambur in many ways: (*i*) it was a fretless instrument, (*ii*) it had a wide flat bridge not present in the Persian Tambur, (*iii*) the new Tambura was a drone instrument, to provide a basic note (adhara swara) to the singer while the Persian tambur was a melody instrument and (*iv*) the Tambura is held vertically and the Persian Tambur was held horizontally.[99]

In the early 19th century, the Tanpura got its present structure through the Tanpura makers of Miraj, and its evolution and journey from a simple body structure to a sophisticated instrument for classical music accompaniment, was achieved.

Curt Sachs refers to an instrument called Tamburi, which he says is derived from the Persian Tambur, and is used as a drone and not a melodic instrument.[100] The description given by him fits that of the Tanpura as we know it. The body of the Tanpura is hollow and acts as a soundbox. The front of the Tanpura is called the sound board (tabli), which is slightly convex. There is a long broad neck ending in the peg box. At the other end is the tumba (gourd). Along the front of the soundboard run four strings attached to the four pegs at one end and passing over the bridge (ghurach) they are fixed to the anchor (langot) at the tumba end. The strings are made of steel (3) and brass (1). The other parts of the Tanpura are the Manaka, the fine tuners, the ghurach (bridge), fingerboard, upper bridge (aad), and targahan. The plucking is done by fingers and gives rise to a rich series of harmonics.

Here a significant factor to be noted is that irrespective of whether the instruments prevalent on the Indian music scene in the 17th and 19th centuries, were influenced by the instruments of the Persio-Arabian Region and the Middle East, or not, there is irrefutable pictorial evidence, that the Indian instruments like the Veena (the zither with two gourds), Flute, Dholak were played along with the incoming instruments like Rabab, Khemencha, Santur, Duff and the Sehtar, in ensembles in Courts at Punjab, Delhi and the Deccan. There was synthesis of cultures between the Arabo Persian and Indian. This is borne out by the following pictures of that time.

Hazrat Nizamuddin Aulia and Amir Khusrau, Hyderabad, approx. 1750-70 A.D.

Kalavant Tansen, approx. 1590 A.D.

Assembly of Sufis, approx. 1630-40 A.D.

Twelve musicians playing Indian and Persian instruments. "Sāqī Nāmah" of Zuhuri. Deccan, 1985. By permission of the British Library. BL Or. 338 f. 54 b. [Ref., Sitar and Sarod in the 18 th, 19th centuries, Allyn Miner, after Pg. 30]

Khusrau Parviz listening to music. Panjab, 1719. By permission of the British Library. BL Add. 18804 f. 325 b. [Ref., Sitar and Sarod in the 18th, 19th centuries, Allyn Miner, after Pg. 30]

A group of women in a garden with musicians. Deccan, early 18th century. The Freer Gallery of Art. 07.263 ID 21. [Ref., Sitar and Sarod in the 18th, 19th centuries, Allyn Miner, after Pg. 30]

SITAR

The Sitar is one of the most popular musical instruments in Hindustani music. It is a chordophone of the lute variety and belongs to the Tata-Vadya class, according to the Hindustani classification system.

There are many theories, regarding its origin and evolution. It would be appropriate to mention here, that during the period of the 16th and 17th centuries, in the Mughal Courts and provincial seats of power, 'the internal and external forces had learnt to work together to bring about a cohesion in society."[101] A well synthesized system of music practice, that combined Arabo-Persian and Indian elements, to evolve new musical forms and instruments, was already prevailing. This is borne out by the Sanskrit and Persian literature of that period: The Tuhfat-ul-Hind (Mirza Khan 17th century) and Amir Faqirullah's Raga Darpana (approx.1665 A.D.), a translation of a Sanskrit work Manakutuhala, written during Raja Mansingh's time in Gwalior (early 16th century). The development of the Sitar was a reflection of the cultural synthesis that was taking place at that time.[102]

In Ahobal's 'Sangita Parijata' (1665 A.D.), there is reference to an anibadh or unfretted and a fretted or nibadha Tamburam. Maharaja Sawai Pratap Singh of Jaipur in his 'Sangitsar' (1790 A.D.) says that the nibadha Tambura is the instrument called Sitar. A Persian translation of 'Sangita Parijat' was made by Pandit Dinanath in 1724 A.D., called 'Parijatak' and Sir William Ouselev (late 18th century) wrote an article, 'Anecdotes of Indian Music' in which he made a drawing of a fretted Tambura, which he copied from 'Parijatak'. This shows the neck and fingerboard to be broad and thick.[103] This was different from the Tambur used in those days with thin neck and fingerboard.

While referring to the nibadh Tambura as Sitar, Sawai Pratap Singh says that it is similar to the anibadh Tambura, the drone instrument, except for the presence of frets. Its small size is similar to the Tamburas of the 18th century paintings, but the frontal as well as lateral pegs, a neck (fingerboard) that does not taper towards the end, a gourd body and a flat surface bridge are features that set this instrument apart from the Tambur. However the evolution of the Nibadh Tambura into the Sitar remains an inconclusive surmise.[104]

The Persian Tambur maintained its features till the 16th century after which it acquired some features of Indian instruments like the Veena or Bin; and a new instrument, the Sitar, emerged from this process. The emerging instrument continued to evolve, over a period of a hundred years, and many varieties were developed.[105]

The earliest reference to the Sitar is found in Muraqqa-e-Delhi (1739-41 A.D.), a treatise written by Dargah Quli Khan, during the reign of Muhammad Shah Rangeele. There is mention of Niyamat Khan's (Sadarang) nephew Feroze Khan (Adarang) being skilled in playing the Sitar and composing new notations. According to Sulochana Brihaspati in Khusrau Tansen Tatha Anya Kalakar, K.C. Brihaspati has suggested that Niyamat Khan's younger brother Khusro Khan is said to have invented the Sitar.[106] K.C. Brihaspati has done pioneering studies of the Persian and Urdu treatises relating to music in the Raza library at Rampur, in the 20th century. The confusion that Amir Khusrau invented the Sitar probably arose because Captain Augustus Willard (1834 A.D.) has made an ambiguous statement in his work that the Sitar was invented by Umeer Khusrau of Delhi (Ibid:84). He was referring to the Amir Khusrau who did pioneering work in inventing new Ragas by combining Persian Maqams and Indian Ragas, and lived in the 14th century in Allauddin Khilji's Court (1296-1315 A.D.).[107]

Amir Khusrau (14th century) has not made any reference to the Sitar in his works, though he was a Persian and Indian music scholar and wrote extensively on poetry and music. In any case, the earliest reference to the Sitar is made in Muraqqa-e-Delhi (1739-41 A.D.). So, accoding to one opinion perhaps Amir Khusrau is being mistaken for Khusrau Khan, as the inventor of the Sitar. However, the theory about Khusrau Khan being the inventor of the Sitar cannot be accepted as being authentic.[108]

As we have said before, the first mention of a Sitar in Muraqqa-e-Delhi (Dargah Quli Khan – 1739-1741), and the earliest visual representation dates back to about 1790 A.D.. This was in Maharaja Sawai Pratap Singh's 'Sangit Sar'. As mentioned before this fretted Tambur differs from the Tamburas of the 18th century paintings in the following ways: presence of frets, frontal as well as lateral pegs (one on each side of the neck), a neck that does not taper towards the end, a gourd body and a flat surface bridge. Since the early Sitars resemble the Tamburas depicted in the 18th century miniature paintings, one school of thought suggests that the Sitar was a modification of the Tambur. However, Allyn Miner says that this may not be a certainty as the two instruments existed side by side, during the period in question, as is borne out by the poetry of Shah Alam in his 'Nadirat-i-Shahi'.[109]

So, perhaps we have to look for other predecessors of the Sitar. One theory about the origin of the Indian Sitar is its possible descendence from the long necked lute like instruments found in the 9th and 10th century Indian temple sculputre. Indian temple sculpture, of the Calukyan period dating back to the 10th century A.D. is found in Pattadakal; and that dating back to the 12th century is found at Chidambaram. This would suggest that the Sitar was in existence in India from early times, and supports an opinion that modern Indian instruments are actually products of pre-Muslim Sanskritic traditions. However, later musicologists would like to believe that there is a 'Central or West Asian influence in the origin of the Sitar'.[110] The contemporary Indian Sitar could trace its ancestry, according to Allyn Miner, to the earlier Persian Setar, the Persian Tambur and the Uzbek Dutar. There are pictorial and written evidences to support this conjecture. Allyn Miner also informs us that according to some musicologists, the Sitar can be directly associated in its ancestry to some long necked lutes of Persia, Turkey or Central Asia, that arrived in North West India and the Mughal Courts with the Muslims, who came from these lands.[111]

In tracing the ancestry of the Sitar, a very popular opinion relates it to the Kashmiri or Persian Sehtar, as its likely immediate predecessor. The Kashmiri or Persian Sehtar is represented in Mughal paintings of the 12th to 16th centuries. This was a small instrument with a pear shaped resonator and a comparatively long thin fingerboard with gut frets. It was made of wood, had a thin bridge and was played by a plectrum worn on the right hand. The Iranian Sehtar played solo or in ensembles even today resembles the Sehtar depicted in the above mentioned Mughal paintings. However the Sehtar played in Kashmir today has seven strings instead of three.

Another theory which would propose that the Sitar or Tambur had indigenous ancestry, is the evidence of lute type instruments in temple art from 2nd century B.C. to 6th century A.D.. According to Abhinavgupta (10th century), the commentator on the

Natyashastra (approximately 4th century B.C. to 4th century A.D.), the Chitra Veena, Kachhapi or Kurmi Veena (both tortoise shaped) and five others that he names as Samvadini, Tantri, Kinnari, Parivadini and Vaisesika are chordophones (mentioned by Bharat) with tortoise shell like gourd or tumba. This evidence found in iconography and ancient texts, of the presence of lute type chordophones, proposes the theory that the Tambur and Sitar were not imported from West Asia.[112] It may be mentioned here that after the 6th century A.D., no presence of lute like instruments were found as epigraphical evidence.

In 1872, Sourendra Mohan Tagore in 'Yantra Kshetra Dipika', one of the earlier books on the Sitar, proposes that the Sitar was related to the ancient Tritantri and Kacchapi Veena of Sarangdeva's Sangitratnakar (13th century) and Bharat's Natyashastra (4th century B.C. to 4th century A.D.). S.M. Tagore, while making these observations was showing his keenness at finding Sanskritic origins for modern Indian instruments. He wanted to spearhead the theory that there was minimal influence of countries of the Persio-Arabian Region, on the development of Indian instruments. Sangitratnakar's commentator Kallinath (15th century) says that the Tritantri Veena was later called a Jantar. Tritantri disappeared after the 15th century as a name, and the Jantar is mentioned in the 16th century 'Ain-i-Akbari' of Abul Fazl. This had a low wooden neck with sixteen frets, and a half gourd fastened at each end. This was a stick zither, the prominent North Indian Vina of the time. Perhaps Sarangdeva's Tritantri, Kallinath's interpretation as the Veena being Tritantri and Ain-i-Akbari's Jantar were the same stick zither type of instrument. Allyn Miner is of the opinion that the Jantar or Tritantri Veena has no relationship to the Sitar.[113]

In the previous paragraphs we' ve been discussing the origin and ancestry of the modern Sitar, from the point of view of finding out whether the instrument was influenced in its development by countries of the Persio-Arabian Region; or whether it was an imported instrument from Persia, Afghanistan or Central Asia; or it developed from indigenous sources. Now, we'll dwell on the development of the Sitar from the point of view of how it acquired its additional strings, especially, the sympathetic strings or 'tarab', and the use of the plectrum or 'mizrab' in the Sitar. According to Sadiq Ali Khan's 'Sarmaya-i-Ishrat' (1875 A.D. –Delhi) one of the most informative books of the 19th century, the Sitar till then had three strings, baj, kharaj and pancham. During the period under scrutiny, the Sitar had acquired five main strings, at least two cikaris and seven, nine or eleven tarab strings, practically all the characteristics of a modern Sitar.[114]

Tarab is a Persian word meaning 'excitement' or 'joy' which has been used in the context of enjoyment of music since medieval times. At what point of time the sympathetic strings came to be called by this name is not known. But, they were in existence in the Sarangi, from the early 17th century. The Sarangi was the first instrument to possess sympathetic strings. Rahim Beg's Naghmah-i-Sitar (1894 A.D.), gives information about a tarabdar Sitar belonging to one Ghulam Muhammad Khan.[115]

The mizrab is an Arabic word derived from the root zarb, 'to strike'. It was used for the plectrum of the Arabic and Persian Rabab, and later also used for certain Persian Tamburs. The mizrab for the Tambur was a flat hand held plectrum, but in the Persian Setar, the mizrab referred to the back-and-forth rhythmic stroking pattern with index finger, and it is in this context that the word mizrab was used for the Sitar.

By the 1830s the Sitar was known for solo performance as well as dance accompaniment. While as the late 18th century and early 19th century was formative for Sitar, by mid 19th century, the gat toda, a form of Sitar playing and presentation, had developed into a solo-genre, and many techniques of the Bin were being imbibed, lending it versatility and popularity. In his Madan-al-musiqi of 1856, Hakim Karam Imam describes the Sitar with detailed information about 6 strings, the last one being of steel and 'tuned to M or to any note one wishes'. This string is called 'cikari', and according to Allyn Miner, it is the earliest reference to the word till then. The cikari are generally drone strings, also found in the Bin.[116]

Many artists and craftsman have, over the years contributed towards the development and popularising of the Sitar. The Jaipur Senias are one such group which include names such as Maseet Khan, Rahim Sen, Amrit Sen and Dulhe Khan. Sahabdad Khan and his descendants, Imdad Khan, Inayat Khan and the twentieth century Sitar maestro Vilayat Khan are names of illustrious Sitar players. Pandit Ravi Shankar and Shri Nikhil Banerjee have earned world renown in the field.[117]

The following is a broad description of a modern day Sitar. The instrument has two parts; the fingerboard and the resonator.

The fingerboard called dand, is hollow and made of tun or teak wood. The resonator or tumba made of gourd is hollow and covered on the top with a wooden plate called tabli. The fingerboard or dand is joined to the resonator or tumba by a joint called gulu. The other end of the dand has got the peg box. The most important parts of the instrument are the gourd, its covering the tabli and the joint or gulu, because they form the main resonating chamber. The two bridges are placed upon the tabli or soundboard, the main strings passing through the bigger bridge called ghurach and the sympathetic strings passing through the smaller bridge, placed just befor the Jawari or main and bigger bridge. The five main playing strings are tied at the lower end with a holder called Langot, which then pass through the Jawari, and passing over the dand and another bridge, the meru, are tied to their respective pegs on the peg box. The two chikari strings are also tied at the lower end string holder and passing through the Jawari are tied to two pegs at the side, just below the peg box. The sympathetic strings are tied to the string holder, like other strings, and passing through the small bridge, meant for them, reach their respective pegs on the side, by passing through holes drilled into the covering of the dand or fingerboard. The main bridge or ghurach is vital to the tonal quality of the instrument and requires constant maintenance. There are nineteen to twenty frets on the fingerboard, tied with silk or nylon thread. To strike the strings of the Sitar, a wire plectrum called mizrab is worn on the right hand forefinger.[118]

KAMANCHA-BOWED LUTE

Origin of Bowed Instruments

Till now we have discussed about the lute variety of instruments, which are, played either by plucking with fingers or with a plectrum, like the Sitar, Tanpura. Now we shall describe the bowed variety of Lute-like instruments. A bowed Lute is also called a Fiddle.

The origin of bowed instruments can be traced to India as well as Central West Asia. While as visual representation is found in the 17th century A.D., wall reliefs of these instruments have been found seven hundred years earlier. It has to be pointed out that there are atleast fifty tribal and folk instruments of the bowed variety found in various parts of India. These Ektara type of instruments have been mentioned in the section on Rabab.[119]

According to Henry G. Farmer, an authority on Arabian Music, bowed instruments can be definitely traced to the 10th century, when Al-Farabi – a musicologist of that time, who was a Turk but wrote in Arabic[120]-makes a clear mention of a Rabab being bowed.[121] The origin of fiddle like instruments could also be traced to 800 and 900 A.D., and according to one opinion certain Persian fiddles originated in Kurdistan. Indian fiddles have a relationship with Turkestanic instruments.[122]

Varieties of Bowed Instruments

The bowed instruments of the Middle East or countries of the Persio-Arabian Region are the Kamancha (Arabic Kamanjah), the Gheichak, shaped like the Indian Sarinda and the Rabab with a variety of shapes and one to three strings.[123]

In India, the Kamaicha, the Sarangi and Sarinda fall under this category of bowed lute-type instruments. Instruments of the Sarinda variety have been found in Vishnupur in Bengal and some temples of West India have reliefs of the Sarangi. The Kamaicha is the oldest bowed instrument in world literature, except the Ravana hatta of Gujarat and Rajasthan. The Ravan hatta is a popular fiddle like folk instrument, very common in Gujarat and Rajasthan.

The Indian Kamaicha

B.C. Deva refers to a bowed instrument called the Kamaicha which perhaps is the Indianised name for Kamancha the instrument popular in the Persio-Arabian Region. It has its origin in Egypt as well as in Sind. Its name is perhaps derived from the Arabic-Persian word Kaman, meaning 'bow'. It is a matter of conjecture whether the ancient instrument originated in Sind and travelled to West Asia and Egypt or vice-versa; and also whether it was similar to the one now found in Iran and the countries of the Persio-Arabian Region as well as the one found in Monghniar, Rajasthan, which borders on the Sindh province of Pakistan.[124]

The Kamaicha, used by the Monghniar community of Rajasthan today resembles the Indian Sarangi and is different in shape, from the Kemenche used in the countries of the Persio-Arabian Region, specifically Iran, in the present times. It consists of a big bowl shaped skin covered resonator, extending into a rectangular fingerboard and further into a peg box. There are three main gut strings and eight drone steel strings attached to a metal hook on one end of the resonator. The strings pass over the bridge and are tied to the pegs. The bow is made of shisham wood and horsehair. It is used as an accompaniment to songs.

Kamancha, of the Persio-Arabian Region

The Kamancha of the Persio-Arabian Region has been referred to as a 'hemispherical – chested viol, with a long iron foot'.[125] It may have been the instrument referred to by Ibn al-Faqih, in 902-903 A.D., as having been used by the Copts of Egypt and the people of Sind. This instrument commonly had two strings, which were 'tuned a fourth apart'. A similar instrument called the Ghichak of Persia, had a larger sound chest than the Kamancha, and being more elaborate had eight sympathetic strings.[126] A variety of the instrument which had a shallow, rectangular sound chest is popular as a folk instrument, and the ancient poets may have used it to accompany their poetry. The Kamancha has been depicted in the frescoes of Qusair 'Amra (eighth century A.D.), though here it is a plucked instrument. 'Abd al-Qadir b. Ghaibi (d.1435) also mentions about the shape of the instrument.[127]

The Persian Kemenche

In 20th century Persian art music, one of the six instruments which is most popular and widely used is the Kemenche, the others being the Setar, Tar, Santur, Nay and Tombak.[128] The Kemenche is an instrument, very popular in Iran today being played solo or as an accompaniment to music. This is a spiked variety of fiddle with three or four strings and has a bowl shaped wooden or gourd resonator. The top of the resonator is covered with a membrane or skin, which forms the sound box.[129]

Before World War I, there existed in Egypt a traditional ensemble called 'takht' which means platform. Here, we could mention that in Hindustani music in India, a recital on a stage is called 'manch pradarshan', which could be considered similar to the idea of the 'takht' as 'manch pradarshan' means performing on a platform. The ensemble called 'takht' consisted of instruments such as 'Ud, the Qanun, the Nay, the Riqq and the Kamanjah (the Arabic name for Kamancha-NOHM p. 445). The Kamanjah was a spike fiddle, which continued as a folk instrument under the name of Rababah.[130] The picture of an instrument called the Rababah on Pg. 137 of the Genius of Arab civilization[131] shows an instrument which resembles the spiked fiddle or Kemenche of Iran today, and also the 'Ektara' type of folk instruments found in Gujarat and Rajasthan like the Ravanhatta.

According to one opinion, the Kaman or Kamanjah is considered to be identical to the Western Violin, in the Arabian Region, the violin having adapted to the requirements of Arab music, in matters of tuning and playing technique.[132]

Spiked fiddles are found all over the Islamic world including Siam and Cambodia. The Malayan and Egyptian fiddles have only one or two strings. Egypt has several species, the Kamanga a 'guz or 'old fiddle' tuned to a and e (dha and Ga) and another similar instrument called Kamanga farh or Sogair or 'part of a fiddle', tuned to e' and b (ga and Ni). Both these instruments have a small coconut body and two hair strings. Besides these two types of Kamanga there is a related instrument called Rabab, which has a quadrilateral frame drum, replacing the coconut body. With one string it is called the Rabab assa'ir or poet's fiddle. As such it accompanies narration. Where the instrument has two strings it is called Rabab al-moganni, or 'singer's fiddle' and is used as an accompaniment to music.[133]

The Kemenche, as found in Iran and other countries of the Persio-Arabian Region belongs to a variety of spiked fiddles, also called 'pierced fiddle' as the cylindrical fingerboard projects through the body and protrudes at the lower end, forming a foot or spike on which the instrument is rested. The pegs are lateral, and the spike may be of wood or ivory or even iron.[134] It has four strings and a range of 3 octaves.The sound box is round and deep and covered with parchment over its surface. The bridge is placed above this parchment covering.[135]

In South West Asia, the Kamanga a 'guz, has three or four strings and in some places like Turkestan in Central Asia and Kashmir in the Indian sub-continent, a set of sympathetic wire strings is also found, placed behind the main strings. The tuning for the three main strings is the base note, its fifth and its octave or the ninth.[136]

Saz-e-Kashmir

An instrument of the spike fiddle variety is found in Jammu and Kashmir, in India, which resembles the Iranian Kemenche. This is called Saz-e-Kashmir. This is a bowed instrument with a round resonator of soft wood, covered on the top with skin, extending to a cylindrical fingerboard. In addition to the three main gut strings, there are fourteen sympathetic strings of steel. The instrument is played with a bow and decorated with ivory work.[137]

We may surmise from what has been stated above, that the spike fiddle varieties of bowed instruments have comparable traits in the music of the Persio-Arabian Region and Hindustani Music. It may be of special interest to note the great similarity in the names of the instruments of the two regions.

SARANGI

The Sarangi is a small bowed Indian instrument which can be said to be similar to the bowed instruments from countries of the Persio-Arabian Region, especially Iran, called Kamancha, Kemenche or Kamanga. India has a history of bowed instruments as can be seen from Indian texts on music.

A North African type of Rabab is a short necked bowed fiddle, an instrument of special interest for its possible relationship to the Indian Sarangi. This complex relationship has yet to be explored.[138] A description of a Rabab is given by Al-Farabi, the noted Arabian theoretician (872-950 A.D.) in Kitab al Musiqi Al Kabir, which is similar to the description of the Tanbur of Hurasan. Its features resemble the Indian Sarangi.[139]

The Sarangi was mentioned by Sharangdeva in the Sangitratnakara (13th century) and scholars have tried to trace its origin to the Ravanhatta Veena or Ravanastra in various texts from the seventh century onwards. It is mentioned as a stringed instrument in Kathakoshprakaran, written by Jeneshvarasuri in 1052 A.D. Apparently two types of bowed instruments were prevalent in India between the seventh and fifteenth centuries.[140] One variety includes instruments like the Sarangi, Kamaicha and the Sarinda, the other variety are the Ektara type of instruments, with one two or three strings like the Ravanhasta Veena or Ravanhatta of Gujarat, the Banam of Orissa and Kingri of the Pradhans in Andhra Pradesh and Maharashtra. The difference between the two lies in the manner in which they are held while playing. The Sarangi type of instruments are held with the resonator below and the pegs above, while as the other variety, like the Ravanhatta, which belongs to the violin category is played with its resonator above and the pegs below.[141]

The Sarangi has its roots in the Indian folk traditions, while at the same time it is a popular instrument, very much in demand, as an accompaniment to classical vocal concerts. The folk Sarangis are of many types, almost ten in number; the Gujeratan Sarangi, Jogi Sarangi, the Sindhi Sarangi, the Dhani Sarangi etc. The Sindhi Sarangi is closest to the classical music variety.[142] Its emergence as a classical musical instrument occurred in the 17th or 18th centuries, when Khayal form of music gained in popularity over the Dhrupad form. The Veena which was being used as an accompaniment to Dhrupad was found unsuited to Khayal accompaniment.[143]

During the period between Ain-i-Akbari (1579A.D.) and Madanu'l-Musiqi (1857 A.D.) 3 categories of musicians formed the socio musical basis of Hindustani music. They were the Kalavant the Qawwal and the Dharhi. The Kalavant sang Khayal as well as Dhrupad, the Qawwal sang Khayal in a slightly different style, beginning the Khayals with Tarana in Persian. The Qawwal also sang Sufi devotional music such as Qaul, but did not sing Dhrupad. The Dharhi community played the Sarangi, to accompany the courtesan singing girls, in their Khayal and Thumri singing. The Sarangi was never used to accompany Dhrupad singing.[144]

The Sarangi can reproduce all the embellishments of vocal music, of any form, like the Dhrupad, Khayal, Thumri, Tappa or Bhajan. Some very great musicians were first trained to play Sarangi and later took to vocal music; *e.g.* Abdul Karim Khan., Bade Ghulam Ali Khan and Amir Khan.[145] Some of the great Sarangi players of the past were Mamman Khan, Bundu Khan, Abdul Aziz Khan and Bade Sabir Khan. Among the present Sarangi players of distinction we are mentioning a few: Ramnarayan, Hanuman Prasad Mishra (Varanasi), Sultan Khan (Mumbai) and Bharat Bhushan Goswami (Delhi).[146]

The Sarangi is carved and hollowed out from a single piece of wood; generally tun wood is preferred but teak or mango wood may also be used. There are three parts to the instrument; the body, which is the resonator or soundbox (also called belly or pet), the neck or fingerboard (also called the chhati) and the peg box (also called the magaj). The sound box is waisted and covered with goat skin, the main bridge or ghurach being placed on it. There are three main strings, made of gut, used for playing melody, and several sympathetic strings made of steel or copper. The pegs for the main melody strings are found on the sides of the peg box, while as those for the sympathetic strings are found on the fingerboard in a lateral position, and on the upper front part of the peg box. Out of the three bridges, one is for the main strings, and two flat small bridges for the sympathetic strings. The gaj or the bow is curved and has horse hair for the string. The bowing hand is held with the palm upwards.[147]

The Indian Sarangi has been found to be similar to the Kamancha and Kemenche of the music of the Persio-Arabian Region; though it may be pointed out that the latter have not developed and evolved into sophisticated concert instruments like the Sarangi.

HARP

As we have mentioned before, one of the sources of data we get about Indian instruments is from reliefs on the walls of temples and burial mounds. Under the influence of Greek sculptors, Indian artists in northern and central India worked on reliefs on the stupa at Bharahat from the 2nd century B.C. onwards. These include musical scenes, with trumpets, drums and harps. The arched harp has figured in reliefs from the Bharahat stupa to reliefs on temples built around 800 A.D. At this period the arched harp had a small narrow body extending into the long neck to form a semicircle, and the upper end of the neck was bent outward to form a beak or a scroll. The strings were close to each other and attached to the neck by simple loops without pegs. The crowding of the strings left the two ends of the instrument free. According to Curt Sachs, the name of this instrument was Vina. Mahabharat mentions the playing of Vina by girls by resting it on their thighs, which would suggest that the instrument could have been only an arched Harp, which rests on the lap. The Vina would rest on the shoulder and on the ground (if it was a stick zither). Bharat mentions the presence of two Vinas, in connection with his experiments, which had 22 strings. This again points to an instrument like the harp and not the stick zither Vina. Perhaps it was the main Vina of Bharat known as Mattakokila, which would have been a vertical harp like instrument with 21 strings.[148]

Persian Harp

There is evidence of three types of Persian harps, as depicted on Sasanian reliefs at Taqi-i-Buston (c.600 A.D.). Out of these, a vertical variety is the first evidence of the harp used till recently in modern Persia. 'The body, often gilded and inlaid, tapered and curved forward at the upper end to form a hook or a scroll. The strings were attached at the lower end to a horizontal bar without pegs, and beyond this bar the body projected downward to form a curled tail upon which the instrument rested while the player knelt on the floor'. The number of strings varied from thirteen to forty, and were arranged in pairs.

The harp was plucked with the fingers of both hands. A plucking device on the thumb can also be distinguished in one of the miniatures. This instrument was obtained from the Persians by the Arabs at Al-Hira, near Babylon, and introduced into Arabia, a few centuries before Islam. The Arabs called it by its Persian name Cank, which in Arabic was spelled as Gank or Sang (as the letter c does not exist in Arabic). The harp was still being used in 1554 in the Arabian speaking countries. It, however did not enter Europe during the middle ages.[149]

Other References to the Harp

- Khusrau's works give information on musical instruments – The Chang, a 16 stringed Harp appears as one of the most prominent instruments of the time. Muhammad Shah, was the lead player.[150]
- Mughal Period pictorial sources show the Harp, Chang mentioned by Amir Khusrau.[151]
- In ancient times, there were instruments such as the Veena and Flute which were used to accompany the singer and these may have functioned as drone instruments. The

> Veena during Bharat's time was a harp-like instrument. Kallinath (15th century) describes a harp like polychord named Swarmandala which according to him was the Mattakokila Veena, the main Veena of Bharat. Even today vocalists use the Swarmandala as voice accompaniment.[152]

The Rigveda, the religious hymns of the Aryans mention 4 instruments, Aghati, Bakura, Gargara and Vana. Gargara is a stringed instrument-probably was the horizontal arched Harp-the only string instrument depicted on Indian reliefs before the Christian era. In the Yajur Veda, the term Vina is mentioned which must have supplanted Gargara.[153]

According to the New Groves Dictionary, the Natya Sastra describes playing techniques for the Vina. Some of these playing techniques clearly make reference to an instrument with open strings, to be plucked with both hands. This instrument could be the Harp.[154]

According to what we have mentioned above, it is evident that harp-like instruments were in existence in India as well as in Persia from ancient times. In India harp like instruments like the Santoor and Swarmandal are in popular use as a concert instrument and as drone accompaniment to vocal recitals, respectively. Similarly, in modern Iranian concert ensembles the Santoor is a favourite instrument along with the Kemenche, the Setar and the Tar. In the countries of the Persio-Arabian Region the instrument Qanoon corresponds to the Swarmandal in India.

SWARMANDALA

The Swarmandala belongs to a class of string instruments of the polychord variety, which are harp like and played vertically. In ancient Indian texts we find references to bow-harp like instruments which may have been precursors to this instrument. The Swarmandala is similar to the instrument known as Qanoon, which has its origin in countries of the Persio-Arabian Region or West Asia.

We will dwell on references to the harp like instruments found in our ancient texts. In the Rigveda (approx. 1300 B.C.) the following process of constructing an instrument called Vana has been described. "Make a structure of Audambara wood and cover

Ancient *Saptatantri veena*; from a sculptural relief
(Mus. Instr., Pg. 113)

A prehistoric harp, from an Indus valley seal
(Mus. Instr., Pg. 109)

Pictures of Ancient Harps of Hindustani Music

it with skin of an ox. Make ten big holes in the wooden structure – the holes should be made in such a way that ten strings can be tied to each groove. In this way, one hundred strings of Dub (grass) or Munj (a special kind of silken cord) are fixed to the Vana". These were instructions to make the Shattantri Vana, which was another name for the Vina of a hundred strings.[155] This description would fit a harp like string instrument of the polychord variety, and it would be a conjecture that it was a vertical harp. In ancient times, the Chitra, Vipanci and Saptatantri Veena were all harps which belonged to the polychord variety of stringed instruments.[156] The Chitra Veena is mentioned by Bharat in the Natyashastra (approx. 2nd to 5th cent. A.D.) The Chitra and Vipanci Veena are mentioned in the epics, the Ramayana and the Mahabharata (approx. 200 B.C. to 500 A.D.). The Vipanci Veena was nine stringed, the Veena with seven strings had many names, like the Parivadini, Saptatantri and Chitra.[157] A possible construction of the ancient harp, the Saptatantri Veena is given here from a sculptural relief. [Previous Page]

The Saptatantri Veena appears to be the most ancient of string harp like instruments, where the body was a boat shaped wooden bowl covered with a wooden plank. Projecting out of this was a curved wooden holder, the danda. The strings emanating from the body were tied to the danda.[158]

Some harp like instruments, with five strings have been depicted in sculptures and reliefs at Bharhut and Budha Gaya. Similar instruments with seven strings have been found near Ajanta (3rd century B.C.), Sanchi in Madhya Pradesh (2nd century B.C.) and Amravati and Nagarjunakonda in Andhra Pradesh (3rd century A.D.).[159]

In the Indian Museum, Calcutta, there is a representation of a seven stringed instrument called the Parivadini Veena, dating back to the Nagarjunaconda Caves (3rd century A.D.). The importance of the bow-harp like instrument is described in the following passage, especially its connection with the Gupta Dynasty (4th-5th century A.D.).

"In ancient days, music occupied a very important place in the daily life of the nobility, members of which had to learn to play a bow-harp. Quite a few kings during the Gupta era (4th-5th century A.D.) were expert performers themselves. Even Emperor Samudra Gupta, confident of his ability as a performer, had himself depicted on his gold coins, clasping the Parivadini Veena.

Members of the nobility always kept one close by, hanging it on the bedroom wall, taking it with them wherever they went, playing it sometimes as they strolled along-in which case it was slung from one shoulder with a strap".[160] The above description clearly shows the Parivadini Veena or Saptatantri Veena to be a vertical bow-harp of the polychord string instrument variety, and appears to be similar to the Swarmandala of today, in the way it was held.

These harps belong to a class of polychords which were bow shaped or arched with a resonator and a danda or arm. These were presumably vertically held, like the Swarmandala of today. There is another category which is the box type, where there is no arm or danda. A wooden chest acts as a resontaor and the playing strings are stretched on this box or chest. In India two such instruments are found even today, the Santoor and the Swarmandala. The Swarmandala is held vertically while playing with fingers and the Santoor is played horizontally with sticks.[161]

The Swarmandala is a variety of polychord belonging to a harp like instrument family of the box type, but played vertically. There is an assumed connection between the Swarmandala and the Mattakokila Veena of Bharata's Natyashastra.[162] This was the most favoured (Mukhya) Veena of Bharat possessing 21 strings; it could produce notes of all three 'sthanas' or octaves. The Chitra and Vipanci were subsidiary or of lesser importance. The Mahati Veena is associated with Narada, but since it also had twenty one strings, it was another name for the Mattakokila Veena. Kallinath (15th century) the commentator of Sharangdeva's Sangeeta Ratnakar (13th century) specifies that the Mattakokila Veena of Bharat's time was in his time called the Swarmandala.[163]

In the above pages we have talked about the similarity of the Swarmandala to the ancient Veenas of the harp like variety. Now, we shall discuss the resemblance of the instrument to the instrument called Qanoon, which has its origin in countries of the Persio-Arabian Region or Western Asia. In Syria, it's known as Qithoro; it was first mentioned by the Syrian lexicographer, Bar Bahlul (about 963 A.D.) The word Qithoro was taken from the Greek Kithara. It also finds mention in the 'Arabian Nights'(10th century). The Qanun is a flat trapezoid shaped box; the soundboard being half of wood and half of skin. It has 26 triple gut strings, and the instrument is played by plucking the strings with wire plectra.

Abul-Fazl's Ain-i-Akbari (16th century) talks about the similarity between the Qanoon and the Swarmandala. The Swarmandala has been described as having twenty one strings, made of steel, brass and gut.[164]

According to Prof. Lal Mani Misra, the Iranian instrument Qanoon and the Swarmandala are exactly similar, the differences being the following; the Swarmandala by tradition had twenty one strings and the Qanoon had twenty eight (acc. to some sources-26 triple strings); the Qanoon was played with fingernails or two thin wooden sticks and the Swarmandala is played only with fingernails. The Qanoon is kept horizontally while playing, while the Swarmandala is held vertically. Sometimes it was also played with a small wooden piece, just like in the case of the Ektantri Veena.

The Swarmandala today is played as an accompaniment to vocal music, especially classical music. It consists of a wooden sound box, on which strings are mounted horizontally. They are tied down on one side with nails, and on the other side also with nails, which also act as pegs. These pegs can be tightened or loosened by a small hammer shaped tuner. In dimensions, the Swarmandala is about one and a half to two feet in length, one and a half feet in width and three to four inches in depth. The strings are tuned to the swaras of the Raga being sung by the artist and are played with bare fingers or with a wire plectrum worn on the index finger. The instrument is placed on the lap, while playing.[165]

PERCUSSION INSTRUMENTS

Percussion instruments are those in which the "sound is produced by a membrane stretched and tightened over the opening of either a frame or a hollow body of any shape. It was struck upon with bare hands until later times when hands were replaced by sticks."[166] These are also called Avanadha or Vitata Vadya in India; the Drum has become a generic word for each and every type of rhythm instrument used. Curt Sachs has classified drums on the basis of material, shape, fastening of the skins, the playing position and the means of playing. In India the drums are classified according to their shapes.[167] The percussion instruments enjoy the status of concert instruments, as their sound can be made definite;

it can be varied in tone colour and pitch; and the sounds can hold for a certain duration. So, they are more musical than idiophones or Ghana Vadya.[168]

Percussion Instruments of the Music of the Persio-Arabian Region

We shall be discussing the drums or percussion instruments of the Persio-Arabian Region under three heads: the frame drums, the cylindrical drums and the kettledrums.

Frame Drums

These were first used in Pre-Islamic times; women used them while rejoicing and mourning, and professional singing girls used them to accompany their singing and dance. These were also called Duff (related to the Hebrew Tof); and were octagonal drums with a shallow frame, two skins and inner snares. Round drums have the general name Daira or 'circular'. The frame drums, in their modern form appeared around the beginning of the Abbasid period (750 A.D.-1250 A.D.) and were of two types: with or without jingling disks. The drums without jingling disks are called Bandair (large sized), Tar (middle sized) and Req (small sized). The drums with jingles are called Mazhar. They are played by striking with the fingers; with the sounds tum, ka and tak being produced according to whether the finger is struck in the middle, border or intermediate area. The Egyptians hold the instrument with both hands; the Tunisians with the left hand only.[169]

According to Ibn Khurdadbih, Tubl B.Lamak is to be credited with the invention of the Duff or Tambourine, and the Tabl.[170] The Tar, a frame drum with small bells or iron rings inside the frame, accompanies dance songs like Saut and Bastah.[171]

Cylindrical Drums

These are made of wood and are shallow and double-headed, the length of the cylinder being smaller than the diameter. The two sides have skins stretched on them; the barrel shaped drum is worn on the shoulder with the heads facing sideways. The skins are beaten with two sticks, or with a stick on one side and with the hand on the other side. The dull sounds (dum) are produced by hitting the centre; clear sounds (tak) by striking the border. The Tabl Baladi is the name given to the smaller variety of a shallow drum. The Tabl Turki is the large variety. These drums originated either in Turkey or Arabia.[172] The double headed barrel shaped drum, is played with traditional folk dance songs of the Arabian Gulf, called Sawt and Bastah. A small double headed cylindrical drum, called the Muruas accompanies the songs of the Naham, who are professional singers performing for the entertainment of the oyster pearl divers.[173] The Tabl Dawul, Tabl Baladi and Hadjir are shallow double-headed drums, which generally accompany processions and open air ceremonies.[174]

These Drums could be compared with the Dholak, a barrel shaped, double sided drum, used on occasions of marriages, celebration of Holi festivities and as an accompaniment to the folk dance 'Garba' in Gujarat (India).

Kettledrums

These are open receptacles; hemispherical with a skin stretched over the opening. Originally clay was used, which afterwards was replaced by metal. An encyclopaedia, first mentions the kettledrum in the 10th century. Here, there is mention of Qasa, the bowl drum, Tabl-al-Markab, a deep kettledrum, also called Naqqara and the Kus. One can see a representation of a kettledrum on a relief at Taq-i-Bustan in Iran, dating to 600 A.D. This might be Tas mentioned in Persian texts of the time. There is a drum found in India by that name, even now.

Kettledrums are depicted in the temple of Borobudur in Java erected by the Indian settlers in about 800 A.D. A type of kettledrum shown here has a flat bottom; may be the rounded bottoms developed later on, taking the shape of an egg, for portability. Later on the shape became hemispherical; the largest diameter being at the head. This may have been due to the change in the material being used from clay to metal.[175]

Ibn Sina (980-1037A.D.) in his Al-Shifa gives us an idea of the new type of instruments having come into use during this period, due to foreign contact. The Abbasid Caliphate was breaking up and new centres of power were emerging; Baghdad had been taken over by the Saljuk Turks and the changing political milieu was influencing the cultural pattern of the time. The Kettledrum has been mentioned by Ibn Sina; according to him one of the drums in use was the pair of Naqqarat (made of single skin), a type of Kettledrum, which was part of the military bands of the Mamluk Turks.[176] In modern times, the following varieties of kettledrums are found in the countries of the Persio-Arabian Region.

- "Naqqarya: two large flat kettles played on the back of a camel....struck with two sticks. Naqrazan: two smaller kettles played on the back of a donkey, shallow, but nearly hemispherical, struck with two sticks.
- Naqqara: two small kettles, played with two sticks.
- Tabl Sami: One kettle of a very shallow shape, carried by the player and struck with two sticks.
- Tabl al-gawig or sawis: one shallow kettle played on horseback, struck with one stick.
- Tabl migri: one shallow kettle, struck with thongs.

All these kettles are made of metal and tightened with chords".[177]

It would be necessary here to mention two vase-shaped drums of the Persio-Arabian Region:

1. *Darabukka*: Single headed vase-shaped drum played with urban dance songs of the Arabian (Persian) Gulf area.[178] This is made of wood or clay, placed under the left hand or between the legs and beaten with both hands. Men and women play the instrument in rural as well as urban areas.[179]
2. *Tombak*: a vase shaped drum generally made of wood and played with the fingers. It is also called Zarb (beat). It is a popular instrument, now being used in ensembles of Sufi classical Music in Iran, along with the Daff. In the 20th century, Persian art music includes the following instruments as being popular and widely used: Setar, Tar, Santur, Kemenche, Nay and Tumbak.[180]

Percussion Instruments of Hindustani Music

Percussion instruments have held an important place in the music life of the Indian subcontinent. Since Vedic times there is mention of Dundubhi, Bhoomi-Dundubhi, the former being used for yagnas and martial purposes.[181] The Natya Shastra and the Mahabharat mention the Pataha, which is the ancient Sanskrit name for a frame drum.[182]

If we go by their shape, the Indian drums may be classified into 3 types:

1. Tubular drums
2. Kettle drums
3. Frame drums

1. Tubular Drums

These are drums in which the body is a tube: it may be a deep drum if the body is longer than the diameter of the skin or a shallow drum if the body is shorter than the diameter of the skin. The type of tubular drums are:

(*a*) Cylindrical drums: *e.g.* Dhole or Dholak
(*b*) Barrel drums: *e.g.* Pakhavaj
(*c*) Kettledrums (Conical Drums): *e.g.* Khol used in kirtans in Bengal
(*d*) Hourglass drums: *e.g.* Damaru[183]

(a) Cylindrical Drums

A cylindrical drum made out of hollowed wooden trunks might have been the earliest drums. Even today instruments of this type are in use: the Kharram of Assam, the large Dhole of the Andhra Reddis and that of the Dhangars of Maharashtra. Bheri is a drum of this category mentioned in the Ramayan, Mahabharat, Jataka and Sangita Ratnakar (13th century).[184] Today large cylindrical drums of various sizes are comprehensively called Dhole when large, or Dholak when small in size. A common feature amongst the variety of these instruments found in different regions of India, is that they are two headed (faced) drums, each face covered with stretched hide. While playing, they are either suspended from the neck, kept on the lap or tied to the waist; they are played with hands or sticks.[185] This finds similarity with the double-sided barrel shaped drum found in the Arabian Gulf Region, where it is used to accompany traditional folk dances, the Sawt and Bastah.

(b) Barrel Drums–Pakhavaj

The bulging or barrel drums of Indian music instruments are ancient in origin. The Mridangam and Pakhawaj fall under this variety. Mridang was and is a general name for two headed drums: the Mridangam of South India, the Pakhawaj of Hindustani music and the Khole of Bengal fall under this category, though they are different in shape and structure.[186] We have to mention an important factor here, about the development of music in India: the categorization into Hindustani music and Carnataka music was a development only after the 13th century A.D. Around the 15th century A.D., the Pakhawaj and the Mridangam developed separately in the Hindustani and Carnataka systems, respectively; the term Mridang is sometimes used as a synonym for Pakhawaj.[187] The Pakhawaj acquired a place of great importance and reverence in Hindustani Music; being used as an accompaniment to Dhrupad and Veena. With the Dhrupad losing popularity to the Khayal performing style in the 18th and 19th centuries A.D., the Phakawaj also lost its supremacy and made way for the Tabla. The strokes of Pakhawaj are played with the open hand (thapi), which could not accommodate to the delicate style of khayal singing, the rendition of Thumri, as well as the Sitar.[188]

The Pakhawaj is a classical music instrument, which still accompanies Dhrupad style of singing. It is a barrel shaped instrument, which has "an asymmetrical convexity towards the left. In fact, the drum has a barley shape (yavakriti), one of the shapes referred to in Bharat's Natyashastra and it is hollowed out of a block of wood." The right face is smaller in circumference and emits a higher pitch. The parchment covering the two faces is called 'pudi' and consists of two layers, the inner complete skin and the outer peripheral ring; the two layers are held by braids (gajra), which are connected by leather straps. Between the braces, there are eight tuning blocks, which can be adjusted with a hammer. A special characteristic of Indian drums is application of dough on the face, to change its pitch; a dough preparation is applied to the left face of the Pakhawaj at the time of the concert, and scraped off after the programme. The instrument is played, sitting cross-legged on the ground, the Pakhawaj being kept on the ground or in the lap and played with the palm and fingers.[189]

In the music of the Persio-Arabian Region, there is no exact resemblance of any percussion instrument to the Pakhawaj; the shallow cylindrical drums, the Tabl Baladi and Tabl Turki, in which the length of the instrument is smaller than the diameter, are not comparable, specially because they are used in folk music and dance, as also in processions of marriages and other open air ceremonies. The Pakhawaj is an instrument of classical concert music.

The Damaru is a bifacial drum with a waist which looks like an hourglass. There are a large variety of these found in different regions of India.

2. Kettledrums (Conical Drum)

(a) Nagara

There is a possibility the kettledrums would have evolved from pots, pans, troughs and such other vessels. The earliest variety may be the Dundubhi and the Bhoomi Dundubhi, mentioned in the Vedas, and later epic literature where the Dundubhi was used as martial instrument. The present versions of the Dundubhi are the Dhumsa, Nissan and the Nagara. The Nissan is found in Gujarat and Rajasthan, the Dhumsa is a huge instrument with a narrow bottom and a wide mouth, found among the Santhals of Chota Nagpur.[190]

The Nagara, a type of Kettledrum may have had its origin in the Persio-Arabian Region, as the corresponding instrument the Naqqarat, has been mentioned in the 10th century, in a music encyclopaedia. Ibn Sina (980-1037 A.D.) in his treatise Al-Shifa also refers to it. Here, we may mention that the ancestry of the Indian instrument Nagara has been traced to the Dundubhi of Vedic times, which is considered to be its predecessor. The earliest visual representation of this type of instrument is found at Bharhut (2nd cent B.C.). Therefore, it is not necessary to find out whether the Nagara evolved from the Naqqara of the music of the Persio-Arabian Region; instead we have to accept a situation that both the instruments are similar. This throws light on the commonality of cultures.

The Nagara consists of a pair of two conical bowl drums struck with sticks; the smaller of the two is higher in pitch and represents the 'madi' or female, the larger with a deeper tone is called the 'nar' or the male. This drum is used in folk dramas, marriages and religious processions; however in the medieval period the traditional place for it was the Naubatkhana. During the days of princely splendour, a special place was reserved above the gateway to the palace or fort, where an ensemble, consisting of many instruments including the Nagara performed. Abul Fazl (16th century A.D.) in his Ain-i-Akbari gives an indication that some of the instruments used in this ensemble were of the Persian variety; like the Surna and Nafir (wind instruments). This gives an indication that Persian instruments were also being used during that period along with the indigenous ones.[191]

The Dukkad or Khurdak is also a conical instrument of the same family as the Nagara, but smaller in size and more sophisticated. It is played with the Shahnai in concert presentations.[192]

(b) Tabla

The Tabla (a type of kettledrum) takes its name from the Tabl of Arabic origin; tabl meaning an instrument facing upwards with a flat surface. Some scholars are of the opinion that the word Tabl may have originated from the Latin word Tabula. Initially, egg-shaped or hemispherical instruments, with skins stretched over the opening (also called kettledrums), were called Tabl. They were played as martial drums in the armies of the Mohemmedans. These were made of metal and had originated from the pot drums of ancient days. Later, the term Tabl became a generic term for all types of percussion instruments of the Persio-Arabian Region *e.g.* Tabl Baladi, Tabl Turki, Tabl Naqqara etc.

There is a need to mention here, that, there are various opinions about the origin of the Tabla. Firstly, that the Tabla (kettledrum) existed in ancient India, in the form of Dundubhi, Bheri, Nisan etc. Secondly, according to reliable sources, the Tabl and its varieties were introduced to Indian music by the Mohemmedan armies. The word Tabla is a distorted version of Tabl. The third probable theory about the origin of the Tabla is, that the conical drums called Dukkad (popular in Sindh and Punjab), because they faced upwards, were renamed as the Tabla by the Muslims. Finally there is another theory which substantiates its Indian origin, that, it is an evolution from an ancient instrument, Mridang. It is interesting to note here that till the beginning of the 14th cent. A.D., we do not find the word Tabl mentioned in Indian music.[193] It is therefore probable that, while identical instruments existed in both the systems of music, the name Tabla may have been imbibed from the Mohemmedans.

The Tabla was initially used for light music in North India and was introduced as a classical music instrument during the time of Mohammad Shah Rangiley (18th cent. A.D.).

The Tabla consists of two drums; the 'bayan' or the left drum and the 'dayan' or the right drum. The 'bayan' is spherical, made of clay or metal, the 'dayan' being made of seesam or some other wood. The playing surface of the 'bayan' is double that of the 'dayan', though both are almost of the same height. The goat skin stretched across the top is made of many layers, being tied at the edges to a plaited strip called the gajra. The gajra is fixed to the mouth of the drum by leather braces called 'baddhi'. These braces are tied to another ring at the bottom of the instrument. The most important part of the top surface or parchment is the black paste called 'syahi'. This is a mixture of iron powder, glue, flour and charcoal powder.[194]

3. Frame Drums

The frame drum is an instrument where the skin (or hide) is stretched over a frame of wood or metal. The diameter, in these types of instruments is much larger than the depth. In some varieties the hide covers only one side of the frame; in others both sides are covered; also there are variations in the size of the instrument. This instrument is found in all parts of India as an accompaniment to folk and tribal music; especially among the nomadic tribes. Though it has a variety of names in different regions, the most common ones are the Daff, Dappu and Dafli.

The frame drums of India are similar to the frame drums called Daff (octagonal shaped) and Daira (circular) of the music of the Persio-Arabian Region. Generally, the frame drum was and is a folk music instrument; however recently it has been included in classical music ensembles in Iran, where Sufi classical music is sung to the accompaniment of percussion instruments like the Daff and the Tombak (a vase shaped drum). In Iran it is one of the most popular percussion instrument.[195]

The ancient name for the Indian frame drum was Pataha, as mentioned in the Mahabharata (approx. 500 B.C. to 200 A.D.) and Natyashastra (approx. 2nd century A.D. to 4th, 5th century A.D.).

Other names include Dayara, Chang and Karachakra. The term Dayara is also used for frame drums in the Persio-Arabian Region.

The Khanjari is a frame drum, smaller in size to the Daff, used in light and folk music in Northern India. The corresponding instrument Khanjeera of South Indian music is used in classical concert music, in an ensemble with other instruments. The Khanjari has a circular frame, made of wood, brass or iron, covered with parchment and is played with the palms and fingers.[196] In the countries of the Persio-Arabian Region, it is called the Tambourine and is associated with the gypsies.

Here we may mention about a popular folk instrument, Chang, which belongs to the Daff family, and is used in Rajasthan and Gujarat. It is a large drum with a circular wooden frame covered with parchment on one side; it is associated with the Holi festival and used as a rhythmic accompaniment to community singing and dancing.[197]

WIND INSTRUMENTS

These instruments use air to produce sound. In India they are known as Sushir Vadya. According to one belief, it is supposed that primitive man heard the sound of the wind passing through holes in the bamboo, and this whistling sound might have given the idea of making the first wind instrument.

Music of the Persio-Arabian Region

Ibn Sina (980-1037 A.D.) in his Al Shifa mentions about new forms of instruments evolving as a result of foreign contact; this was the assimilation of Arabian music with Persian and Turkish influence. These instruments were the Mizmar (Arabic name) Surnay (Persian name), both of which were classical names for the Oboe, the conical flute. The Dunay (double pipe) and Arghul (melody pipe and drone) are also mentioned by Ibn Sina.[198]

We now give further details about the wind instruments of the Persio-Arabian Region. These can be broadly classified into (1) Flute (2) Oboe.

1. Flute

There is only one wind instrument used in Arabian art music, the simple vertical flute; this has been traced to 3000 B.C. in Egypt. In

Algeria, it is still known by its oldest Arabic name, Qasaba (Qasabat:plural). The Persian name Nay is used for the same instrument.[199] The Nay is a generic term for all kinds of flute. They are essentially folk instruments, but one type the Nay-e-Haftband is widely used in art music. The instrument is held obliquely; it is made of wood, with the rim blown out, six finger holes and one thumb hole.[200] The Nay is also used by some Dervish Sufi groups to accompany their chants, the munshid. The Qasaba (reed) or Nay is 60, 70 cm long with five or six finger holes arranged in two groups. Traditionally made of reed or cane, flutes are now often made of simple metal tubes or pieces of pipe. Shephardesses in Beduin society play them in Iraq, Lebanon, Palestine and Jordan.[201]

2. Oboe

This variety of flute is conical in shape, the end towards the mouth being narrow and the one away from the mouth being broad, expanding at this end to form a bell. The earliest evidence is found on Jewish coins of the 2nd century A.D.. The classical names of the Oboe are Surnay in Persian and Mizmar in Arabian. With the Mohemmedan conquests, the instrument spread to many parts of the world, including India.[202] The popular and revered Indian instrument Shahnai is considered to be similar to the Surnay. According to some opinions, when the Muslim influence was getting absorbed with the indigenous music, the Muslims found a great similarity between their instruments and the ones locally available; and they gave Arabic and Persian names to the Indian instruments. May be, the Persian name Shahnai was given to a conical flute already existing in India.[203]

The Oboe belongs to an ensemble of instruments called tabl baladi, which is played at weddings; the instruments included are many large and small Oboes, a pair of Kettledrums, Naqrazan and the drum, Tabl Baladi, after which the ensemble is named.[204] The Surnay is also called Shawm.[205]

In ancient literature Mizmar occurs as a general term for all wind instruments and sometimes as a designation for all reed instruments; or it may refer to the Oboe. This confusion continues to persist even in modern times. The double reed instruments are known by the following names: Zurna, Zamr, Ghayata, and Mizmar (rarely). The Muwiz or Mijwiz, Maqruna, Mutbiq or

Mutabbiq are generic names for single reed instruments, composed of two pipes. When one of the pipes is longer and serves as a drone, the instrument is called Arghul.[206]

Hindustani Music

Wind instruments use air to produce sound and are called Sushir Vadya. These are also called Mukh Veena in ancient texts, which means the melody instrument played with the mouth. The wind instruments are classified according to how the vibrations of air are generated. Vibrations may be produced by reeds-single, double or free. Among musical instruments, wind instruments are the oldest in India, dating back to the Indus valley excavations where whistles have been unearthed.[207] The Nadi, Venu, Tunav and Bankura are mentioned as reed instruments in the Vedas.[208] In the 13th century, Sarangdeva mentions wind instruments such as the Vansi, Pava, Murli, Madhukari etc. and describes 15 varieties of Vansh (flute).[209]

During Akbar's reign (16th century), there is mention of players of Sarna, Karna and Nay. The Sarnas were the Surnas or Shahnai of Indian and Persian origin; the Karna was the long straight trumpet. It was during this period that the Surna came to be known as Shahnai.

Hindustani Flute

The Bansuri or Hindustani flute held an exalted place as a wind instrument in the Indian music scenario in the ancient period of history. The Vansh or Venu is mentioned as an important instrument in the Vedic and post Vedic period treatises. Bharat's Natyashastra has given the first and systematic description of the Vansh or Venu. In sculptures and paintings such as the Ajanta frescoes (2nd cent. A.D.), long flutes are known to exist. In Sanchi, Ellora & Ajanta and in various temples of Karnataka, visual evidence of the horizontal flute has been found. The Ashtha chap cult of Vaishnavites, flourishing during Akbar's time, have made repeated references to Bansuri, Vanshi and Murli in relation to Lord Krishna, who was an accomplished player of this instrument. It was an instrument played by the common people, and was not a classical music instrument, during this period.

Gradually, the flute lost its position as a popular instrument; especially during the eighteenth and nineteenth centuries, when the descendants of Tansen gave importance to only string instruments like the Veena and Rabab. In the 20th century, Pannalal Ghosh (1911-59 A.D.) realised its potential and re-established its lost position of glory.[210]

The flute is a simple bamboo tube of uniform bore, closed at one end. It has six finger holes and one blowing hole. The length of the flute is normally between 2½ feet to 3 feet, depending on how thick the wall of the flute is, and the density of the bamboo used.[211]

There appears to be a similarity between the Hindustani flute and the Nay or Qasaba of the music of the Persio-Arabian Region.

Shahnai

Among the various wind instruments prevalent in India, the Shahnai is found to be similar to the Surnay, a wind instrument of the Persio-Arabian Region. "Shahana, Shahanay and Shahanai are all said to be synonyms of Surna, which is described as follows: it is a wind instrument made of special wood and is accompanied by Duhul. The instrument is found in Iran in different shapes, and its size is half a metre."[212] Though the name Shahnai is of Persian origin, reed instruments have been found in India since ancient days. The wind instrument Nadi or Nali, which according to some opinions is a reed instrument, finds mention in Vedic literature. Matang's Brihaddeshi also mentions a reed pipe called Mahuvari or Mohori.[213]

Since ancient days these instruments in various shapes and sizes have been played on auspicious occasions. There are plenty of instruments in use in different regions of India, which resemble the Shahnai, like the Pendre and Shahnai of Bihar, Tute and Surnas of Jammu and Kashmir, Nafiri of North India, Nagaswaram and Mukhveena of South India etc.[214] Shahnai, Nagaswaram, Sundari and Nafiri have structural similarities and are different in their sizes. Nagaswaram is the biggest, Shahnai is medium sized, and Sundari and Nafiri are small sized. These instruments have a special mechanism for the entry of air into the instrument *i.e.* the reeds. In Shahnai, the reed is made of a type of cane. The instrument consists of:

(*a*) A main body, the tube, which is conical in shape, widening at the end away from the blowing end,
(*b*) The reeds which act as the valve for passing of air, and
(*c*) The metallic 'bell' or pyala at the farthest end.[215]

The Shahnai was played in an ensemble called 'Roashan Chauki' in the Western and northern regions, consisting of two Shahnai players, a drone and a Naqqara player. This ensemble formed an important part of social festivities and the artists played both folk and classical music. The Shahnai ensembles were also called Naubat, which performed in specially made balconies above the gateway to palaces and forts, called Naubatkhanas or Naqqarkhanas. These formed part of royal festivities.[216]

It is necessary here, to mention about the three likelihoods that could be accepted about the origin of the Shahnai:

(*i*) Shahnai was imported from Persia, with the Mohemmedan armies, as they came and occupied territories in Northern India
(*ii*) The Persian name Shahnai was given to an existing Indian instrument, because of the similarities found between the two
(*iii*) It evolved from earlier indigenous instruments.

The Shahnai has undergone a great extent of transformation from the 15th and 16th centuries; it has emerged as a greatly respected and revered classical music concert instrument. However, it continues to be a great favourite as part of an ensemble for wedding festivities.

The Shahnai players of today go through rigorous classical music training and their presentations include the 'ragadari' concept of slow and systematic progression of the 'swars' (tones) for Raga elaboration ('badhat'). For this purpose, there has also been a conscious effort to improve the tonal quality of the instrument.[217]

IDIOPHONES

Idiophones or Ghana Vadya would perhaps be the oldest musical instruments used by man kind. We are informed by Bharat in the Natyashastra (approx. 2nd cent. A.D. to the 4th, 5th cent. A.D.)

that melody comes from 'tata' and 'sushira', while as 'ghana' gives the metre and 'avanadha' adds extra colour and performance.

Persio-Arabian Region

In the Persio-Arabian Region, very few varieties of idiophones exist. Among these two varieties of concussion idiophones are common: Kasat (cymbals) are used mainly in religious processions, usually together with the cylindrical drum. In the course of the zikr rituals of certain Dervish Sufi orders, tiny finger cymbals (Sunuj or Sajat) attached to the thumb and middle finger of each hand are used by the dancers. Another type of idiophone is the percussion idiophone; the following are the varieties being used in common everyday life:

(*i*) the copper plate played by women in yemen,
(*ii*) oilcans used as drums,
(*iii*) the mortar which is pounded in lively rhythmic patterns while grinding coffee,
(*iv*) Empty jars which pearl fishermen beat with their right hand.[218]

A Bedouin instrument, the Mihbaj perhaps can be treated as a percussion idiophone. This is a wood coffee-grinder consisting of approximately a foot tall base and a two foot pestle. It serves a double purpose; as a household item and in the hands of a professional artist it becomes a percussion instrument as well. The Mihbaj is also a sign of a person's social status and reflects the much cherished Arab virtue, hospitality.[219]

Hindustani Music

In Vedic literature, the cymbal, the most common, and popular 'ghana' vadya of Indian music, is referred to as Aghati. In Vedic rituals, a member of the group of singers was known as 'ganaka'; this person gave rhythm to the ceremonial recitation by clapping hands. In Karnataka music concerts, vocal or instrumental, even today, a person keeps 'tal' with the hands in addition to the percussionist, who gives rhythm on the percussion instrument. The Ghana Vadya was developed to fulfil this need to give rhythm with the hand; and instruments such as clappers, castanets, danda, bells and the cymbals developed.

The simplest of these instruments is the Danda or Dandiya, used in the Garba and Dandiya Ras (dance) in Gujarat. These are beautiful lacquered sticks, about 30 cm in length, struck together to the rhythm of the dance. The Dahara or Laddi Shah, an iron rod with metal rings, shaken to the rhythm of the fakir's song, is used by the Laddi Shah singers of Kashmir.[220]

The Cymbal, a concave, cup-shaped instrument, may be as small as 5 cm., like the Manjira, or Jalra; or 30 cm. large across, such as the Bortal of Assam. Two such cup like instruments are beaten against each other. Here, we must point out that the deepness of the concavity also varies.[221] The Manjira is very popularly used in Bhajan singing, a devotional light music style of presentation.

The Jaltarang is an example of an idiophone. It consists of a number of China bowls filled with water arranged in a semi-circle, which are struck with a small bamboo stick.[222]

The Cymbals or Kasat of the music of the Persio-Arabian Region which are used for religious processions may be compared with similar Cymbals called Majira of Hindustani music.

PERSIAN INSTRUMENTS

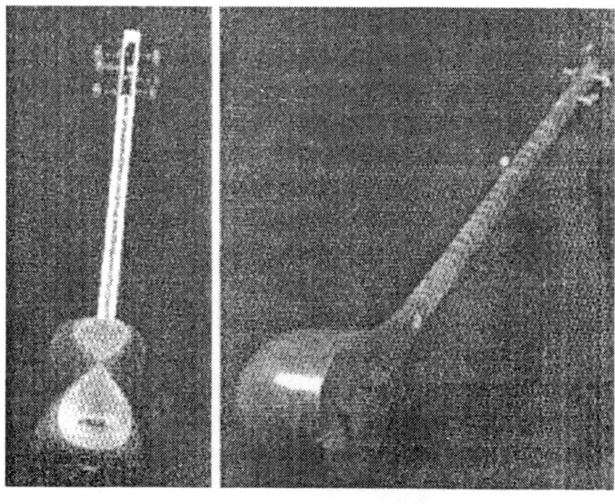

Tar Setar

INSTRUMENTS OF THE PERSIO-ARABIAN REGION

Kemenche

Gheichek

Persian Instruments

INSTRUMENTS OF THE ARAB WORLD
[Ref.: The Genius..., Pgs. 136 to 141]

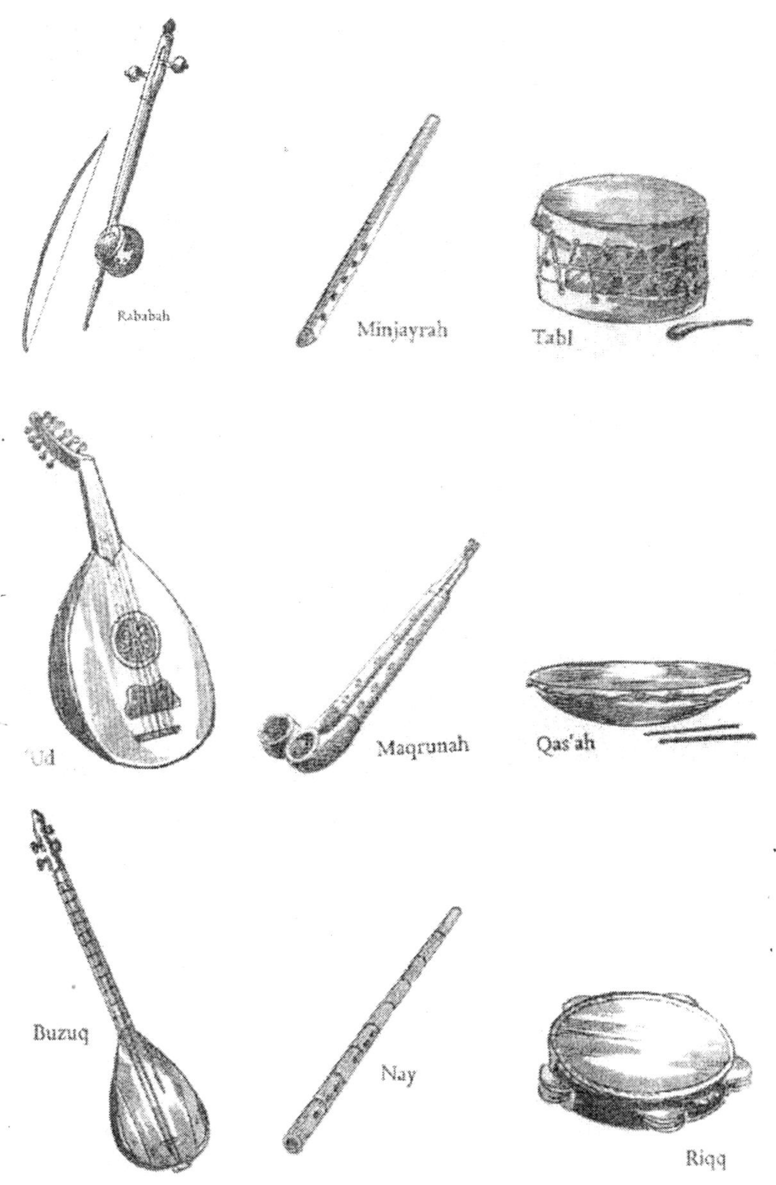

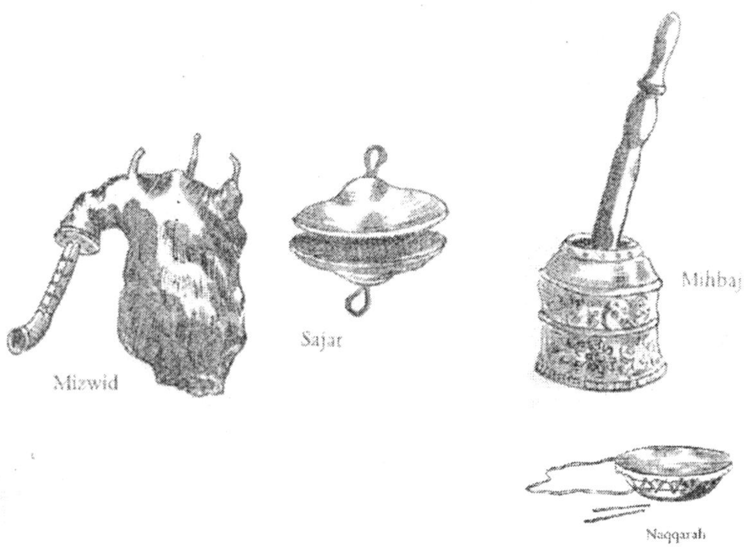
Mizwid
Sajat
Mihbaj
Naqqarah

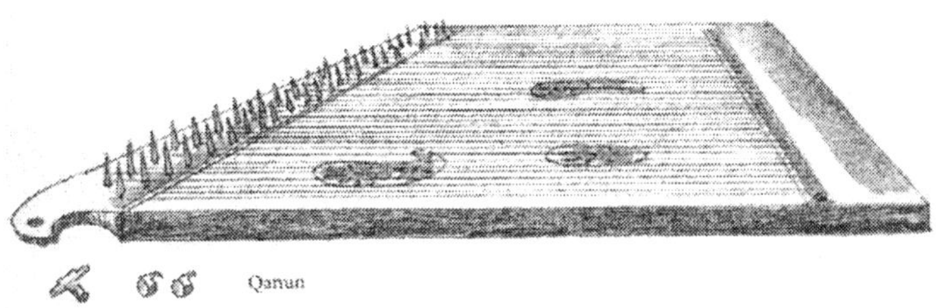
Qanun

INDIAN INSTRUMENTS
[Ref: Vadya Darshan]

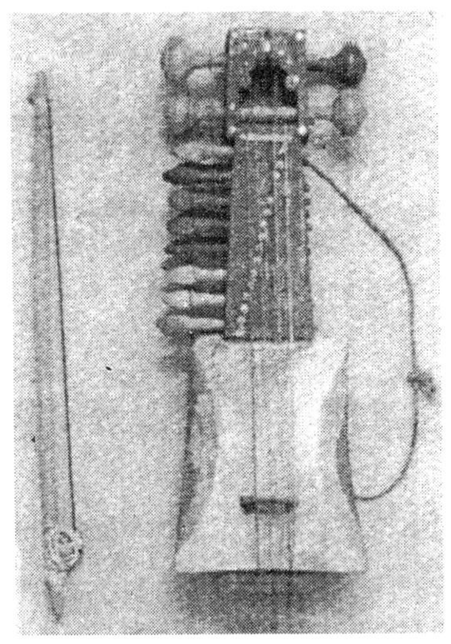

Sarangi

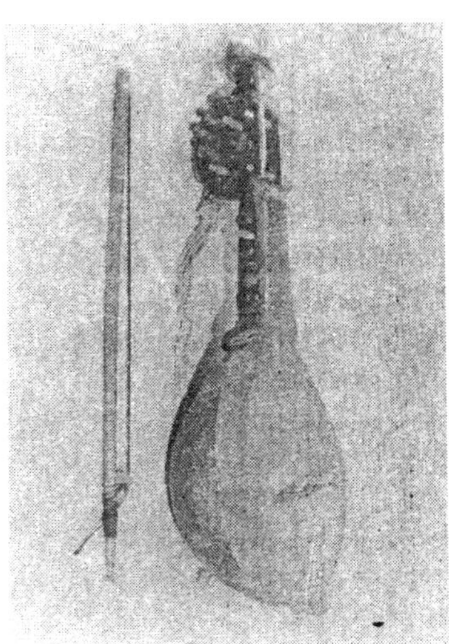

Kamaicha, Rajasthan

Rabab, Jammu and Kashmir

Rudra Veena, North India

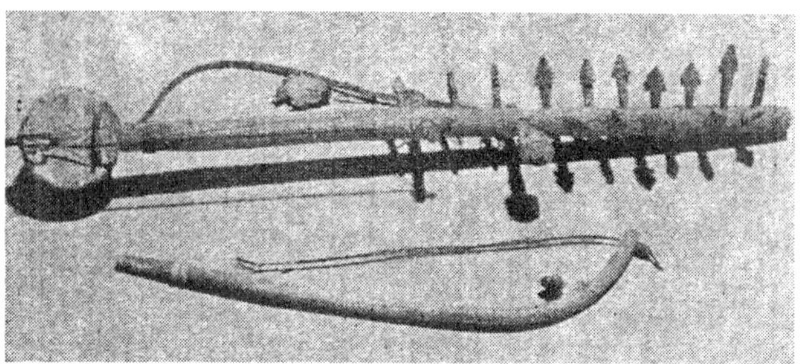

Ravanhata, Rajasthan

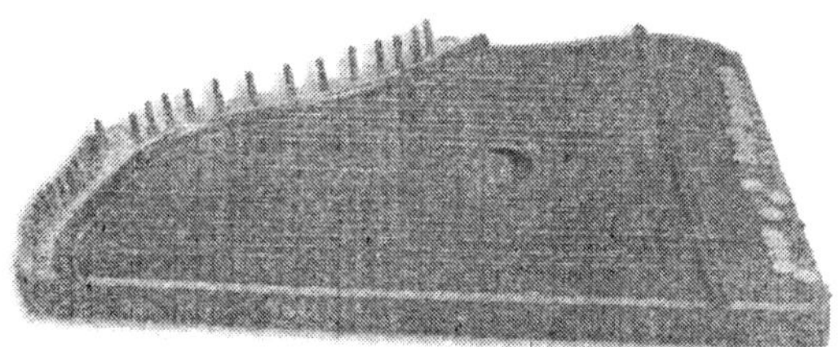

Swarmandal, North India

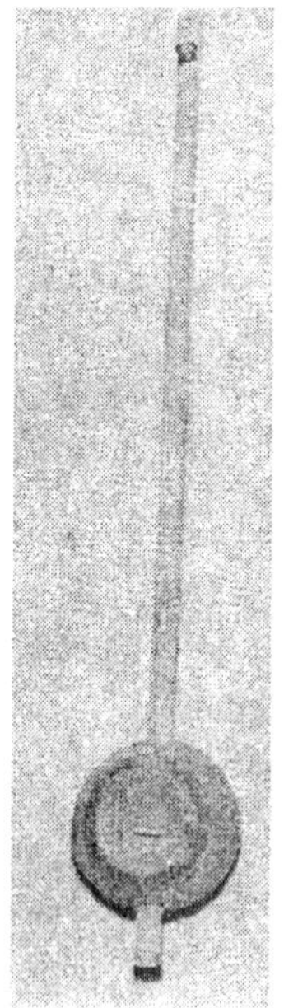

Ektara, Maharashtra

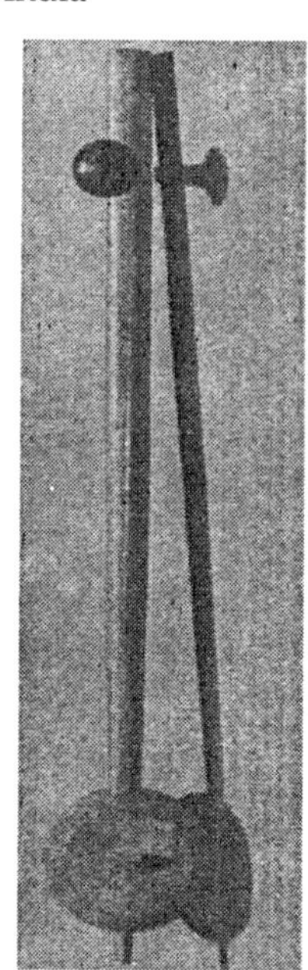

Tumbi, Punjab

Santoor, Jammu and Kashmir

Saz-E-Kashmir,
Jammu & Kashmir

Nagara

Tabla, North India

Sarod, North India

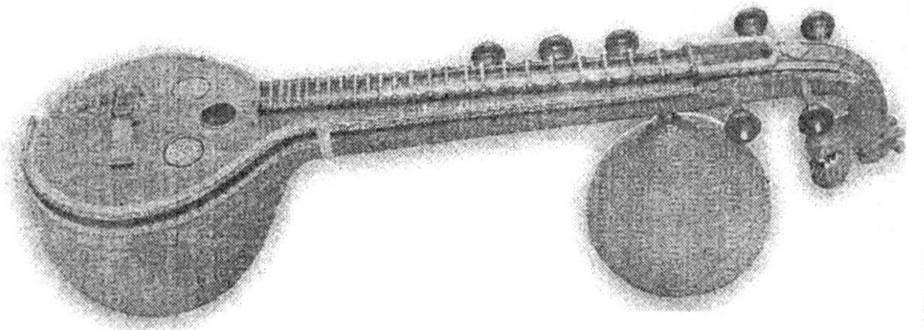

Veena, South India

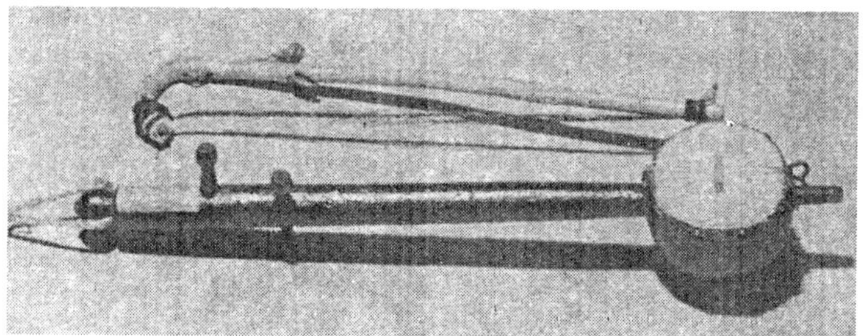

Ravanhata, Gujarat

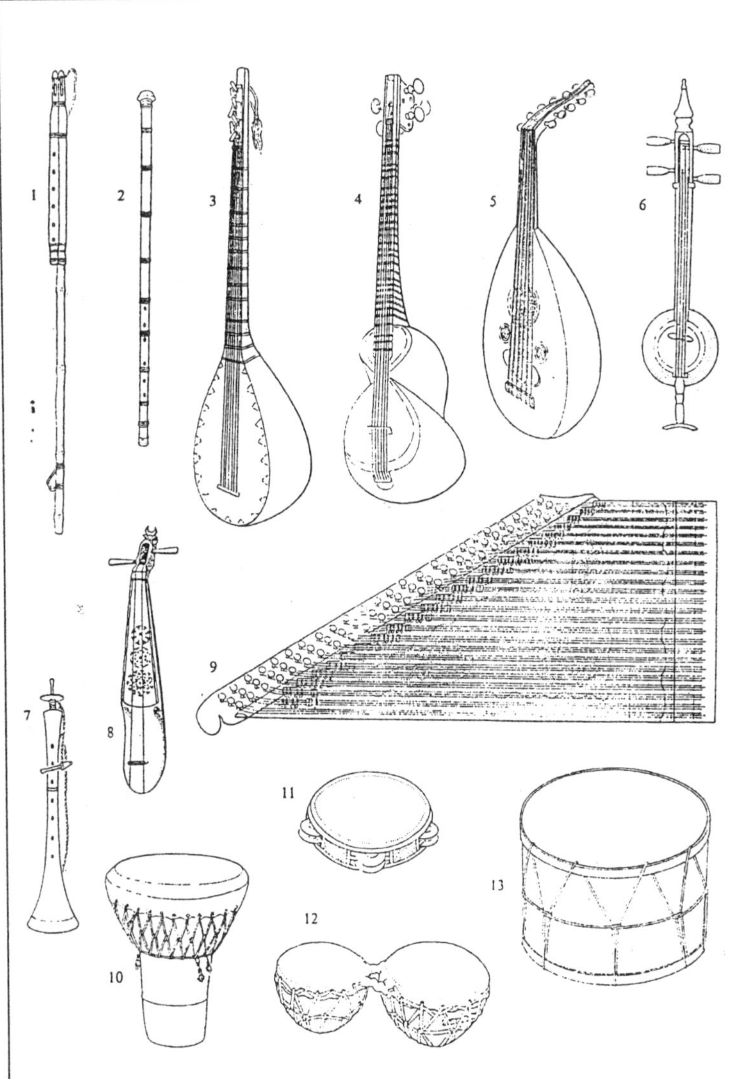

Instruments of the Near and Middle East: 1. Arghūl. 2. Nāy. 3. Saz. 4. Tār. 5. Ūd. 6. Kamānjah. 7. Zūrnā. 8. Rabāb. 9. Qānūn. 10. Darabukkah. 11. Daff. 12. Naqqārah. 13. Davaul (shown half size in relation to others) [Ref: Harvard Dict., Pg. 533]

INSTRUMENTS OF THE PERSIO-ARABIAN REGION
[Ref: New Grove IX, Pg. 298]

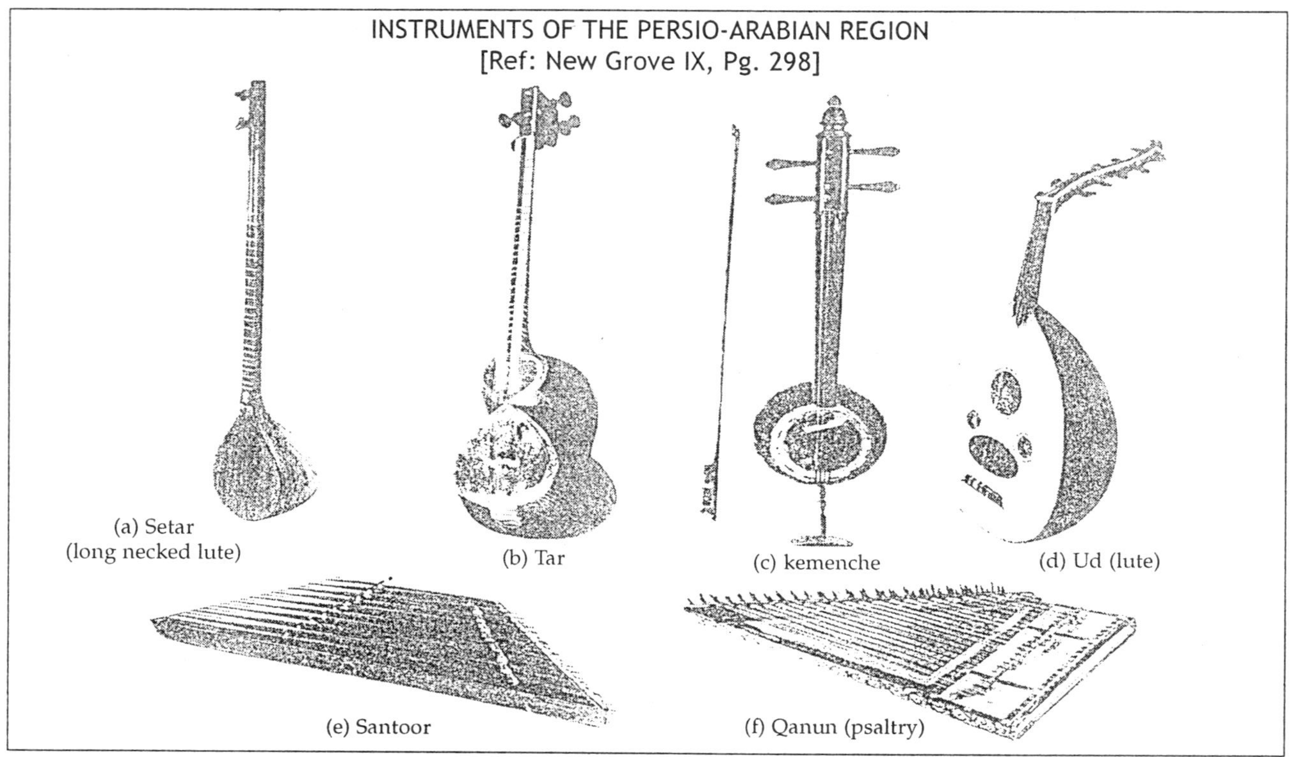

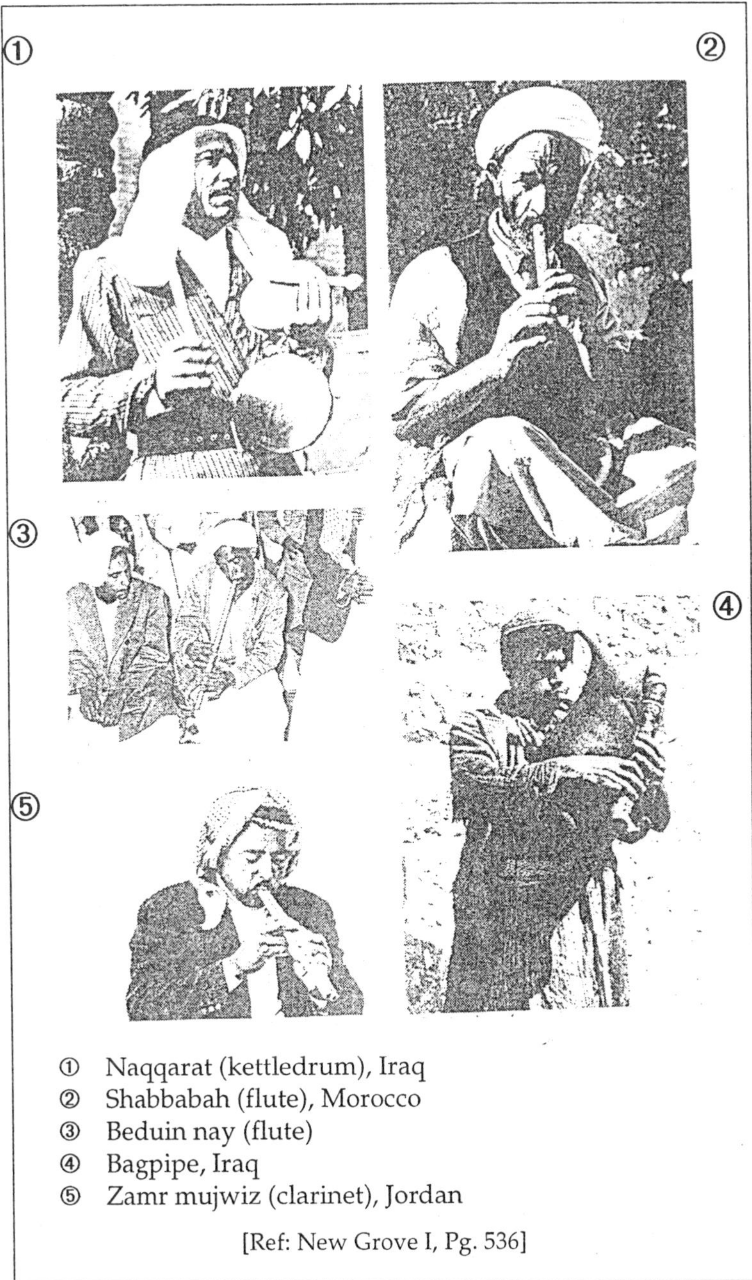

① Naqqarat (kettledrum), Iraq
② Shabbabah (flute), Morocco
③ Beduin nay (flute)
④ Bagpipe, Iraq
⑤ Zamr mujwiz (clarinet), Jordan

[Ref: New Grove I, Pg. 536]

REFERENCES

1. A.M., p. 28.
2. New Grove IX, pp. 70-71.
3. *Ibid.*, p. 71.
4. *Ibid.*, p. 72.
5. New Grove I, p. 521.
6. T.H.M.I., p. 229.
7. New Grove IV, p. 487.
8. C.M.I., p. 5.
9. *Ibid.*
10. *Ibid.*, p. 6.
11. T.H.M.I., p. 244.
12. *Ibid.*, p. 246.
13. New Grove I, pp. 520-21.
14. New Groove IX, pp. 78-81.
15. *Ibid.*, p. 77.
16. C.M.I., p. 6,7.
17. T.H.M.I., p. 222.
18. C.M.I., p. 103.
19. Mus. Instr., p. 98.
20. *Ibid.*, p. 99.
21. *Ibid.*, pp. 107, 117-18.
22. Mus. Instr., p. 118.
23. *Ibid.*, p. 99.
24. C.M.I., p. 103.
25. *Ibid.*, pp. 103-05.
26. *Ibid.*, p. 105.
27. T.H.M.I., p. 253.
28. New Grove I, p. 515.
29. N.O.H.M., p. 428.
30. M.I.W., p. 78.
31. T.H.M.I., pp. 254-55.
32. *Ibid.*, p. 253.
33. N.O.H.M., p. 446.
34. T.H.M.I., pp. 253-54.
35. The Genius..., p. 136, T.H.M.I., p. 254.
36. N.O.H.M., p. 446.
37. The Genius..., p. 136.
38. M.I.W., p. 78.
39. T.H.M.I., pp. 253-54.
40. New Grove I, p. 520.
41. The Genius..., p. 136.
42. T.H.M.I., pp. 159-60.

43. Mus. Instr., pp. 127-28.
44. T.H.M.I., pp. 159-60.
45. A.M., p. 61.
46. T.H.M.I., pp. 160-61.
47. *Ibid.*, pp. 251-52.
48. *Ibid.*, pp. 252-53.
49. New Grove I, p. 537.
50. A.M., p. 61.
51. N.O.H.M., p. 445.
52. A.M., p. 61.
53. *Ibid.*, p. 62.
54. *Ibid.*
55. *Ibid.*, pp. 61-62.
56. *Ibid.*, pp. 64-66.
57. C.M.I., pp. 154-56.
58. A.M., pp. 66-67.
59. Mus. Instr., p. 130.
60. C.M.I., pp. 167-68.
61. A.M., pp. 67-68.
62. C.M.I., p. 169.
63. A.M., p. 68.
64. C.M.I., p. 169.
65. *Ibid.*, p. 171.
66. *Ibid.*, p. 172.
67. *Ibid.*, p. 173.
68. The Genius..., p. 138.
69. New Grove IX, *Handout of Iran Culture House*, N.D. (3.07.2003), pp. 297-98.
70. *Ibid.*
71. *Ibid.*
72. C.M.I., pp. 112-13.
73. *The Veena*, by C.S. Anantapadmanabhan, Gana Vidya Bharati, New Delhi, 1954, pp. 1-2.
74. T.H.M.I., p. 152 .
75. *Ibid.*, pp. 153, 224 .
76. Mus. Instr., p. 119.
77. T.H.M.I., p. 224.
78. *Ibid.*, pp. 224-26.
79. *Ibid.*, pp. 231-32.
80. *Ibid.*, p. 253.
81. New Grove IX, p. 78.
82. T.H.M.I., p. 221.
83. C.M.I., pp. 113-14, 235.
84. *Ibid.*, pp. 114-16.
85. *Ibid.*, p. 120.

86. *Ibid.*, pp. 123-24.
87. *Ibid.*, p. 123 .
88. *Ibid.*, pp. 231, 233-34.
89. A.M., p. 28.
90. T.H.M.I., p. 257.
91. C.M.I., p. 233.
92. T.H.M.I., pp. 255-57.
93. A.M., p. 28.
94. *Ibid.*, p. 29.
95. *Ibid.*, pp. 29-30.
96. *Ibid.*, p. 30.
97. *Ibid.*, p. 31.
98. C.M.I., p. 238.
99. *Ibid.*, p. 238.
100. T.H.M.I., p. 232.
101. *Tarjuma...*, Introduction, p. LVIII.
102. A.M., p. 30.
103. *Ibid.*, p. 31.
104. *Ibid.*, p. 32.
105. C.M.I., p. 144.
106. *Ibid.*, pp. 142-43.
107. A.M., pp. 21-22.
108. C.M.I., p. 142.
109. A.M. pp. 32-33.
110. *Ibid.*, pp. 18, 26.
111. *Ibid.*, p. 18.
112. C.M.I., p. 139.
113. A.M., p. 25.
114. *Ibid.*, pp. 46-48.
115. *Ibid.*, p. 49.
116. *Ibid.*, pp. 40-43.
117. *Ibid.*, pp. 146-48.
118. *Ibid.*, pp. 148-49.
119. Mus. Instr., p. 138.
120. T.H.M.I., p. 255.
121. N.O.H.M., p. 445.
122. T.H.M.I., p. 216.
123. Harvard Dict., p. 532.
124. Mus. Instr., p. 141.
125. N.O.H.M., p. 445.
126. *Ibid.*
127. *Ibid.*, pp. 445-46.
128. New Grove IX, p. 298.
129. *Ibid.*, p. 306.

130. The Genius…, p. 136.
131. *Ibid.*, p. 137.
132. *Ibid.*
133. T.H.M.I., p. 255.
134. *Ibid.*, p. 255.
135. New Grove IX, p. 298.
136. T.H.M.I., p. 255.
137. Vadya Darshan, p. 37.
138. A.M., p. 61.
139. C.M.I., p. 156.
140. *Ibid.*, pp. 176-77.
141. Mus. Instr., pp. 138-41.
142. *Ibid.*, pp. 143-45.
143. C.M.I., pp. 177-78.
144. New Grove IX, p. 88.
145. C.M.I., p. 179.
146. *Ibid.*, p. 181.
147. *Ibid.*, pp. 182-85.
148. *Ibid.*, p. 156; C.M.I., pp. 113-14.
149. T.H.M.I., p. 259.
150. A.M., p. 20.
151. *Ibid.*
152. C.M.I., p. 235.
153. T.H.M.I., pp. 152-53.
154. New Groves IX, p. 78.
155. S.I.N.I., Vol. I, p. 6.
156. Mus. Instr., p. 112.
157. *Ibid.*, pp. 111-12.
158. *Ibid.*, p. 112.
159. *Ibid.*, pp. 116-17.
160. S.I.N.I., Vol. I, p. 36.
161. Mus. Instr., pp. 117-18.
162. *Ibid.*, p. 119.
163. C.M.I., p. 228.
164. Mus. Instr., p. 119; T.H.M.I, pp. 257-58
165. C.M.I., pp. 226, 228-30.
166. *Ibid.*, p. 10.
167. *Ibid.*, pp. 11, 13.
168. *Ibid.*, p. 36.
169. T.H.M.I., pp. 246-47.
170. N.O.H.M., p. 423.
171. New Grove I, p. 513.
172. T.H.M.I., p. 249.
173. New Grove I, p. 513

174. New Grove I, p. 537.
175. T.H.M.I, pp. 249-51.
176. C.O.H.M., p. 195.
177. T.H.M.I., p. 251.
178. New Grove I, p. 513.
179. *Ibid.*, p. 537.
180. New Grove IX, p. 297.
181. Mus. Instr., pp. 39-40.
182. *Ibid.*, p. 43.
183. C.M.I., p. 13.
184. Mus. Instr., pp. 47-48.
185. *Ibid.*, p. 55.
186. *Ibid.*, p. 52.
187. C.M.I., p. 26.
188. Mus. Instr., p. 53.
189. C.M.I., pp. 26-30.
190. Mus. Instr., p. 63.
191. *Ibid.*, pp. 63-64.
192. C.M.I., p. 47.
193. *Ibid.*, pp. 36-38.
194. *Ibid.*, pp. 41-42.
195. *Handout of Iran Culture House*, New Delhi, on the occasion of a Classical, Sufi Music programme on 3rd July 2003; Mus. Instr., pp. 42-45.
196. Mus. Instr., pp. 42-45.
197. *Vadya Darshan*, a brochure of the Sangeet Natak Akademi, New, Delhi, March, April 2002, pp. 8-9.
198. C.O.H.M., p. 195.
199. T.H.M.I., p. 247.
200. New Grove IX, p. 298.
201. New Grove I, p. 537.
202. T.H.M.I., p. 248.
203. C.M.I., p. 90.
204. T.H.M.I., p. 248.
205. N.O.H.M., p. 423.
206. New Grove I, p. 537.
207. C.M.I., pp. 63-65.
208. *Ibid.*, p. 65.
209. *Ibid.*, p. 66.
210. *Ibid.*, pp. 70-74.
211. *Ibid.*, p. 79.
212. *Ibid.*, p. 86.
213. *Ibid.*, pp. 86, 88.
214. *Ibid.*, p. 89.

215. *Ibid.*, pp. 93-94.
216. *Ibid.*, p. 90.
217. *Ibid.*, p. 92.
218. New Grove I, p. 535.
219. The Genius..., p. 138.
220. Mus. Instr., pp. 21-23.
221. *Ibid.*, pp. 30-31.
222. *Ibid.*, p. 33.

7

Tasir and Rasa — Comparative Analysis of their Emotive Qualities

The meaning of 'Ethos' in Greek is the ability of a melodic scale (harmonia) to evoke emotions, depending on its particular structure. To the extent that each melody is different from another, they have different effects on the listener; one melody may make a person sad, while another may make a person happy. Pỹthagoras, the Greek philosopher believed that music not only influenced God, but man also. He introduced a principle of classification, in which one mode would be relaxing for the mind, another would reduce sorrow, a third would be romantic. He called the principle "Ethos', and this was very similar to the ability of Indian Ragas to evoke emotions or 'Rasa' in a listener. This also relates to the concept of Tasir, as found in the music of the Persio-Arabian Region.

The Concept of Tasir of the Persio-Arabian Region

In the melody modes of the Persio-Arabian Region called Maqamat, the Greek principle of 'Ethos' is called Tasir. According to Al Farabi, the Maqamat evoked, 'such emotions as satisfaction, ire, clemency, cruelty, fear, sadness, regret and other passions'. According to Curt Sachs,[1] maqamat is considered to be a systematized pattern of melody. The inherent ability of each of these Maqam to produce in its listener a definite feeling or emotion is called Tasir.

In Hindustani Music, the main goal of Raga presentation is the production of emotion or 'Bhava', which gives 'Anand' or happiness to the listener. The expression of various feelings and emotions, by mankind, which reside within his innermost being, is termed as 'Rasa' by musicologists. Ancient scholars like Bharat (Natyashastra, approx. 2nd cent. A.D. to 4th,5th cent. A.D.) have described how Rasa is produced and how the rendition of a Raga by various techniques of Alap and Tana can produce different emotions and "Rasa"; there are approximately nine 'Rasa' which have been identified.[2]

Ibn Sina, the well known scholar of the Persio-Arabian Region mentions the corresponding ta'thir (ethos) of twelve primary modes – Rahawi, Husain, Rast, Busalik, Zangula, Ushshaq, Hijaz, Iraq, Ispahan, Nava, Buzurq, and Mukhalif (Zirafgand).[3]

The 12 principal Maqam used in the Arabic influenced regions, as well as their Persian, Turkish and other variants have long since been not just a scale of notes but also the basis for composition: each has an identifying melodic pattern and is associated with particular moods.[4] Maqam is 'a pattern of melody, based though with a certain freedom on one of the modal scales, and characterized by stereotype turns, by its moods and even by its pitch middle, high and low....'[5] The Maqam Rast named after the scale note Rast (the 'direct' note) begins with the note, ends with it, does not go higher than the octave above it, and is quiet and restrained, in its emotive qualities. Its ornamentation is also subdued.[6]

The initial note too is important in setting the mood of the Maqam; for *e.g.* the Maqam Rast starts from the tonic and Mahur from the fifth, Rast is slow and sombre, while Mahur is faster.[7] The Maqam Bayati, very popular in the Middle East is associated with tenderness; and is used for both secular and religious music.[8]

At this point we could compare Rast which starts from the tonic and is slow and sombre, with Raga Bhupali, which is expanded more in the lower octaves and has a peaceful or 'Shant' Rasa associated with it. On the other hand the Maqam Mahur starts with the higher note, fifth, and is of faster tempo. This could be compared with Raga Adana which is elaborated in the Madhya Saptak (middle octave) and Tar Saptak (higher octave), has a faster tempo and is of 'chanchal' prakriti (nature).

Plato (429-347 B.C.), the Greek philosopher, associated Greek modes with certain qualities, for e.g. the Lydian scale or mode was female in character, the Phrygian was robust, etc. The Greek principle of ethos, was borrowed from a similar ancient Semitic principle, in which the melodic modes were associated with the elements of nature, the celestial spheres and with the ability to evoke emotions. When experiments were conducted to find out the cause of this effect it was found that in Greek music the high notes had produced a romantic, exciting effect and low notes had a calming, sedative effect. In oriental music, the 'ethos' of a melody depends not on its high or low quality, but on the intervals between notes, on the note permutations and combinations, on their rhythm and also on certain musical compositions.

The Arabian Maqam are also associated with certain curative properties, which would be related perhaps to their qualities to evoke emotive responses. The healing properties were the following;

Rast healed the eyes: Iraq cured palpitation of the heart and dementia, Isfahan helped in colds, Rahawi in headache, Buzurk in colic and Zangula in heart disease.

In Indian music, many scholars are carrying out research on the therapeutic effects of music. For example: Raga Bhairavi has a soothing effect.

Persian Region

In present day Persian music, certain features and descriptions have been ascribed to the Dastgah and constituent Gushe, which correspond to the Maqam of the Persio-Arabian Region and Ragas of Hindustani Music. These descriptions, by their 20th century music scholars, Safavat and Morteza Varzi, are not documented 'facts' but assumptions.[9] They find similarity with descriptions of Hindustani Ragas given by many musicologists of the 20th century; like Pandit V N Bhatkhande in his 6 part series, 'Kramik Pustakmalika', Pandit V D Paluskar in 'Raga Vigyan'(7 parts) and Pandit Ramashray Jha in 'Abhinav Gitanjali'. Here, each Raga has been ascribed a distinct Rasa, or emotive quality and mood.

The following is an example of the features of the Dastgah Shur:

DASTGAH SHUR

Mood : burning pining, sympathetic, sorrowful, tender, consoling

Colour : red
Element : fire

The mode Shur is characterized by burning and pining; it is sympathetic, sorrowful, tender, consoling, while it represents intensity and concentration.

The Rasa Concept of Hindustani Music

The Greek concept of ethos and that of Tasir in the music of the Persio-Arabian Region finds a striking similarity with the Rasa theory of Indian music.

The Rasa theory is an important aspect of Indian culture and thinking. The presentation of a Raga evokes happiness and certain feelings and emotions; these are called the Rasa of that particular Raga. Rasa is the source of all happiness (anand); the aim of all forms of art is the evocation of Rasa. The first mention of Rasa is found in Bharat's Natyashastra in the context of drama.

Rasa is the soul or vital energy of music, poetry and drama and manifests itself in the form of sound or 'dhvani'. Bharat said that Rasa is that which can be relished – 'Rasyate iti rasah'. The relishment of Rasa is known as flavour which creates ecstatic joy in the mind and leaves an impression of wonder (chamatkar) and that is the source of uncommon delight or lokottara – ananda. (vide S.N. Shastri, The Laws and Practice of Sanskrit Drama, Vol. I (1961), pp. 258-59.)

Bharata asks the question, 'Ras iti ka padartha:?' What is Rasa? To this, Bharat himself replies that Rasa is realized by the tasting or relishment of all varieties of art with the help of Sthayi bhava. Rasa or emotional content is essential in all aspects of appreciation of art [Vide Natyashastra (Kasi Ed., p. 71)].[10]

Bharat said in the Natyashastra that without Rasa nothing is fruitful. Rasa is manifested with the help of bhavas. (Bhavas are emotional moods and Rasa is aesthetic sentiment). Bhavas are the components or parts ('avyav') of Rasa: these are sthayi bhava, vibhava, anubhava and sanchari or vyabhichari bhava. The sthayi bhava are the most stable and important, the others being subordinate.[11] According to the Natyashastra the following relationship between sthayi bhava and Rasa is accepted in the art of drama and music:[12]

Sthayi Bhava (emotional Moods)	*Rasa (Aesthetic sentiments)*
Rati	Shringar
Has	Hasya
Shok	Karun
Krodh	Raudra
Utsaha	Vir
Bhaya	Bhayanak
Jugupsa	Bibhatsa
Vismaya	Adbhuta

In current music theory the existence of Shant (peaceful) Rasa is also accepted.

In Indian music the various swar patterns of Ragas, as represented by alankaras, gamakas, sthayas (musical phrases or group of identifying notes of a Raga) evoke various emotions or Rasa in a listener. Each Raga portrays a particular Rasa: *e.g.*

1. Raga Bhupali is peaceful (Shanta Rasa)
2. Raga Bageshwari is romantic (Shringar Rasa)
3. Raga Bhimpalasi evokes feelings of separation {Virah-Karun Rasa)

The Concept of Ragadhyan and Ragamala Paintings

There is another important aspect of Raga and Rasa that requires to be discussed; that is Ragadhyan and the Ragamala Paintings.

The Ragadhyan tradition in Indian music is a unique aesthetic concept, in which the Raga is conceptualized in the form of poetic verse, and this poetry is depicted in the form of pictures called the Ragamala paintings. Ragamalas were the composite art of painting the Ragas in human forms, to create an imagery of the Raga, which would evoke some feelings and emotions (bhava) and aesthetic sentiments (Rasa). This was part of the tradition of classifying Ragas into Stree (Female) Purush (male), Putra (Son) and Napunsak (Genderless) categories.

Every Raga has a set of swar combinations which give rise to some emotions or Rasa: this sentiment was translated into poetry, which in turn was translated into pictures. The Raga is brought to life in male, female form or in the image of Gods and Goddesses;

this image can be seen by the singer while rendering a Raga. The Rasa, nature (prakriti), mood, time and season ascribed to the Raga gets depicted in the Ragadhyan of the Ragamala paintings: also called the Garland of Ragas.

The depiction of Ragas and Raginis in the Ragamala paintings was perhaps an established art by the 16th century; by this time the 'dhyan' (images) or motifs had been more or less decided. The oldest pictures are found in a manuscript called 'Kalpsutra' (1550 A.D.) in the Devshanopada Gyan Bhandar in Ahmedabad.

Pandit Damodar's Sangit Darpana (1625 A.D.) became very popular because it contained the Ragadhyans of 6 Ragas:-Bhairav, Malkauns, Hindol, Dipak, Shri and Megh. Here Raga Bhairav has been described as Lord Shiv, which evokes the emotion of awe, respect or fear. Raga Malkauns has been described in red colour, wearing a garland of skeleton of heads of the enemy. This would inspire the feeling of bravery or Vir Rasa.[13]

Over a period of time this tradition spread to other centres in India and a variety of Ragamala paintings emerged. In the 17th and 18th centuries many schools or traditions of paintings flourished: Rajasthani, Pahadi, Dakshini, Mughal etc.

In the Ragadhyan concept, different swar combinations convey different states of the mind and are related to particular moods and emotions or Rasa. The male Ragas convey surprise, bravery and anger; the female Ragas, love, happiness and sorrow; the genderless Ragas depict fear. The pictures of seasonal Ragas would depict the emotions evoked during that season; e.g., joy and euphoria at the arrival of rains in Raga Megha. The picturization would include the clouds and peacocks. Asavari is a sorrowful Raga; Bhairavi depicts love and devotion.

In the Ragadhyana pictures depicting Gods and Goddesses, the idea was that the singer, by singing the related Raga exhorts the Divine Beings to appear before them. Poetic verses or Sanskrit slokas were made to describe the Ragas and these were picturized into paintings. In this manner, music, poetry and painting were combined to present a very unique musical art form: it was an excellent means of portraying the aesthetic relationship of Rasa and Raga.[14]

Keeping in view the above discussions on Maqam, Dastgah and Tasir, and Raga and Rasa 'Siddhantha' (principle) and the associated Ragadhyan concept, we can see that there are many comparable traits and similarities between the two systems of music, of the Persio-Arabian Region and Hindustani Music.

'Raga Dhyan' Concept, Ragini Gaur (Jaipur, Rajasthan) (1710 A.D.)

Raga Vibhas
Hyd., approx. 1700 A.D.

Raga Basant
Golconda, approx. 1690-1700 A.D.

Raga Megh, Malwa,
Artist: Madhodas, 1680 A.D.

Ragini Devagandhari, Kangra,
approx. 1785-90 A.D.

Raga Dhyan concept associated with the Rasa Sidhantha (Principle) of Hindustani Music

Courtesy : National Museum — Janpath, New Delhi.

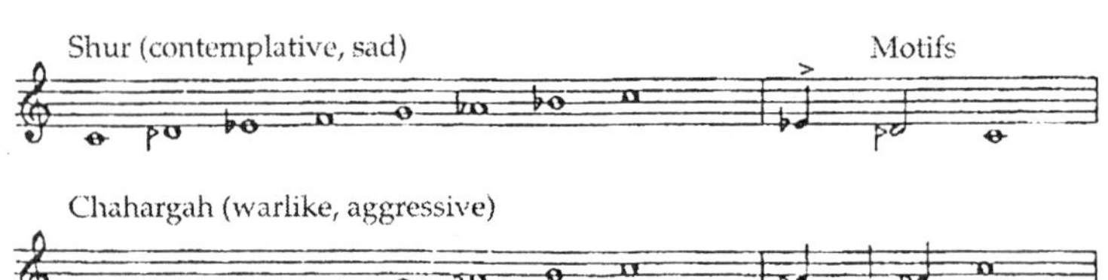

Three Persian *dastgahs*: scale, character, and characteristic motif

Emotive Elements of the Persian Dastgah

Harvard Dict..., p. 531.

REFERENCES

1. *The Rise of Music...*, Curt Sachs, p. 285.
2. *Sangita Visharad*, p. 192.
3. Groves Dict. Vol. VI (old), p. 678.
4. COHM, p. 198.
5. *The Rise of Music...*, Curt Sachs, p. 285.
6. COHM, p. 198.
7. *The Rise of Music...*, Curt Sachs, p. 285.
8. COHM, p. 198.
9. M.S.P., p. 74.
10. H.D.I.M., pp. 238-39.
11. *Ibid.*, p. 251.
12. *Saundarya Shastra*, pp. 79-80.
13. *Bhart. Sang. Ka It.*, p. 64.
14. *Bhart. Sang. Me Ragon ke Saath Devtaon ki Kalpana*, (an article) Jagdish Mittal, Nibadh Sangita, Ed. L.N. Garg, Sangita Karyalaya, Hathras, 1978, pp. 376-78.

8

Forms and Other Comparable Aspects of the Music of the Persio-Arabian Region and Hindustani Music

FORMS OR PERFORMING STYLE

In this chapter, we shall describe the Forms or Performing style prevalent in the Persio-Arabian Region and India, and discuss their comparable traits.

Forms of Music of the Persio-Arabian Region

The Abbasids who became the rulers of the Caliphate in 750 A.D., were enthusiasts for music, especially their ruler Harun al-Rashid, who loved not only court music but also music popular among the people. The form of concert music called the Nauba, which is of Central Asian origin, began to be adopted under the early Abbasids. Al-Asfahani (896-97 A.D.) mentions a group performance called 'Nauba'. This form was already known to the Chinese, and consisted of a series of vocal and instrumental pieces of different types. It remains even now the most important and common form of Islamic music.[1]

A word may be said here about the combination of the text and melody of a form of presentation. Every verse in Arabic poetry contains a complete thought, and a short melody was composed for it; the same melody being used for subsequent verses. Ibn Muhriz (d.c. 715 A.D.) introduced the practice of giving a different tune to the second verse. This practice came into popularity in the Zajal form in Spain. These short melodies were repeated many times, especially in the classical ode[2] Qasida; however the singer was allowed to vary the tune and also introduce the 'gloss' or 'fioritura', to exhibit his originality and artistry. The above description has been given for vocal music; the same practice was used in instrumental music also.[3]

It is not until the 14th, 15th century, in the works of Abd-al-Qadir, (d.1435 A.D.) that a clear picture emerges with regard to the descriptions of the Presentation styles or Forms of the music of the Persio-Arabian Region.

Nashid and Basit

These are two of the forms described by 'Abd al-Qadir. In Basit, an Arabic verse is set to music with an instrumental prelude; the Nashid al-arab consists of an Arabic verse (with a Persian language counterpart Nashid-al'ajam) with free rhythm and fixed rhythm sections alternating with each other. Some information is available from the 10th century text Kitab al-Aghani wherein we get the picture of a song form, wherein Nashid, with one or two lines of verse, constitutes the first part in free rhythm, and the Basit constitutes the remaining part.[4]

In the Abbasid period (750-1250 A.D.), a music performance in the court required that a fixed order was given to the music pieces being performed. Perhaps, due to this, even the constituents of a Form of Presentation had a fixed sequence of appearance. This requirement perhaps resulted in the development of the most complex form of all, the Nauba (meaning:turn). It consisted of four movements, which may have gone through a process of crystallization, and eventually developed into a sequence of fixed music forms, which were different from each other. The first two of these were called Nashid and Basit; and the progress was from slow (or heavy) pieces to faster (or light) ones.[5]

NAUBA

Abd al-Qadir (d.1435 A.D.) mentions four sub-parts of the form Nauba:

1. Qawl
2. Ghazal

3. Tarana
4. Furudasht
5. Mustazad

The Qawl and Furudasht are Arab poetry set to music, the second, Ghazal is Persian poetry set to music, and the Tarana may be in any language. The rhythm used was usually one of the following three: thaqil awwal, thaqil thani and thaqil al-ramal. A fifth sequence piece called Mustazad had been added to the Nauba by 'Abd al-Qadir, but there is no clear information of its having been accepted.[6]

We have mentioned before that the Nauba was and is the principal art form prevailing in the Region. Some information about its early history and development has been given and now we proceed to give further details about its structure and composition. "It is a suit of movements performed as a unit". There are two major types of Nauba:

(*i*) the Eastern Nauba performed principally in Egypt and Syria, and
(*ii*) the Andalusian Nauba, further differentiated into three types (Moroccon, Algerian and Tunisian) which has derived from the traditions of Muslim Spain.[7]

1. The Eastern Nauba

This consists of eight pieces of music based on a single mode, arranged in a fixed pattern of succession of rhythmic modes. The complex patterns of rhythm appear in the beginning and simpler patterns towards the end. Each constituent piece is described below.

(a) Taqsim

An improvised solo instrumental prelude, it is a piece of music, where the player can display his special abilities; and he also, explores and defines the particular identifying notes of the Maqam being presented. This is usually a piece without rhythm. A vocal counterpart of a Taqsim is the Layali [solo vocal virtuoso improvisation, on the words 'ya layali ya ayni ('oh, night, oh my eyes')].

The Mawwal, a vocal un-rhythmic improvisation, based on a popular poetic form of the same name, with a similar structure like the Taqsim, may sometimes replace it.[8]

2. *Bashraf (Beshrev, Peshrav)*

This instrumental piece follows the Taqsim and the name has been taken from the Persian word Pishrav, which means coming before.[9] This section is based on a long and complex rhythmic pattern. The presentation of this form goes through 4 sections called 'Khana', in which a) the related Maqam is presented, explored; b) related Maqamat are introduced; c) identifying group of notes are played in lower and higher octaves and d) finally the composition descends to the lower notes.[10] This exploration of the notes of a Maqam, while presenting the 1st, 3rd and 4th 'Khana' of the Form Bashraf, closely resembles the elaboration of the notes of a Raga in the Sthayi, Antara, Sanchari and Abhog sections, in the Alap (a vocal piece without words) of the Form Dhrupad of Hindustani music. The introductory instrumental Alap in Indian music also follows the same pattern, after which it is followed by 'Jod' and 'Jhala'. The second section, where related Maqamat are introduced by using note modulations, resembles the practice in Hindustani music of 'Avirbhav' (appearing) and 'Tirobhav' (disappearing), where groups of notes of similar Ragas are brought in and then taken away to enhance the aesthetic beauty.

3. *Samai*

It consists of 4,5 sections; the first 3,4 being based on the metre Samai thaqil and the last on the metre, Darij Samai or Sanguin Samai.

4. *Tawashih*

This consists of vocal pieces with texts from the poems of the same name, a genre originated in Andalusia, but popular in the entire Persio-Arabian Region. The members of the ensemble sing the piece based on rhythm comprised of either single, double or more than two rhythmic modes.

5. *Qasida (Plural Qasaid)*

This is a solo vocal piece in which verses of classical Arabic poems of the same name are sung. The musical rhythm matches the poetic metre of the poems. Poems include genres such as hymns, elegy and satire. The singer himself plays the Ud, generally.[11]

This ends the classical section of the Nauba. The next section is lighter in character and has three parts.

6. *Tahmila*

An instrumental piece, in which solo players and ensemble playing are alternated. The ensemble pieces are precomposed.

7. *Dawr*

This is a vocal folk form, Egyptian in origin, based on Zajal, a genre of popular poetry. The principal singer presents phrases, with instrumental prelude.

8. *Darij*

In this ending piece, a series of Tawashih are sung in fast tempo. The Eastern Nawba is performed in the form of an ensemble (takht) with instrumental accompaniment like the Ud, Qanun, Violin and Nay; the percussion is provided by the Darabukka. These days the Naubat are performed in concerts, along with certain other musical forms, which were not originally part of the Nawba. These are the Layali and Mawwal, vocal presentations and Dulab and Lunga (Turkish origin), instrumental presentations.[12]

The Western or Andalusian Nawba

Spain was under Muslim rule from the 8th to the 15th century. At first the court music of Spain followed the Eastern Damascus tradition. However, in 822 A.D, Ziryab, the pupil of the Baghdadi musician Ishaq al-Mawsili arrived, and he started the process of developing an independent Andalusian style, and 24 Andalusian Nawbat, each in a different mode came into existence. He treated the subject with mystical and musico-therapeutic concepts. In the

Eastern Persio-Arabian Region, music was the preserve of the ruling class and the elite and performed by specialists; while as in the Western Persio-Arabian Region it reached the masses, and was choral in character. New poetic forms came into existence; the Muwashshah (court poetry) and Zajal (popular poetry), the Muwashshahat supplying the text for most of the Andalusion Nawbat.[13]

The gradual reconquest of Spain by the Christians, saw the Muslims of Spain migrating to North Africa, mainly Morocco, Tunisia and Algeria. The Nawbat in these areas are based on traditional Maqamat of the Persio-Arabian Region and follow the principle of the time of the day when a particular Nawbat with its related Maqam has to be sung. In Moroccon Nawba each constituent section is based on a different Maqam.[14] The Moroccon Nawba belongs to the category 'ala' (instrumental, secular classical music). A second category of classical music, Sama, exists, whose texts Madih (religious poems) glorify Prophet Mohammad. This is a type of religious vocal music, without instruments, but is also secular in spirit. When Sufism took its roots in India, the Sama music was practised as a religious ritual by the Sufi Shaikhs.

Forms of Music in Persia after the 19th Century

We have mentioned in the chapter on Melodic Modes, that in Persia, their structure was reconstituted in the 19th, 20th century, to form the Dastgah and constituent Gushe, the Gushe-he forming a chain called the Radif. The traditional presentation forms also underwent a change, though, they continued to rely on tradition, to a great extent. Till the 16th century, the Persian and Arabic music had reached a fair degree of synthesis, but political developments in Persia, thereafter, caused it to develop on independent lines.[15]

The three instrumental forms are:

1. Pishdaramad
2. Reng
3. Chaharmezrab

The vocal form is the Tasnif. These forms were in existence before, but their new pattern, having been composed by 19th and 20th century musicians, had 'more or less defined forms and proportions' and they were rhythmically stable, falling into regular metric patterns. In the erstwhile traditional music, improvisation within a given frame of reference was encouraged and so an instrumentalist could perform only singly at a time. With the influence of European music, in the late 19th century, ensemble music was introduced and hence a need was felt to develop fixed (as different from improvised) performing styles of melody and rhythm.

Pishdaramad

To meet this need, an instrument form called the Pishdaramad was invented by Gholam Hoseyn Darvish (1872-1926 A.D.). It was meant as an overture to go before the Daramad section of the Dastgah. The musical composition of the Pishdaramad is based on the important Gusheh-ha of the Dastgah for which it is composed, has modulations and it concludes in the mode of the Daramad section. The rhythm used is in duple, triple or rarely in quadruple time. The piece is played in medium tempo and lasts two to four minutes.[16]

Pishdaramad may be considered to be a sort of prelude which prepares the listener for the melodic mode (Dastgah), which the succeeding pieces are to feature. Among these Humayun, Shur and Mahur are very popular. The rhythmic modes (Mizan) used are those that are based on Western standards, though some are of folk origin.[17]

Reng

This comes as a section to end the performance of a Dastgah, and is a dance number. Its tempo is fast, normally in 6/8 time. The structure and form is similar to the Pishdaramad, and the musical content is based on some important Gushe-ha (plural of Gushe) of the Dastgah being played.

According to some opinions, the larger structure of the Qawwali form of Indian Sufi music which became very popular in the 17th and 18th century, contained Rang as a constituent form, apart from Qaul, Qalbana, Naqsh, Gul, and Nigar.[18] Whether the two forms of music, the Persion Reng and Rang, a constituent of Qawwali which had their origin in the Persio-Arabian Region bore any similarities, needs to be explored. The Qawwali form of Indian Sufi music can be traced to the 10th century Nauba of the Persio-Arabian Region.

Chaharmezrab

This is based on a recurring musical motif (or groups of identifying notes) of a Dastgah and is in fast 6/8 tempo. It is not an ensemble piece, and here the solo performer displays his abilities. "Older Chahermezrab compositions are monothematic, but more recent ones tend to be more extensive and involve modulations." This performing style can be placed anywhere in a Dastgah presentation; it's position is not fixed and it may be repeated more than once in a performance. The melodic form of Gushe-ha used in the Chaharmezrab is the same as the one used in the preceding or following section. This is a fixed composed piece, and indicates the extent of Westernization of Iranian music, as opposed to the improvisatory nature of the traditional music.[19]

Improvisatory sections of music are very common throughout the rendition of a Raga, in Hindustani Music, both vocal and instrumental. For example, an Alap (groups of notes which delineate the structure of a Raga) may be played or sung in the initial stage before the composition begins, during the presentation of the composition, and even afterwards, to enhance the thematic structure of the Raga. Perhaps, a parallel could be established between the Chaharmezrab and the Alap.

Tasnif

According to one opinion, the Tasnif is a ballad,[20] a vocal form, accepted everywhere; "many an example being set to the words of Sa'di and Hafiz. It sometimes precedes the Rang in the Naubat-i-Maratib". Among other vocal compositions are pieces sung in dramatic representations e.g., the operat-i-laila va majnun.[21] About its inclusion as a Form, in the repertoire of Iranian music of the 19th, 20th century onwards, we learn that it is similar to the Pishdaramad in structure; consisting of a vocal piece with instrumental accompaniment. It is placed at the end of a Dastgah, just before the Reng. The best known Tasnif are composed by poet musicians, Aref, Sheyda and Amir Jahed of the 20th century; though older Tasnif compositions also exist. The modern Tasnif are known as Taranah and incorporate western harmony and orchestration.[22]

Forms of Hindustani Music

The popular forms or performing styles of Hindustani Classical Music are mainly Dhrupad, Dhamar, Khayal, Thumri, Tarana, Trivat, Tappa, and Chaturang. Sufi Music forms an integral part of North Indian music and represents the synthesis that took place between the various influences of the Persio-Arabian Region and India, from the 13th century to the 18th century, according to information available from scholars and musicians of the medieval period. For the purpose of this work, we will discuss only those Forms prevalent, which reflect this synthesis.

A popular Sufi Music Form is Qawwali. However, this has not been described separately in the manuscripts of the 17th and 18th century. The following two forms are considered to be components of the larger structure of Qawwali; Qaul and Qalbana.

Some other popular Forms of that period such as Naqsh, Gul, Nigar, Baseet, Rang and Gazal[23] are also considered to be components of the larger structure of Qawwali. All these are described in the manuscripts of the 17th and 18th century, mainly Raga Darpana by Faqirullah (approx. 1665 A.D.), Tohfat-ul-Hind by Mirza Khan (17th century) and Shamsul Aswat by Ras Baras, son of Khushal Khan Kalawant (translation of Hindi work). Another Persian manuscript of this period is Maarafat-un-Nagham, by Abul Hasan Qaiser.

Since the purpose of our work is to compare the Forms of the Persio-Arabian Region and Hindustani music, and the subject matter of Hindustani Classical Music Forms is very extensive and exhaustive, we have discussed here, only those Forms which reflect the synthesis which took place between the indigenous music and the music of the Persio-Arabian Region.

Tarana

In the present times, Tarana refers to a form of singing which contains certain selected syllables without any meaning, which are interwoven and presented as a style in a Raga.[24] In Tohfat-ul-Hind, it is described as having "Arabian and Persian couplets in which few meaningless syllables are repeated in various melodious forms. The principles and structure of this style have been derived from Hindustani Geet."[25] Natyashastra by Bharat (approx. 2nd century A.D. to 4th, 5th century A.D.) mentions a type of Geet with meaningless syllables. Among the 6 Angas of Prabandha described by Pandit Sarangdeva (13th century) in Sangit Ratnakar, Tenak is an Anga formed by combining meaningless syllables.

In the music of the Persio-Arabian Region, there is a form of presentation called the Nauba. This was of Central Asian origin and was imbibed into the music of the Persio-Arabian Region during the early Abbasid rule (750-1250 A.D.). Abd-al-Qadir (d.1435 A.D.) mentions that it comprised of four parts, the third one being the Tarana. Even today, in Andalusia (Spain), Tarana is the name of a kind of dance and song, performed in a classical style. Therefore, we can say that a form called Tarana existed in Arabic Music even though it was different from the Hindustani Tarana. Amir Khusrau, the noted scholar musician during Allahuddin Khilji's time (1296-1315 A.D.) introduced this form in Hindustani music on the basis of similar patterns existing in ancient Hindustani music and music of the Persio-Arabian Region.

Though now Tarana is composed of meaningless syllables and is sung in the pattern of the Khayal style, in its earlier form, (during the 13th and 14th century) it included Persian and Arabian couplets and Rubaiyat, interspersed with syllables like Ta, Re, Na, De, Re, Tom etc.[26]

During the 17th and 18th century, the Tarana also included Urdu couplets along with Persian Rubaiyat.

Tarana was popular in Sufi religious assemblies and some Taranas were even composed by the Sufi musicians.[27]

Qawwali

This is a popular form of music today, in which, a group of people sing together, where the text used are couplets in Persian, Urdu or Hindi. However, this Form was popular even in the 13th and 14th century A.D. and has undergone many changes.

Al-Asfahani's (9th century) book Al-Aghani gives us information about groups of singers who sang one after another in teams, and this style was called Nauba ('turn') in Arabic. In due course their singing was also called Nauba, and this developed into the most complex style of presentation of the music of the Persio-Arabian Region.[28]

The Nauba performing style may be favourably compared with the Qawwali. Qawwali was also used, as it is used now to convey the mystic message of the Sufis through music. Sheikh Nizamuddin Chisti (13th century) and Sheikh Qutbuddin Bakhtiar Kaki (1236 A.D.) were prominent Sufi saints who were greatly affected by Qawwali music.[29]

In Ghunyat–ul-Munya (1374-5 A.D.) the oldest book available on Persio-Arab and Indian synthesis, we are informed that female singers were also included in the singing group.

According to one opinion the Khayal form of music that developed was influenced by Qawwali; and Khayal singers were called Qawwals. The larger structure of the form Qawwali was considered to include component forms like Qaul, and Qalbana. Naqsh, Gul, Nigar, Baseet, Rang, and Gazal[30] were some other popular forms of that period.

In the 14th, 15th century description of the Nauba prevalent in the Persio-Arabian Region, Qaul and Gazal are the two constituents given; these are also constituents of Qawwali, which is a form of Sufi classical music in North India. Similarly in the Persio-Arabian Region an independent form of vocal music Baseet existed, in which an Arabic verse was set to music. This has been described by Abd-al-Qadir (14th, 15th century). One of the constituents of Qawwali is also called Baseet. Again we find a similarity in names between Rang, which is a component of the larger structure of Qawwali and Reng, which is a Form of Iranian Music of the 19th, 20th century, this being a fast dance number.

Qaul

The word Qaul has been derived from the Arabic word Qaulah, which means to speak or give an opinion. Qaul was a poetic composition, in which an Arab saying from Prophet Mohammed's teachings or a verse from the holy Quran was included, and the words set to a Raga. While setting the Arab prose to verse, a few syllables of Tarana were added. Sometimes Persian words were also used. Qalbana, Naqsh, Gul are different categories of Qaul. Faqirullah, in his Raga Darpana has stated that it was an innovation of Amir Khusrau (14th century). However, Qaul has been mentioned in the 16th century in Sanskrit books also. This was the period when the Arabo-Persian music had been imbibed into the Indian music and Qaul and Geet were equally popular forms of music. There is the story of Amir Khusrau singing Qaul and Baseet (which he had learnt in Persia) in a competition with Gopal Nayak of South India, who was performing the Form called Geet.[31]

This was the period when the Kalavants and the Kavval, the Rababiya or the Binkar were equally representative of the age; and the system of music which by that time had assimilated every incoming influence, still had its infrastructure intact.

Qalbana

This was another form popularized by the Sufis and differs from Qaul only in two ways: (1) Qaul comprises of Arabic words with Tarana syllables while Qalbana has Hindi words with Tarana syllables, along with Arabic compositions. (2) The second difference is that Qaul is set to only one Tala, while in Qalbana, the Talas keep changing in the same composition. The adoption of Hindi in this performing style, would have been an attempt to make the incoming music from the Persio-Arabian Region, adjust to the existing structure.[32]

Naqsh - Gul and Nigar

This was a form of musical composition in which the verses were in Persian. A song with only one line in Persian was called Naqsh, and a song which contained a Persian Rubai was called Naqsh-Gul. These songs describe the beauties of nature and are composed on Ragas which are sung in the Spring season, e.g. Basant. This form was an answer to the Hindustani Geet, namely Man, which was an earlier form. The Nigar is similar to Naqsh-Gul except that it's words describe the monsoon, and hence it is composed on Ragas sung in the rainy season e.g. Ragas of Malhar Ang.[33]

Baseet

There is mention of this form of music as early as the 10th century, in texts such as Kitab-al-Aghani, by Al Asfahani, and the treatises written by Abd al-Qadir (14th, 15th century). Here the Basit is described as an Arabic verse set to music with an instrumental prelude. Another presentation form of that period was considered to have two sections; the initial one being called Nashid, and the second, Basit.[34]

Baseet was also a song form based on an earlier form Chhand mentioned by Faqirullah in Raga Darpana (17th century). Whether the Form of Baseet sung during the 17th, 18th centuries in India was based on the earlier Form sung in the Persio-Arabian Region is not known. It consisted of four parts, each part being composed in a different Raga.[35]

We now describe three Forms of music, popular during Amir Khusrau's time; these were the Sohela, Reng and Sama.

Sohela

One of the presentation styles was called Sohela; it was a part of Khayal gayaki, sung in the same Ragas in which Khayals are sung, but unlike the Vilambit (slow) Madhya (medium) and Drut (fast) talas (rhythm) used in Khayal singing, the Sohela presentation employs only madhya and drut talas like Sulfakta and Jhaptala. The composition consists of a sthayi (first part of the song) and a number of antaras (the second part of the song) which are recited in the form of verses. This was sung at the time of marriages.[36]

Reng

According to Ustad Chand Khan, the Reng is a famous composition associated with Amir Khusrau, and performed in the same manner even now, as it was performed at Amir Khusrau's time (14th century A.D.). It is a favourite form of music preferred by the musicians in the Kavval mehfils, on the occasion of Urs. The texts of this composition are special from the point of view of laying bare the innermost feelings of devotion and respect of Amir Khusrau towards his Pir, Nizamuddin Aulia. According to Ustad Chand Khan, the intensity of feeling in this song form leaves everybody touched and moved.

The composition consists of a sthayi and many antaras, each of the antaras being of a different variety.[37]

Sama

This was also a devotional form of singing among the Sufi Kavvals, in which the participants danced in devotional ecstasy.

Zakri

A form prevalent during the 17th and 18th centuries was the Zakri. This consisted of a few verses and phrases and was popular among the Muslims of Gujarat. The text of the songs conveyed philosophical ideas. Qazi Mohammad Gujarati was the one who introduced this style. The songs of this style spoke of love, passion and death.[38] It would be in order to mention some more Forms of Sufi music, practiced even in the present times. A form of Indian Sufi vocal presentation used in the present times is the Nauha and Sozkhani. This is a vocal form, a kind of recitation, sung and recited either by an individual or in groups, during Moharram. The language used is Urdu and the subject matter is always the heroic deeds and martyrdom of Imam Hasan and Husein.[39]

Another Muslim devotional practice which has some connection with classical Hindustani court music, is the music used by Shia Muslim groups in the month of Moharram, lamenting the martyrdom of Hasan and Husein. This is a form called Marsiya; some classical musicians specialize in presenting this style.[40]

ORNAMENTATION

Ornamentation or embellishment along with melody modes and rhythms, are one of the three important characteristics of the music of the Persio-Arabian Region.

Tarkib

Ornamentation is also called fioriture (zawaid, tahasin, zuwwaq) and consists of shakes, grace notes, the drawled scale, appoggiatura, (a musical process by which a grace note is shown; which, includes the note above and below, of the note being considered), and the Tarkib. This embellishment called Tarkib has many connotations; one of them being an instrumental process in which a melody was occasionally decorated 'by striking certain notes simultaneously with their fourth, fifth or octave'. This arabesque or festooning was a device by which the artists could display their special abilities. In the vocal device of this name, Tarkib, special syllables were set apart such as ta and ya or the conventional ya laili. Ibn Sina (c 1035 A.D.) is credited with giving the name Tarkib to this instrumental embellishment.[41]

The use of this embellishment of tarkibat, *i.e.* simultaneous striking of the fourth, fifth or octave with other notes, however infrequent it may have been, raises the question by many scholars whether the Muslims possessed the principle of harmony, in the middle ages. This subject has been discussed by Dr. H.G. Farmer and other scholars on Arabian Music.[42]

Alkindi (c.790-c.874) has described an embellishment technique of the Lute, where some notes are struck simultaneously with the melody. It is necessary to note here, that no Arabic Music was written down, till the 13th century. The intricacies of the art of music were passed down orally from master to pupil and emphasis was laid on the quality of the voice and production of subtle ornamentation, grace notes, trills with the voice, as the melody was developed. This is similar to the use of various types of 'Gamak' in Hindustani Classical music, where the voice is trained to produce intricately woven group of notes, to enhance the performance of a Raga.[43]

During the 10th and 11th centuries Arabian and Persian Music had been influenced by Greek, Byzantine music, due to geographical and political circumstances, but what marked and differentiated Arabian, Persian music from the others was its profusion of ornamentation.[44]

Tahrir

We shall now discuss how ornamentation is used in the contemporary music of Iran. The main ornamentation in Persian music is called Tahrir, which is a "falsetto break or cracking of the voice in the form of a grace note above, and in between the notes of, the melody line". (falsetto: singing on high notes by men) Tahrir is widely used in the music of countries of a geographical area covering from the Far East to Spain. In Europe it is called yodelling. It may be of Indo Iranian, Indo-European or possibly Asiatic origin. In Hindustani music the corresponding techniques employed to bring about embellishment in the voice are called Gamak (vibration produced in the voice), Meend (sliding of notes gracefully), and Kan-Swar (Grace notes). The Kan-Swar in Hindustani music are smoother and take the form of slurs and slides, rather than the Arabian and Persian counterpart, where ornamentation is produced by a cracking of the voice between notes. Here it must be emphasized that Iran and Azerbaijan which have similar cultures, possess the most intricate and highly elaborate form of Tahrir in the world. Safavati, a Persian musicologist of the 20th century has listed various types of Tahrir: *e.g.* Tahrir-e-bolboli (nightingale Tahrir), and Tahrir-e-Chakoshi (hammer tahrir).[45]

Tahrir, an important component of the vocal technique of Persian art music, is unique to this region. As mentioned before, this is a type of embellishment with a quasi-yodelling effect and high falsetto notes. Qamar Taherzade an outstanding musician of the 20th century excelled in this art form and later musicians have not been able to maintain the same level of proficiency. Tahrir is a difficult art, in which the singer improvises the line and the instrumental accompanist simultaneously imitates the vocal piece as closely as possible. There is a pause by the singer, followed by the instrumentalist repeating the entire phrase alone.[46]

This perhaps could be compared to the Jugalbandi technique in Hindustani music, wherein, during the rendition of a vocal classical piece, both in slow motion Alap and fast moving Tana, the vocalist and the instrumentalist, alternatively sing and play, the latter copying the section sung by the vocalist. Many vocal and instrumental techniques of embellishment are used by both musicians.

Another type of ornamentation in Persian music is a 'slow wave vibrato' (quivering, trembling), which comes in the form of waves, accentuating secondary notes on the modal scale. It hardly ever rests on the tonic, 5th or 4th (Sa, Pa or Ma), but it does fall on the 7th or the 2nd (Ni or Re). For instance in Isfahan, it seems like a slow play between the 2nd and minor 3rd, or the 7th and tonic. Traditional music should be presented in a steady tone, interspersed with vibratory rests or waves on some notes. This technique also has parallels in the way the notes of a Raga are stressed in Hindustani Classical Music, using voice techniques (quivering, vibrating, sliding etc. which are known as Meend, Gamak) as the Raga is presented.

The vocal syllables used during the free-rhythm Gushe (corresponding to the Hindustani music Alap) to embellish the singing are yo, yar (beloved) and the Arabic ya (Oh). Other syllables or words used are Aman (Oh,) Jan or Jun (soul), Janam (my soul), Dele (heart) Aziz-e-maw (my dear) ey, ay or vay (Oh!).[47]

Arab, Persian and Turkish melodies can now be written in European notation with half-flats and half-sharps for the microtones, to provide for the nuances of the music. The improvisation of music, specially for making it more ornamental is the essential feature of the music of the Persio-Arabian Region. The Nauba, the principal form of music presentation in the Persio-Arabian Region has much scope for this variety of improvisation. In the Turkish Taqsim, in the opening piece, the principal instrumentalist improvises an ornamental piece. In Morocco, the overture[48] (Taushiya) is preceded and followed by an instrumental piece called the 'Bughya', where there is ample scope of embellishment of the music.[49]

In Hindustani music, melodic ornamentation is an indispensable part of its presentation. The rigidity of music is broken by 'gamaks', a 'style that is characterized by numberless shadings, graces, slides, tremolos, rising and falling'. This makes the music ornamental and is the 'life and soul' of Indian melody. In Somnath's words 'music without 'gamaka' is like a moonless night, a river without water and a creeper without flowers'. In all Indian music this melodic ornamentation goes hand in hand with a rhythmic pattern of beats, which is almost indispensable.[50]

As we have seen in the previous discussions, ornamentation forms a very intrinsic part of Persian and Arabian music. We can therefore say with a degree of certainty that there is a commonality between the ornamentation of the music of the Persio-Arabian Region and that of Hindustani Music.

FOLK MUSIC AND SOCIOLOGICAL ASPECTS

Persio-Arabian Region

The folk music of any region is closely associated with the sociological circumstances prevalent in any society. The folk music of the countries of the Persio-Arabian Region (or the Middle East), does not differ substantially from the art music of the area. The folk musicians are specialists, in their respective fields; for example those who recite epics, or those who specialize in wedding songs. The instruments used by art musicians are also used by the folk musician community; and some performing styles are also related.[51]

We get some information from reliable sources about the pre-Islamic days or the beginning of the Islamic period, with regard to the cultural ethos prevailing at the time. Mention has been made of some 'hadith' (traditions of the Prophet: sayings and practices that had acquired the force of law) which tells us that although Prophet Mohammed banned music in general, he specifically allowed folk music and instruments, which would be of benefit to society. Ikhwan-al-Safa (a brotherhood which flourished in the second half of the 10th century) had in its fifth epistle on music, described many forms of folksongs. This manuscript was called Al-Risalah-al-Khamisa fi al-musiqi. These songs exhibit a diversity of ethnic repertories and types of styles that existed. There were special trumpet tunes to express the joy of the inhabitants of an island at the arrival of a boat carrying water; or an ensemble of trumpets and drums playing tunes on the occasion of the opening of a dyke on the Nile.[52]

In this pre-Islamic time, we also get information about a very popular fair being held in Ukaz (now Western Saudi Arabia), where musicians and poets congregated to exhibit their art and contest with each other. The 'treasured poems', the Mu'allaqat were sung and recited.[53] The odes called Qasaid were sung in the desert. The Qasida (plural: Qasaid) is a type of sung poetry; it is very sophisticated and one of the ancient forms, originating from the Beduins in the desert. It is performed at gatherings, where events are narrated and the poet singer is the spokesman for the moods and aspirations of the people.[54] Singing at that time was called Ġhina and it originated from the caravan songs called Huda. Further, forms of music like the lament called Biqa and the elegy Nauh were developed. The lament and elegy would have been sung on occasions of mourning for the dead. Finally the song form Nasb came into existence, and perhaps this was the beginning of the music forms of the Persio-Arabian Region.[55]

The number of forms and genres of sung folk poetry of the Persio-Arabian Region is impressive and the poet musician enjoys a distinguished position. The Ataba, Ubudhiyya and Muthamman are other forms of sung poetry common in Lebanon, Syria, Palestine and Jordan. The Ataba and Ubudhiyya are improvised solo song types. These are very rhythmic and include hand clapping and response from the audience.[56] Epic songs are sung by bards or poet musicians called Shair to the accompaniment of the Rabab. The Shair is the walking archive of the community and interpreter of memorable events, customs and manners.

Ibn Khaldun (d.1406), in the chapter on music in his Prolegomenes, describes the difference between art music and folk music. The former is bound by rules and regulations and long training is required to acquire the skills, while as folk music is spontaneous and does not require the observation of much instruction. Scholars did not pay attention to folk music in the countries of West Asia till the early 19th century. Villoteau in 1809, devoted many pages of his works to folk songs and dances; while as Lane, in 1836 has written about Egyptian folk tradition. The Cairo Congress on Arab Music in 1932, gave special attention to folk music and many eminent scholars gathered and initiated a comprehensive investigation of ethnic music.[57]

The music of the Islamic folk was not very different from what it is today. The toil song was practised by the boatman, the sailor, the porter, the weaver, and other workmen. The swaying lilt of this form of music lessened the sweat of hard work, as well as lent a rhythmic pattern to the work. On the domestic scene there were lullabys, the bridal songs and the elegy.[58] A popular type of song performed at wedding festivities by a double chorus, without instrumental accompaniment is called Rezif.[59] These forms of music were not only enjoyed by the common folk, but the ruling class as well; as we have instances where Caliph Harun (ruler during early Abbasid period, 8th century) was supposed to have enjoyed this from his Court minstrels.[60]

Another song form of the Persio-Arabian Region is the song sung by shepherds in the desert, who sometimes play a small double Clarinet, widely known in the Arab world, called either Zummara or Zifti (a Turkish derived word). The war dances of the Beduins are called Arda or Ayala. Like most Beduin dances, the war dances are associated with festive occasions and are accompanied by a percussion ensemble consisting of one or two Tabl, several Tar (frame drums) and a pair of Tus (small cymbals).[61]

The most refined music in the folk genre is that of the pearl divers. As they are required to stay on the oyster banks for two three months at a stretch, they are accompanied by one or two professional singers (Naham). In the camps of the pearl divers on the oyster banks, other songs, Fijiri are performed at night, and the rhythms of the Fijiri are cyclic and of remarkable length: in some of the sub-genres (*e.g.* Bahri and Adhani) each cycle may have a time unit of 32 beats. In the work routine of the pearl divers, every separate stage has got a special type of song associated with it, sung by the professional singers, Naham. The divers and sailors produce a vocal drone in very low octaves which are two octaves below the normal pitch of the Naham.[62]

There are work songs for agriculture and camel driving. In the village and rural areas, many women take an active part in music; they are singers, composers and poets.

In North eastern Iran, some musicians specialize in singing epics like Ferdowsi's Shahnameh, or the story of Hossein's martyrdom. "A folk music genre is likely to consist of severely limited melodic material, and a singer may make his career from performing variants of one tune type. In Iran, thousands of lyrical quatrains are sung to variants of a single melody called the Chaharbeiti tune."[63]

In the traditional urban music of the Arabian (Persian) Gulf, dance songs Sawt and Bastah are performed. There are private houses, called Dar, where musicians live in a group or community, and performances of these dance songs are also held here. The Sawt dance form originated in Yemen and the Bastah in Iraq. Sawt and Basta may also be accompanied with the percussion instruments Tabl and Tar. The Sawt is traditionally performed by a musician, who is also a proficient Ud player and two drummers. Each song form has a separate rhythmic pattern.[64]

North Indian Folk Music

The folk music of India is varied and touches every aspect of life in its various provinces or regions. There are folk songs for different activities of rural life, like sowing, reaping; the wedding ceremonies in the rural as well as urban regions are incomplete without the appropriate songs for each ceremony; further the festivals and various seasons have their own special genres. In each region the folk music is sung in the language of that region, and these are based on classical Ragas, in many instances; though the rules and regulations binding classical presentations are not strictly followed.

We observe from the history and development of Hindustani music that after the Vedic period, cultural and sociological differences emerged in society. This led to the birth of two branches of music, classical and folk; the former being adopted by the specialists and the latter by the common folk. The two genres have always depended and borrowed from each other.[65] We give below the names of some folk music styles sung in regions of Northern India, and we will observe that there are many similarities between the occasions and events for which folk music is performed in the Persio-Arabian Region and India; even though the structure and composition would be different.

Folk Music of Uttar Pradesh

1. Wedding songs are performed for each and every ceremony; they are called 'Ghodi' for the ceremony in which the bridegroom sits on the horse; 'Banna' and 'Banni' are sung during the entire duration of the wedding festivity by women of the household and guests; 'Bhat' is sung during a wedding feast, and many 'Mangal Geet' and 'welcome songs' are sung to welcome the wedding party.

The other genres are given below:

1. Virah – sung by the Yadav community, on weddings, to the accompaniment of drums.
2. Nirwahi – A song sung during the sowing activity.
3. Sohar – these are songs sung by women on childbirth to the accompaniment of 'Dholak'.
4. Narua Bhakkad – this is a song of the barber community, sung on weddings.
5. Alha – the story of Alha Udal's historic fight is set to music. The village folk are filled with sentiments of courage and bravery, on hearing this.
6. Barahmasi, Savni, Chaiti – these are seasonal songs. In Barahmasi Geet, the 12 months are described, while singing the praise of Lord Rama and Lord Krishna.[66]

Folk Music of Punjab

The region of North India is a treasure house of folk music. Every aspect of daily life is associated with music; of special interest are the songs sung by women on festivals and weddings. The following are some of the varieties popular in Punjab:

1. Tappe Geet – These songs start with the words "Bahari Barsi..........",
2. Giddha Songs – Women sing this while doing the Giddha dance on weddings and special occasions,
3. Bara Maha – These are associated with the seasons; descriptions of the different months of the year are sung,
4. Vara Lok Geet – The singing of this song arouses sentiments (Rasa) of bravery,
5. Dholak Geet _ These are wedding songs and have a lot of variety like, 'Damdi', 'Ghela' and 'Suhag'.[67]

Folk Music of Kangra Valley (Himachal Pradesh)

Kangra Valley lies in the Himachal Pradesh province of India, and is very rich in its folk music tradition. The names of some of the varieties are given below:

1. Sanskar Geet: Sohar, Namkaran, Mundan, Vivah, Mrityu, Sanskar Geet,
2. Dharmic Geet: Upasana Geet, Shitla Ashtmi, Navratri etc.,
3. Praday Geet: Aikal, Dokal and Group songs,
4. Seasonal songs (Ritu Geet): Jhule ke geet, Barahmasa, Chaiti-Phag Geet etc.,
5. Kangra's Lok Katha and Lok Gatha.[68]

Folk Music of Madhya Pradesh

As in other areas, in Madhya Pradesh also, the folk music reflects the social customs and rituals associated with festivals, weddings; as well as the joys, sorrows and toil of daily life and work. Madhya Pradesh consists of various regions like Bundelkhand, Malavi, Nimadi and Bagheli. In the Nimadi area, folk bhajans in the local dialect are sung, based on raga and tala. Some names of folk music compositions in the Bundelkhand region are Saire, Rachre, Malarare, Savan, Divari, Phange, Lori and Dadre.[69]

Muthamman, Maqam bayyati; transcr. A. Shiloah (Shiloah, 1974).

Muthamman is a form of folk music of the Arabian Region (New Grove I, Pg. 533)

REFERENCES

1. C.O.H.M., p. 191.
2. Ode: Poem meant to be sung with or without rhyme.
3. New Oxford Hist. of Music, p. 456.
4. New Grove I, p. 520.
5. *Ibid.*, p. 520.
6. *Ibid.*
7. *Ibid.*, pp. 523-24.
8. Harvard Dictionary, p. 530; New Grove 1, p. 524.
9. Harvard Dictionary, p. 530.
10. New Grove I, p. 524.
11. *Ibid.*
12. *Ibid.*
13. *Ibid.*
14. *Ibid.*, pp. 524-25.
15. New Grove IX, p. 296.
16. *Ibid.*, pp. 296-97.
17. Groves (old), Vol. VI, p. 681.
18. Hind. Music, Ahmad, pp. 133-34.
19. New Grove IX, p. 297.
20. A ballad is a sentimental composition of several verses, sung to melody, with subordinate instrumental accompaniment; a poem narrating a popular story
21. Groves (old), Vol. VI, p. 681.
22. New Grove IX, p. 297.
23. Hind. Music, Ahmad, pp. 133-34.
24. Hind. Music, p. 125.
25. *Ibid.* pp. 126-27.
26. Hind. Music, Ahmad, pp. 126-27.
27. *Ibid.*, p. 128.
28. *Ibid.*, pp. 131-32.
29. Hind. Music, p. 132.
30. Hind. Music, Ahmad, pp. 133-34.
31. *Ibid.*, p. 134.
32. *Ibid.*, pp. 136-37.
33. *Ibid.*
34. New Grove I, p. 520.
35. Hind. Music, Ahmad, p. 138.
36. Mousiqui Hazrat Amir Khusrau, p. 243.
37. *Ibid.*, p. 246.
38. Hind. Music, p. 139.
39. In conversation with Prof. N.P. Ahmad, Faculty of Music and Fine Arts, University of Delhi.
40. New Grove IX, p. 76.

41. N.O.H.M., p. 450.
42. *Ibid.*, p. 471.
43. C.O.H.M., p. 194.
44. *Ibid.*, p. 195.
45. M.S.P., pp. 108-09.
46. New Grove IX, p. 298.
47. M.S.P, pp. 108-09.
48. The beginning of an orchestral piece.
49. C.O.H.M., pp. 198-99.
50. T.H.M.I., p. 221.
51. Harvard Dictionary, p. 529.
52. New Grove I, p. 528.
53. N.O.H.M., p. 423.
54. New Grove I, p. 529.
55. N.O.H.M, p. 424.
56. New Grove I, pp. 529-30.
57. *Ibid.*, p. 528.
58. N.O.H.M., pp. 434-35.
59. New Grove I, p. 513.
60. N.O.H.M., pp. 434-35.
61. New Grove I, p. 513.
62. *Ibid.*
63. Harvard Dict., p. 529.
64. New Grove I, p. 513.
65. *Lok Sangeet Tatha Shastriya Sangeet Ka Parasparik Sambandh*, an article, (Nibadh Sangit), p. 68.
66. *Sangit Visharad*, Garg, p. 170.
67. *Dissertation: Punjab Ke Lok Geet*, Arvind Kumar, 1978-1979.
68. *Kangra Ka Lok Sangita, Vishleshnatmak Adhhayan: Ek Ruprekha*, p. 28, Sangita, Oct. 1990, Sangit Karyalaya, Hathras.
69. *Bhopal Ke Aas-Paas*, Prof. Ramcharan Dubolia 'Vasant', Sangita, March 1996, Sangita Karyalaya, Hathras, pp. 14-15.

Conclusion

It may be stated, without doubt, that there are numerous similarities and comparable traits between the music of the Persio-Arabian Region and Hindustani Music, suggesting that each has been influenced by and benefitted from the other. There are various opinions about whether the two regions borrowed or not from each other at different periods in history; or whether it was coincidental that strong similarities existed between the two systems. These theories have been discussed in their respective contexts, during the course of this work.

Swami Prajnananand says that in order to study Indian Music in its true historical perspective, the study of Arabo Persian Music becomes indispensable, because this was introduced to India by their scholars and poets during the Muslim Rule from 11th century onwards. The races and groups that came from the Arabian Region brought with them Islamic influences and culture. This was made up of a core Arabic tradition which had assimilated the culture and practices of Greece, Byzantine (refers to erstwhile Roman influence), Persia, Turkey, North Africa (Egypt) and Spain. This exposure to the incoming influences from the Arabian Region got gradually absorbed and blended with the indigenous art and music system during the Medieval period. Historians and music scholars reporting on the development of music of that period have recorded this intermingling. Therefore, emphasis has been given in this book, to this blending of cultures, in which contributions of outstanding musicians and scholars like Amir Khusrau and Faqirullah have been discussed.

According to Dr. N.P. Ahmad, the Indian Music that developed during the Medieval period was based on the rich Indian heritage and its interactions with the Persian, Arabian, Turkish and Central Asian influences. As a result of this intermingling, some new forms of presentations like the Tarana, Qawwali emerged, as did some instruments like the concert Tambura from the Persian Tamburi and Sarod from the Rabab.

However, it is necessary to point out that from the published material available so far it cannot be concluded whether the Hindustani Music borrowed from the Music of the Arabian Region or they from us. Swami Prajnananand says that, the Arabian Region also borrowed many of the materials of music from India, just as we imbibed their influence in the Medieval period. When Pythagoras (approx 500 B.C.) travelled to India, he carried back with him knowledge of music, medicine, mathematics etc., and this may have been passed on to the Persians, who in turn had been exposed to the Greek civilization. Moreover there is evidence that Indian instrumentalists were invited to Persia in the Sasanian era (224 to 642 A.D.); Prof Lane affirms that the Arabs borrowed tenets from Indian treatises apart from Greek and Persian treatises to form the system of music which they have possessed for many centuries.[1] Mr. Majid Ahmadi, of the Iran Culture House, New Delhi is also of the opinion that all music originated in India.

During the course of this work, an interesting point emerged that should be highlighted. In the border regions of North West India like Kashmir, musical practices are being exchanged between neighbouring people and races from West Asia due to geographical proximity. According to the New Grove Dictionary of Music and Musicians Vol. IX (p. 72), the husky vocal quality of Kashmiri singers is similar to the classical singers of Persia. The Persian plucked Sehtar and the mallet struck Santur are both played with the same 'rapid repeated note riz', which is characteristic of West Asian string instrument technique.

The Arab world is a land of unity and musical contrasts. There are large geographical areas like N. Africa (Morocco, Algeria), the area of Egypt and the Levant (Syria and Palestine) and the Arab peninsula and Iraq, which have their own identities as well as separate cultural and aesthetic sensibilities. According to the Genius of Arab Civilization (p. 121), the Arabian Region at one time covered "a vast geographical area ranging from the Atlas Mountains and parts of Sahara in Africa to the Arabian Gulf region and the banks of the Euphrates." In the 7th century A.D., the Arabs invaded Persia, which had in turn been influenced by the Greek civilization. The Greeks were probably inheritors of the ancient wealth of knowledge of Egypt and Mesopotamia; this Greek influence with its emphasis on the mathematical sciences and astronomy, including the term 'al musiqi' was imbibed by the Arabs. By exposure to Greek music, its musical nomenclature was also absorbed when the Arabs extensively translated their treatises into Arabian.

During the first centuries of Islam, there was intense exposure to Arabian music from Persia and the Byzantine (erstwhile Roman) provinces. The development of musical practices of the Arabian Region were greatly affected by Persian influences and the organization and classification of the modal systems were affected by Byzantine models, and formed its 'classical' style, as practiced in the Courts. Prof. Mohammad Amin, an eminent scholar of History, stresses the fact that this Persian and Byzantine influence even eclipsed the Arab culture to some extent.

The Arabs were in occupation of Spain from the 8th century to the 15th century. The introduction of Arabian science and literature into settings of wealth and splendour at the imperial courts at Granada and Cordoba were inspirational to new artistic life and further development and evolution in the field of music. A major factor influencing Arab music was the supremacy of the Ottoman Turks over Syria, Palestine, Iraq, the coasts of Arabia and much of North Africa (1517-1917 A.D.). Arabian music interacted with Turkish music and absorbed much by way of new instruments and Forms of presentation (like the Turkish Saz Semai, Turkish Pesrev). It was observed that there was a great overlapping of melodic modes and metric modes.

The most recent influence from outside was the Napoleonic conquest of Egypt (1798-1801 A.D.) and subsequent political and cultural interactions in the 19th and 20th century. During this period in the music of the Persio-Arabian Region, many Western instruments were introduced and due to an attempt at westernization, specially in Egypt and Iran, the Western notation was adopted. It was observed that, due to this westernization, the indigenous music could not develop as may have been expected.

The various historical developments, that took place during the periods of various ruling dynasties *i.e.* Sasanian, Umayyad, Abbasid, had both unifying and diversifying influences on the history of the Region. Under the Abbasids (750-850 A.D.), the Arabian Empire reached its height of glory and cultural and musical achievement. The invasion of the Mongols (1258 A.D.), subsequently lead to the disintegration of the Arabian Empire.

If we trace the development of Hindustani Music during different periods in history, from the ancient to the modern, the Medieval period, stands out, as the blending and amalgamation of the Persio – Arabian music and Hindustani music took place during this time. It was found that a definite change was brought about in the indigenous music by the introduction of new Ragas and instruments. It was also observed that during this period, the incoming and indigenous music were being performed side by side in complete harmony and a spirit of comradeship. Musicians were encouraged and received great patronage from the Muslim rulers, during that period. During the rule of the Khilji dynasty, (14th Century A.D.) Amir Khusrau, (1253-1324 A.D.), a poet musician and statesman made novel contributions to Indian music by combining the Persian Ragas with the Indian, and forming a new set of Ragas, such as Sazgiri, Zilaf and Yaman which are sung to this day. Akbar (16th century A.D.) gave exceptional patronage to music and the arts; Tansen, an illustrious musician was one of the nine gems of his court. Mohammad Shah Rangiley's (18th century) knowledge, love and patronage of music was another instance of the interest shown by the Muslim rulers in art and culture. The example of Sadarang and Adarang, two outstanding musicians in his court, is widely known.

However it was observed, during the process of this work, that inspite of foreign influences, Indian music remained intact in its basic foundation, and in fact flourished and became enriched by absorbing them.

Till the 15th century the Melodic Modes (scales) of the Persio – Arabian Region had a common history for the different areas of the Region, *i.e.* Arabian, Persian, Turkish and Central Asian; after that because of political factors, the Persian region developed its separate cultural identity, and their modes were reconstituted to form the Dastgahs and constituent Gushe. However, the area as a whole had a common political and geographical past, because of which the basic principles of modal structure remained common. The modal structure of the Maqam, and Dastgah is the same as the Indian Raga, which is also based on a modular (like a scale) framework. There are other similarities between the two systems; such as the common pattern of note-scales, presence of identifying group of notes ('sthai' or core components), the style of developing the modal presentation by stress on some notes, etc.

A noteworthy point that has been highlighted in this book is that the Maqam of the Persio-Arabian Region has parallels in Indian music other than its similarity to the Indian Raga. The Maqam System was found to be similar to the Mela That Raga Classification system, and a relationship has also been traced to the Murchhna system of Indian music. Hence the subject of Raga classification has been incorporated in this work.

Learned scholars over different periods of the History of Indian Music have commented upon the development of the Indian Raga. The Indian Raga was traced to the Jatis of Bharat's Natyashastra and the first musician to record the word Raga was Matang in his Brihaddeshi (8th, 9th century). A point to be noted here is that during the Medieval period cultural exchanges were taking place and a definite blending and fusion took place between the incoming Persian music and the Indian Raga resulting in the formation of new Forms and melodies (an approximate period from the 13th century A.D. to 17th century A.D.). The scholars and musicians who contributed towards this were Amir Khusrau (1253-1324 A.D.), Faqirullah (Raga Darpana – 1662-63 A.D.) and Pundarika Vithala (Raga Manjari-approx. 1599 A.D.). Certain eminent scholars have discussed and commented upon this blending that was taking place; these are Mohammed Karam Imam (Madan-ul-Musiqi – 19th century A.D.), Pandit V.N. Bhatkhande (20th century A.D.) and Ustad Chand Khan (Mousiqui Hazrat Amir Khusrau, 20th century A.D.). The Medieval period of Indian history reflects the spirit of tolerance and harmony which existed among the people of that time whether they were Hindus or Muslims, monarchs or courtiers; all participated in the harmonious blending of musical ideas and techniques.

While talking of the blending and fusion of the Maqam of the Persio-Arabian Region and the Hindustani Raga, an important point has to be brought out that during the course of this work, determining the melodic structure and note formation of the Persian Maqam and the Indian Raga has not been undertaken. This is an exercise that could be taken up separately and it was beyond the scope of the present work. It is necessary also to emphasize that the melodic structure and form of these blended Ragas as they existed during Amir Khusrau's (14th century A.D.)

or Faqirullah's (17th century A.D.) period would be different from the present times. Tracing these developmental changes would be an interesting exercise which could be taken up in the future. Ustad Chand Khan has expressed a word of caution regarding the Mishra Ragas which were composed by Amir Khusrau; as the individual characteristics of the constituent Indian Ragas that were combined with the Persian Maqams were different from each other.

The study of the rhythmic modes of the Persio-Arabian Region, and the Indian tala, brings out the strong similarities between the two systems of music. The percussion instruments on which the two systems of rhythm are played are similar; *e.g.* the Tabl, Darbukkah, Tombak of the Persio-Arabian Region and the Tabla of Hindustani music. Both the rhythm concepts have repeated cycles, a pattern of beats, and component units representing units of measurement of time of a particular melodic piece. In both the systems, again, the beats may be strong or low sounding (dum) or weak or high sounding (tak), depending on whether the central part of the surface of the instrument is hit or the peripheral part, respectively. There are rests alternating with these beats, in both the systems. These rests and beats are recognizable by their sound and timbre. So, this chapter highlights the commonality of the music of the two regions.

It was found that strong comparable traits exist between the instruments of Persio-Arabian Music and those of Hindustani Music. This similarity assumes great importance as it was found that similar string instruments existed in the two systems of music from ancient periods. Iconographic evidence shows that harp-like and lute-like instruments – both long necked and short necked, were found from ancient times in the Persio-Arabian Region as well as in India.

It is useful to note here, that the evolution of instruments in India is not matched by a corresponding development in the instruments of the Persio-Arabian Region. An example is the Persian Tamburi which came into India in the early days of the Mohemmedan occupation. This was a small sized crude prototype of the Ektar family in India, used by folk artists and mendicants in rural India; there are many varieties of this in Gujarat and Rajasthan. This has now developed into a rich concert instrument, the Tanpura which is used as an accompaniment to vocal music, or even as a drone for instrumental music. A parallel development does not appear to have taken place in the Arabian Region.

A second example of this instance is the Kemenche and the Sarangi. The Kemenche, a bowed instrument, is one of the oldest bowed instruments of the world, barring the Ravanhatta of India. It was known in West Asia and Egypt, as well as in Sind in the 10th century A.D. Without going into the controversy of whether the Sarangi developed from the Kemenche of the Persio-Arabian Region, after it was introduced in India, or from similar instruments found in India itself; it is to be noted that the Kemenche is still played in the same structure and form, as the older instrument, in concert ensembles in Irani Sufi Classical music. However, the Sarangi, which was originally only a folk instrument has now developed into a sophisticated concert instrument.

As far as the Percussion instruments are concerned, it was found that both the regions have a very large number of these. Though there are similarities in them, and in some instruments a common ancestry may also be found; however it must be pointed out that the drums of the Persio-Arabian Region have not evolved to as high a level of sophistication as the Tabla and Pakhawaj of Hindustani music.

Among the Wind instruments, the Shahnai is considered to have evolved from the Surnay of the Persio-Arabian Region; the Surnay came to India with the marching armies of the invading forces of the Muslims. However, the Shahnai has been developed into a respected and magnificent classical music instrument in India; this trend may not find a parallel in the Persio-Arabian Region.

Among the idiophones, the Kasat (cymbal of the Persio-Arabian Region) and the Manjira (cymbal of the Hindustani music) are similar in appearance, and both are used for devotional music.

Many comparable traits were found between the Tasir of Persio-Arabian music and Rasa of the Indian Raga. In both the systems, during the process of development and elaboration of the presentation of the Maqam or Raga, the use of certain notes, their permutations and combinations, and similar other techniques give the required emotional content to the melody.

There is need to stress on the significant similarities that exist between three very important aspects of music of the two regions *i.e.* performing style, ornamentation and folk music.

Many Performing styles, were introduced to Hindustani music in the Medieval period, *e.g.* the Tarana, Qawwali and other forms of Sufi classical music; and Amir Khusrau made significant contributions in this area. An association was found between the Qawwali and the Naubat, a performing style dating back to the 10th century in the Arabian region. During the Mughal period, this form was also found in India.

It is to be pointed out here that the presentation style of Persio-Arabian Music, having being influenced by Western Music since the 18th century, has not been able to develop and be nurtured as an indigenous art form to the extent that it has happened in India. In India, however, throughout the period of Muslim and Western domination, the classical music Forms continued to develop and evolve from the Prabandha to Dhrupad and then to the Khayal style. The Dhrupad and the Khayal Forms of presentation survive today in their pure indigenous structure, and as highly evolved art forms. The classical music presentation, popular in the Arabian Region, *e.g.* in Egypt, consists of a traditional ensemble known as 'takht' (platform); the traditional instruments used are the Ud, the Qanun, the Nay, the Riqq and the Kamanjah, which was replaced by the violin, due to westernization. In Iran, a similar ensemble of Sufi classical music would have alternating vocal and instrumental Forms, the text for the verses being taken from the celebrated Sufi poets like Sa'di, Rumi and Hafiz.

It is interesting to note that both the systems of music – the Persio-Arabian and Hindustani are highly embellished; infact some techniques of embellishment like 'Gamaka' of Hindustani music (vibration of the voice) may resemble the highly complicated ornamentation, 'jawaid' of Persio-Arabian music.

The Folk music styles of both the regions, form a part of the everyday lives of the common folk and exhibit great similarity, in their sociological aspects, though the names and structure may be different. Both the systems have their seasonal songs, devotional music; songs expressing their joys and sorrows on occasions of birth, marriage, festivals and even their working life like sowing, reaping, pearl diving (in Arabia), fishing etc..

According to what has been discussed till now, it would be noticed that all efforts have been made to cover as many facets of the music of the Persio-Arabian Region and Hindustani music. This work had not been carried out before in one single research work till now. However, since both the topics cover a vast ocean of knowledge, much remains to be done, specially in the areas of melodic modes and instruments. It is hoped that this modest beginning would lead to further and more detailed research, in these two rich and profound music systems.

REFERENCE

1. Music of the Nations, p. 109.

Bibliography

The New Grove Dictionary of Music and Musicians, Edited by Stanley Sadie, Macmillan Publishers Pvt. Ltd., London, 1980, I, IX, XII.

The Harvard Dictionary of Music, edited by Don Randel, The Belknap Press of Harvard University Press, London, England, 1986.

The New Oxford History of Music, Vol. I, (The Music of Islam) – (Wellesz), Oxford University Press, London, 1957.

The Genius of Arab civilization, edited by John R. Hayes, The MIT Press, Cambridge, Massachusetts, 1983.

Music and Song in Persia, The Art of Avaz, Lloyd C. Miller, Curzon Press, Richmond, Surrey, 1999.

Pelican History of Music, Edited by Alec Robertsons and Denis Stevens, Penguin Books, Baltimore 1960 (1970).

Music of the Nations, Swami Prajnananand, Munshiram Manoharlal Publishers Pvt. Ltd., 1973.

A History of Arabian Music, Dr H G Farmer (1929).

The Larousse Encyclopaedia of Music, ed. by Geoffrey Hindley, (*The Music of the Arab World*).

The Rise of Music in the Ancient World East and West by Curt Sachs (The Greek Heritage in Music in Psalm), W.W. Norton and Co., New York 1943.

Hindustani Music, Najma Perveen Ahmad, Manohar, New Delhi, 1984.

Tarjuma-I-Manakutuhala and Risala-I-Ragadarpana by Faqirullah, General Editor, Kapila Vatsayan and Shahab Sarmadee, IGNCA KMS 21, and Motilal Banarsidas Publishers Pvt. Ltd., Delhi, 1996.

Mansingh Aur Manakutuhala, Hariharnivas Dwivedi, Vidyamandir Prakashan, Murar (Gwalior), 1954.

Madan-ul-Musiqi, Mohammad Karam Imam, (Siddiq Book Depot), also published by Sangit Karyalaya, Hathras.

Mariffunnagmat (Pt-I), Raja Nawabali, translated by V N Bhatt, Sangit Karyalaya, Hathras, (1958).

Ustad Chand Khan, Krishna Bisht and V.K. Rangra, Published by Ustad Chand Khan Centenary Committee, Delhi (1999).

Bharatiya Sangeet Ka Itihas, Dr. J.S. Bawra, A.B.S. Publication, Jalandhar, 1996.

A History of Indian Music, (Ancient Period) by Swami Prajnananand, Ramkrishna Vedanta Math, Calcutta, 1963.

The Music of India, by H.A. Popley, Award Publishing House, New Delhi, 1986.

Bhartiya Sangit, Ek Aitihasik Vishleshan, Swatantra Sharma, T.N. Bhargava and Sons, Allahabad, 1988.

A critical study of Sangita Makaranda of Narada, Dr. (Mrs) M. Vijay Lakshmi, Gyan Publishing House, New Delhi 1996.

Music and Song in Persia, Lloyd C. Miller, Curzon Press, Richmond, Surrey, 1999.

Musalman aur Bhartiya Sangita, Acharya K.C.D. Brihaspati, Raj Kamal Prakashan, New Delhi, 1974.

Mousiqui Hazrat Amir Khusrau, Ustad Chand Khan, Kohinoor Printing Press, Delhi-6, 1973 (Mousiqui Book Depot, Delhi, 1978).

Bhartiya Sangita Ka Itihas, Dr. Thakur Jaidev Singh, Sangita Research Academy, Calcutta, 1994 (Vishwavidyalaya, Prakashan Chouk, Varanasi).

Classical Musical Instruments, Dr. Suneera Kasliwal, Rupa and Co., New Delhi 2001.

Musical Instruments, B.C. Deva, National Book Trust, India, New Delhi 1977.

The History of Musical Instruments, Curt Sachs, J.M. Dent and Sons Ltd, London.

The Concise Oxford History of Music, Gerald Abraham, Oxford University press, Oxford, New York, 1985.

Sitar and Sarod in the 18th and 19th centuries, Allyn Miner, General Editor, Farley P Richmond, Motilal Banarsidas Publishers Pvt. Ltd., Delhi 1997.

String Instruments (Plucked Variety) of North India Vol. I, Sharmishta Ghosh, Easter Book Linkers, Delhi (India), 1988.

Musical Instruments of the World by Carl Engel, updated by Arun Joshi, Research Publications, New Delhi., 1999.

Sangita Visharad, Ed. L.N. Garg, Sangita Karyalaya, Hathras, 1980.

Grove's Dictionary of Music and Musicians (old) Eric Blom Vol. I, VI Macmillan and Co. Ltd., London, New York, 1954.

Historical Development of Indian Music, by Swami Prajnananand, Firma K.L. Mukhopadhyay, Calcutta, 1973.

Ragas and Raginis – O.C. Gangoly, Munshiram Manoharlal Publishers Pvt. Ltd., 1935 (Rep. 1948).

Sangeeta Ratnakara of Nissanka Sarangdeva, by R.R. Ayyangar, Wilco Publishing House, Bombay, 1978.

The Sangeetratnakara of Sarangdeva, Ed. By Pt. S.S. Shastri, The Adyar Library and Research Centre, 1943.

Melodic Types of Hindustan, Narendra Kumar Bose, Jaico Publishig House, Bombay, 1960.

Hindustani Sangeet Me Raag Ki Utpatti Evam Vikas, Dr. Sunanda Pathak, Radha Publications, New Delhi, 1989.

Sangeet Chintamani, Ist Part, Acharya Brihaspati, Sangeet Karyalaya, Hathras, 1976.

Bhartiya Shastriya Sangita Aivam Saundarya Shastra, Dr. Anupam Mahajan, Haryana Sahitya Akademi, Chandigarh, 1993.

MAGAZINES (ARTICLES)

1. *Sangeet*, July 1954.
2. *Sangeet*, Feb., 1966.
3. *Sangeet*, May 1969.
4. *Sangeeta*, Sept. 1993, An article, Hindustani Music, Maulvi Abdul Halim Sharer.
5. *Vadya Darshan*, a publication of Sangeet Natak Akademi, New Delhi, March, April 2002.
6. *Bhartiya Sangeet Me Ragon Ke Saath Devtaon ki Kalpana*, Jagdish Mittal, (an article) Nibadha Sangeet, Ed. By L.N. Garg, Sangeet Karyalaya, Hathras, 1978.
7. *Lok Sangeet Tatha Shastriya Sangeet Ka Parasparik Sambandh, (an article)*, Devilal Samar, Nibadh Sangeet, Ed. By L.N. Garg, Sangeet Karyalaya, Hathras, 1978.
8. *Raga Vigyan*, Vinayakarao Patwardhan, an article, 'Raganga Padyati' by N.M. Khare, Sangeet Gaurava Granthamala, Pune (1958).

Index